Exeter, 1540-1640

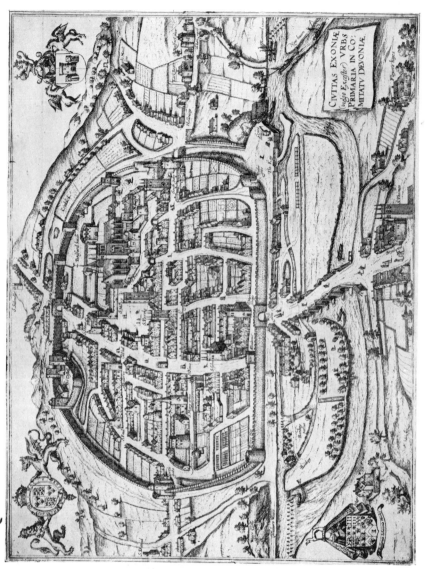

CIVITAS EXONIÆ
(vulgo Excester) VRBS
PRIMARIA IN CO:
MITATV DEVONIÆ.

Exeter, about 1600

Exeter, 1540–1640

The Growth of an English County Town

By

WALLACE T. MacCAFFREY

Second Edition

HARVARD UNIVERSITY PRESS

CAMBRIDGE, MASSACHUSETTS
AND LONDON, ENGLAND

1975

ISBN 0-674-27501-2 (cloth)
ISBN 0-674-27503-9 (paper)

LIBRARY OF CONGRESS CATALOG CARD NUMBER 75-13939
Printed in the United States of America

Acknowledgments

My debts of gratitude are numerous. Harvard University and the University of California at Los Angeles made possible by their grants the inception and continuance of my research. I am grateful to the staff of the Exeter City Library and the City Librarian, Mr. N. S. E. Pugsley, to the staff of the Houghton Library at Harvard, and to the Public Record Office, and the British Museum. I have a very heavy obligation to Dr. W. G. Hoskins. He has been unstintedly generous, both with important information drawn from his own vast knowledge of English local history, and with helpful and friendly counsel. Dr. Joyce Youings of the University of Exeter and Mr. W. B. Stevens were very helpful in providing information from their own researches into Exeter history. To three good friends I own particular debts of gratitude: to Mr. C. K. Croft-Andrew, formerly Archivist of Exeter and now of the North Riding; Professor Sir John Neale; and Professor W. K. Jordan. To each I owe special thanks not only for advice and assistance in the course of my research, but for friendly encouragement and support throughout the long task of preparing the book. Mrs. Madeleine Gleason has been of invaluable assistance in the work of revision. In addition, I am grateful to Dr. Hoskins and to The Devon and Cornwall Society for permission to use the map of Exeter, and to the British Museum for permission to reproduce the print of Exeter as a frontispiece.

WALLACE T. MacCAFFREY

Contents

TABLES

Exeter, 1540-1640

ABBREVIATIONS

ECM Exeter City Muniments

AB   Act Book

RR   Receiver's Rolls

PRO Public Record Office

BM   British Museum

APC Printed Acts of the Privy Council

SPD State Papers, Domestic

HMC Historical Manuscripts Commission Report on Exeter

TDA Transactions of the Devonshire Association for the Advancement of Science, Literature, and Art.

Introduction

My purpose in this study is not to write a "History of Exeter" in the conventional sense. A narrative history of the city in the early modern period could possibly be written, but only as a monument to dullness. Narrative history is perhaps geared to measure the rate of change of societies only of a certain magnitude, and much of local history belongs to that microcosmic world which is too fine for the historian's calipers. Hence I have preferred a topical approach.

My original concern was with the structure of English society as a whole. England in the sixteenth century was still in many ways a federation of small societies, and the status of an individual was defined by his membership in one of them. Society at large was not yet an agglomeration of individuals but a confederation of local communities, owing obedience to the commanding power of the Crown but by no means sacrificing their own sense of identity or their own group interests in doing so. I have, therefore, chosen to study one of these local societies, from a two-fold point of view. On the one hand, I am concerned with the history of the city itself as a separate and complete historical unit; on the other, with its role as a member in the heterogeneous national society of the sixteenth century.

I have deliberately stressed the fact that Exeter was a *community*, that is, not a political or geographical entity merely but a miniature world of full dimensions. It has been my assumption—and I have sought to sustain it throughout—that this borough community retained in the sixteenth century much of the integral, comprehensive quality of earlier medieval urban society, and that it embraced every important aspect of the townsman's life: political, economic, religious, and social in the most general sense. For him the city precincts were the limits of a world, and the greater universe of

England and Englishmen loomed hazily over its parapets. A foreigner was still someone from outside the city walls. Primary social loyalties were still owed to the local community, and the individual reacted to the larger movements of society not as an Englishman but as a townsman of Exeter.

How far this assumption is valid is a question which must be left in major part to the text, but a few general considerations may be mentioned here. A century earlier than 1540 or a century later than 1640 we should certainly face fewer questions. In 1440 the medieval borough was perhaps at the height of its development; by 1740 the chartered borough was little better than an archaism.

On the whole, little attention has been paid to provincial urban life during this intervening period; a generally accepted view is that medieval urban society was vanishing before the new forms of industrial and commercial organization, and that it had lost most of its vigor. This may be true in many instances, but I contend it was not so in Exeter. Here the ancient community life was, if anything, strengthened during the sixteenth century. The new powers bestowed on the civic officials by the Crown not only heightened the prestige of the borough magnates but also increased their actual authority. This authority was used vigorously and for many ends. Economic advantage, social prestige, the protection of the weak and the restraint of the vicious, religious instruction—all were pursued by the urban community.

One trend is evident: the exclusiveness always implicit in medieval urban politics became even more pronounced. A tiny oligarchy monopolized power of every kind, and more and more embodied the active life of the borough. Nevertheless, the borough remained the effective instrument of control and direction in every element of local life. With this in mind I have made my particular topical analysis. Assuming the existence of the community as the central fact of Exeter history, I have tried to examine this protean entity in all its various aspects. Taking as my starting point its political character as a chartered liberty, I have, so to speak, boxed the compass. Successive chapters deal with the politics, the public finance, the economic organization, and the instruments of social control of the civic community. They are followed by a treatment of the major corporate enterprises of the city during our epoch, and by a chapter on the religious revolution in Exeter. Chapter VII places Exeter in the larger world of English politics and administration, while the last chapter is an attempt to describe the inner social structure of the community and to provide a kind of synthesis of the entire study. In this manner I have tried to view the community of Exeter from all possible angles without losing sight of its integrity as a functioning whole.

This study is concerned not solely with one particular city but also with England in its entirety. I do not expect to find in Exeter a microcosm of the English world, but rather that a study of its life will provide a different historical perspective for the whole English scene. The historian of the Tudor monarchy, for instance, quite properly puts in the forefront the great issues of religion, of foreign policy, and of constitutional practice. The Elizabethan Settlement, the war with Spain, and the activities of the prerogative courts are matters of prime importance. But the local historian, by the same logic, has to shift his point of view to match that of his subject. He must attempt to see the Tudor world as the hostmen of Newcastle or the weavers of Coventry or the merchants of Exeter saw it. In this panorama the great motions of the English state form but a dim background, a secondary range of vision; the foreground is filled with the struggle over the Gateshead manor lease, the collapse of the cappers' trade, or the building of the Exe Haven. The great issues are not entirely lost, but they are transformed. The war with Spain becomes a question of burdensome taxation, the Reformation one of a local real-estate boom, and the whole scope of the Tudor monarchy is seen from the level of execution rather than inception of policy.

The book is based on the rich manuscript collection in the Exeter city archives. Primarily I have used official documents: charters, deeds, the act books of the Chamber, the account rolls, the letters, and numerous miscellaneous official papers. But for the first half of the century under study invaluable material is furnished by the collections and by the writing of Exeter's great antiquary, John Hooker. Chamberlain from 1555 to 1600, he was unfailingly industrious in pursuing the history and antiquities of his native city. His work gives a color and glow to this long dead world that no official records could provide.

The year 1540 was chosen as a starting date for various reasons. Records grow more voluminous and informative about this time, but more than that, events brought on a turning point in Exeter's history. Within little more than a decade the Courtenays, Exeter's overweening neighbors for so long, were swept away; the city became a county in itself; the stirring episode of the Prayer Book Rebellion produced a new self-confidence and substantial reward; and finally the city's other great neighbor, the Bishop, was sadly reduced by the storm of religious revolution. All these events opened the way for an era of growth and new life. The century that followed is the subject of this book. The convulsion of civil war in the 1640's provides a decisive break in the flow of Exeter's history although not in its continued growth and prosperity.

Chapter One

The Setting: Geographical and Historical

A book such as this, concerning itself with a mere century in the ancient corporate life of Exeter, breaks into the mid-course of a stream of civic history which had flowed unbroken for the greater part of a millennium. The resulting disadvantages are obvious. We are forced to give a brief and perforce inadequate account of the preceding centuries. But, more important, we are faced with the presence of those glacierlike elements in the city's history which change so slowly, so nearly imperceptibly, that they cannot be measured in the brief span of a century.

Some of these elements are physical in nature, such as the geography and topography of the city. They themselves change very slowly indeed, if at all; but their effects can be changed rapidly and radically. Almost equally slow to change is the historical environment, the deeply rooted complex of tradition. The community of Exeter had long since established a fixed pattern of life. This tough network of habit controlled not only the formal structures of institutions but also the routines of action. No action could be taken except through the channels provided by custom; no new problems could be met except in the terms set by the pattern of tradition. The object of this chapter is, then, two-fold: first, to describe the physical setting and, second, to survey the slow accretion of the community's traditional pattern of life down to about 1500. Only in the subsequent chapters will the bare bones of this description be clothed with flesh, as the character and operation of the traditional pattern are examined in closer detail.

As far as physical environment goes, there is no absolute change to be recorded, no silting up of the estuary as at Winchelsea or encroachment of the ocean as at Dunwich. Nor are there any great relative changes to report, such as the shift in trade routes which ruined Southampton in the sixteenth century or a technological revolution like the later one which has made the Exe a mere pleasure stream. The story of the canal and the consequent shift of the head of navigation from Topsham can most conveniently be considered in a later chapter; it worked no alteration in the important geographic characteristics of Exeter.

A glance at the map reveals the hilly but not rugged nature of Devon geography. An equally prominent feature, more apparent to the traveler's eye than it is upon the map, is the series of rivers cutting transversely from north to south through the hills—Axe, Otter, Clyst, each with its wide, shallow valley dropping gently to the ocean and cutting a path through the long line of shore cliffs. Deepest and longest of these, reaching far up into North Devon, is the Exe. This stream, unlike its sisters to the east, opens out widely into a considerable tidal estuary, and some four miles above the head of this estuary stands the city of Exeter.

The advantages of its situation are immediately evident. The Exe Valley provides a pathway into the heart of North Devon and into western Somerset, while access from the valleys of East Devon is not seriously impeded by the low hills. The tributary valleys of the Culm, Yeo, and Creedy open up additional routes of access. No East Devon valley can boast a haven such as that of Exe, while Dartmouth to the west, despite its excellent harbor, has no such easy routes into a rich hinterland. Plymouth's situation is similar to Dartmouth's. The Exe estuary, moreover, looks out directly across the seas to a wide range of continental coast, from the Seine estuary, around the Breton shores, and thence down the west coast of France to Bordeaux, and even farther, around the Viscayan corner to the Cantabrian and Galician and Portuguese ports, and finally, southwards to Cadiz and the Straits, and westwards to the Atlantic Islands. All these coasts were the resorts of Exeter shipping.

The rich shire of which Exeter is the county town was in this era among the first two or three counties in England in wealth and in population.[1] We can only guess what the population was. If the ecclesiastical census of 1603 can be trusted as an indicator, the combined population of Devon and Cornwall was between 375,000 and 380,000. This would mean a density per square mile of 96; using the same figures, the diocese of London (Middlesex and Essex) would have 180, that of Canterbury about 93, Bath and Wells (Somerset) 92, in the North, York (Yorkshire and Nottinghamshire) about 60. On the basis of muster figures Devon probably counted six inhabitants to Cornwall's four, that is, about 227,000 in the former and 151,000 in the latter county.

Agriculture, wool, and mining provided a diversity of natural wealth, and skillful artisans converted it into goods sold throughout England and on the Continent. That there had been an increase in Devon's wealth during the recent centuries is more than a fair guess. Hooker, the sixteenth-century historian of the city and of the county, in his survey of 1599[2] referred repeatedly to the tradition that the shire had once been much more heavily wooded while now there were few lands not enclosed either for tillage or for sheep. He adds that although Devon was not a land of great flocks, nearly every holder of a few fields had, along with his horses, oxen, and kine, a few sheep, so that altogether, Hooker thinks, the shire might boast

[1] Based on the Diocesan Return of 1603 (Harleian MS. 280) as summarized in Brian Magee, *The English Recusants* (London, 1938).
I am grateful to Dr. W. G. Hoskins for additional information on Devon's relative standing among the counties. In taxable capacity it seems to have stood first in the subsidy of 1524–25 when it paid a little more than Kent. In the benevolence of 1545 (see J. Strype, *Ecclesiastical Memorials,* II, 489) Devon was fourth, following Somerset, Kent, and Essex, but in the seventeenth-century ship money assessments Devon stood second only to Yorkshire among the counties. See PRO, SP 16/422/8. In population Devon ranked second only to Yorkshire in the muster returns: 17,000 in 1573 against 40,187 for Yorkshire in 1573 and 14,178 for Lincolnshire in 1587.
[2] BM, Harleian MS. 5827, "Synopsis Chorographical of Devonshire" by John Hooker, fol. 3–5.

more sheep than any other in England.[3] However this may have been, the Port Books of Exeter bear witness to the flood of woollen goods that poured out of the Devon valleys. Besides this export there was also that of tin, then mined quite extensively in Devon as well as in Cornwall, particularly on the reaches of Dartmoor.[4] There were other items as well as these staples. The apple orchards of the West already produced their famous cider which, according to Hooker,[5] was a favorite item of purchase by shipmasters who were able also to stock their ships with other necessary provisions. The county, if not ordinarily a corn exporter, at least provided its own food grains for bread and beer in most seasons. Hooker's description of farming methods,[6] of fertilizing and irrigation and pruning, suggests a prosperous and enterprising farming population. One wishes for more detailed information, but it is safe to assert that Exeter was the capital of one of the richer provinces of England, and a market in which was centered much of the economic life of the West.

The city was not only an economic center but also a provincial capital. Here in the lordly cathedral was the seat of the large diocese of Exeter, embracing both Devon and Cornwall. Exeter was also the center of secular administration in the West. The Justices of Assize as well as the Admiralty Judge of Devon held court here; and in the 1540's the city was a principal seat of the Lord Lieutenant of the West. And since the county gentlemen of Devon and Cornwall came here so often on business, they found it convenient to carry on their social life in the city also. The era of town houses was yet to come, except for the Devon abbots, each of whom kept a house here, but it was not uncommon for gentry even from Cornwall to keep such feasts as Christmas at Exeter.

The considerations that moved the Romans to their original choice of the site of Exeter had more to do with topography than with

---

[3] *Ibid.*, fol. 7d. Hooker asserted that there were few parishes where the wool tithe did not amount to 20 nobles, and that in some to £20 or better. He added that he could name places where it amounted to £100 or better but feared to offend the holders of these benefices.

[4] *Ibid.*, fol. 8d.

[5] *Ibid.*, fol. 5.

[6] *Ibid.*, fol. 5–6.

economic advantages. The westernmost of their administrative centers, it stood in a highly defensible situation. If we may assume that the present outlines of the walled city are those of the Roman post, it is not difficult to understand the choice of site.

To the west flows the river from which the city rises almost precipitously. On the north it is bounded by the deep stream bed of the old Longbrook, where the modern railway station stands. It is joined to the neighboring parish on the east by a narrow neck of land sloping away on either side from East Gate; and on the south it is isolated again by the lands that slope away from Southernhay. On no side is it easily assailable by a force armed only with hand weapons. Below in the valley the Exe is broken into complex channels which in the Middle Ages served the various water mills, but there is left a considerable flat area of meadows, partly on the eastern shore, partly on Exe Island. Beyond to the west lie the flat lands of St. Thomas parish, stretching towards the foot of Haldon. To the north the great rounded hill of Duryard manor slopes down to the junction of the Exe, Culme, and Yeo, the three valleys of which lead respectively to Tiverton, Cullompton, and Crediton, all prosperous wool towns in the sixteenth century. Southwards towards the sea the Exe Valley widens again, reaching down to Topsham, there to join the broad valley of Clyst. On the west bank the lands of Alphington and Exminster parishes extend along the estuary, dominated by the Courtenay seat, Powderham Castle.

The internal geography of the city is simple. "It is not alltogether four square but declynethe somewhat towardes a roundenes and containeth in circute or compasses 1600 whoale passes after fyve foote to the passe which after 1000 passes to a myle conteyethe a myle and halfe and somewhat more. It is pendant towards the south and west in such sorte that the streetes be they never so fowle or fylthyie yet with one showre of rayn they ar clensed."[7] The dominating height of the castle crowns the northeastern mound to which Hooker refers, and it is balanced on the southeast by the massive

[7] ECM, Book 55 (Freeman's Book), under the title, "The Description of the City of Exeter made, collected, and done by John Vowell alias Hooker, Chamberlayn of the said Citie, 1 Elizabeth, 1559."

structure of St. Peter's Cathedral which with the Close buildings, the Bishop's Palace and gardens, altogether occupies a district perhaps one quarter of the total walled area. Two major thoroughfares, crossing in the middle of the city at the Carfax (Quatrefoix), divide it roughly into four quarters, of which the southeast is almost entirely filled by the episcopal establishment. Much of the rest of this quarter was occupied by the house and gardens of the Earl of Bedford (until 1536 the Black Friars' house). The east-west axis is High Street; the north-south, Northgate and Southgate Streets, separated by the Carfax. In the early sixteenth century four gates gave entrance, one at each prime point of the compass. Besides the walled episcopal area the city included the precincts of St. Nicholas Priory.

We are fortunate in possessing two very similar maps giving the more detailed internal topography of the sixteenth-century city—the earlier dated 1584, the later 1617.[8] The most important feature they reveal is the large open area of gardens and courts within the walls, a feature confirmed by other documents. In the first place, there were the castle grounds and ditches now enclosed in the Rougemont Gardens. Beyond these were the large gardens in the southeast corner of the city, attached to Bedford House, and close by them the spacious grounds of the Bishop's Palace and the cathedral churchyard which reached from St. Martin's parish church to St. Mary Major. In the northwest corner of the city there was another open area where the early medieval site of the Franciscan house was occupied by drying racks (the Friernhay). The area given over to private dwellings was even more restricted by the existence of seventeen parish churches.[9] Possibly a third of the intramural land was occu-

[8] There are two early maps of the city. One, now in the British Museum, is dated 1587. The other, published in Braun and Hohenberg, *Civitates Orbis Terrarum* (Cologne, 1618), lib. vi, is apparently a copy of the earlier map, altered only in details of arrangement. The first is reproduced in A. G. Little and R. C. Easterling, *The Franciscans and Dominicans of Exeter*, History of Exeter Research Group Monograph No. 3 (Exeter, 1927).

[9] Before the Reformation the Hospital of St. John and the Priory of St. Nicholas would have to be added to the list of ecclesiastical buildings within the walls.

pied by ecclesiastical buildings, gardens, the castle, and the Bedford town house.

There was by now some extramural population. On the two islands under the western walls, Shillay and Exe Island, gardens and rack fields seem from the map to occupy most of the space, but we know from subsidy and muster rolls that there was a considerable population here. Similarly, around the other gates clustering suburbs had grown up. The city's jurisdiction had for centuries included St. David's parish to the north and east and Holy Trinity parish to the south of the walled city. (The lands of the two parishes actually met in Southernhay and together they may well represent the twelve plough-lands of Exeter Domesday.) The extra-mural parish of St. Edmund's belonged to the Courtenay manor of Exe Island, which passed into the city's possession in 1550. In the previous year an act of Parliament had formally established the city's bounds so as to include these extra-mural parishes along with St. Sidwell's. The legal enactment merely confirmed what was already social and topographical fact.[10]

What was the population of this whole urban area? The raw data for the sixteenth and early seventeenth century are scanty and highly inconclusive. However, on the basis of the data at hand an estimate that the city may have numbered somewhere between 7500 and 8500 inhabitants in the 1520's probably makes sufficient allowance for error. The military survey of 1522, complete for fifteen of Exeter's nineteen parishes, does at least record the *nil* assessments (those initially listed but then judged too poor to pay), which number 36 percent of the listed population.[11] Presumably the same proportion would hold for 1524 and 1525. Subsidy rolls for those years, which represent the most serious attempt of Tudor government to assess accurately the taxable wealth in land, goods, and wages, are available.[12] If we consider the

[10] Hooker, *History* (see chapter 2, note 2), II, 438–447, and W. G. Hoskins, *Exeter in the Seventeenth Century* (Devon and Cornwall Record Society, n.s. II, Torquay, 1957), xi–xii.

[11] ECM, Book 156a.

[12] PRO, E 179/96/171, 179/96/146–147, 179/96/155, 179/97/188.

950–1000 names listed there as heads of households, we can estimate the size of the average household by using some appropriate multiplier. But this list, with subsidies on wages down to the level of £1 per annum, presumably includes single servants who were members of their master's household—i.e., male adults, not only heads of households.[13]

Evidence for change in size is very uncertain. Muster lists for the 1570's and for 1628 suggest a sizable increase from about 900 able-bodied men to over 1,300, but there is no good reason to assume that a serious effort to enumerate the able-bodied men in the lowest economic strata was made.

Parish register evidence has been carefully tabulated by Ransom Pickard.[14] The evidence comes from only eleven parishes, for the period 1570 to 1640. For this interval Pickard counts a total number of baptisms of 14,186. If we extrapolate for the whole city (assuming the same proportion of population in the missing parishes as is found in the 1524–1525 subsidy lists) we arrive at a total of about 19,360. Averaged for the entire period, this yields only about 276.6 births per annum. If we assume a population of about 8,000 across these seventy years, the raw birth rate per thousand would be 34.3 annually. Burials for the same period totalled 17,360, leaving a natural increase of 1,730. We cannot estimate immigration figures, although all the casual evidence suggests a steady flow.

The next available count is the poll tax of 1660, which taxed everyone over the age of sixteen. The total count here is 6,845 (including 376 listed as too poor to pay, but excluding those on public relief). If we use the assumption that 40 percent of the population was under sixteen, we arrive at a total of about 11,400. Adding those on poor relief the total would be around 12,000.

About the best one can say, then, is that in the century under examination Exeter grew substantially, so that it was perhaps half again as large in 1640 as in 1540.

[13] See Appendix II for suggestions of a variety of different ways in which these data could be utilized.

[14] Ransom Pickard, *Population and Epidemics of Exeter in Pre-census Times* (Exeter, 1947).

How did the population of Exeter compare with that of other provincial cities? On the basis of subsidy payments for three major sixteenth-century levies (1524, 1535, and 1576), Professor Hoskins ranks Exeter fifth or sixth among English cities other than London.[15] It was consistently outranked by Norwich and Bristol and probably by Newcastle (which was excused from the subsidies). Norwich and Bristol seem to have been substantially larger, at a conservative guess, half as large again. Towns of about the same size as Exeter were Gloucester, and, early in the century, Coventry. What is noteworthy is Exeter's consistent position as fifth or sixth on the subsidy rolls. Norwich and Bristol are the only other cities which consistently appear among the first half dozen. Exeter's prosperity was clearly stable in the sixteenth century, in contrast to the fluctuating fortunes of many other urban centers.

The great majority of Exeter's population lived within the walls, as we have seen, but suburbs were growing even early in the sixteenth century. The figures for 1524–25, our only complete breakdown by parishes, suggest that as much as a fourth of the total population lived outside the walls in St. David, St. Sidwell, on Exe Island, and around the Magdalen. The proportion probably increased. In number of births St. Sidwell was easily the largest parish while the partially extramural Trinity was second, and St. Edmund and St. David fourth and fifth respectively. Possibly a third of the births in the decade 1630–40 occurred in these parishes. The rate of infant mortality was probably high in these poverty-stricken districts, however, and their populations may not have formed so large a proportion of the total.

Four hundred years ago Exeter's beauty must have appeared to much greater advantage than now. In the absence of sprawling red-brick suburbs the dignity of its site was not obscured. Cathedral, castle, and city neatly ringed by the walls made a compact whole on the sloping eminence above the river. The embowering hills about

[15] W. G. Hoskins, *Provincial England* (London, 1965), 70–71.

the city and the flourishing gardens within must have removed any suggestion of bleakness from the scene. The characteristic color contrasts of Devon must have been even more apparent when the still unspoiled green of the hills was set off by the dusty red of fallow field, parish churches, and city walls as well as by the quiet gray of the cathedral. Altogether, even at its most bustling, Exeter must have presented a pastoral aspect of great charm in which country and town were inextricably mingled.

Exeter can claim, with more certainty than most English cities, a continuity reaching from Roman times forward, but its developed civic life, like that of almost every other European city, can be traced only from about the end of the twelfth century. In that epoch Exeter felt those impulses which were stirring all Europe to renewed and vigorous urban life. The shock of the urban revolution was absorbed by local institutions in England. The well-ordered feudal monarchy proved flexible enough to accommodate a modest but not unimpressive urban development without major convulsions. English towns, except for London, remained small by continental standards; neither in number nor in size could they compare with their famous contemporaries in Flanders or Italy, or even France. And as their economic consequence remained modest, so did their political stature. For the most part the English medieval city was a small market town of mainly local significance. Seaports had, of course, overseas trade as did some inland cities, but this did little to alter a primarily local character. Likewise, although numerously represented in Parliament, they played a very secondary political role there. Throughout, their subordination to Crown, Church, and baronage is apparent.

There resulted from these conditions a rather uniform pattern of development. On the political side there were steady and ever wider grants of self-government given by the monarch, who was in most cases also the local landlord. The beneficiaries of the charters were the local merchant magnates, who slowly but steadily built up small but strongly based civic oligarchies, varying little in form from city to city. On the economic side, the same merchants secured for themselves a monopoly of the market, which they organized in such fashion that they forced all local trade through their hands. Opportunities for profit were carefully reserved for a privileged few.

Nevertheless, dominating as their position was within the walls of the cities, these urban magnates were overshadowed in the larger society of England not only by the great lords, lay and ecclesiastical, but even by the country gentry. It was not only the inferior status of businessmen in a society of hereditary aristocrats but also the limited wealth of the townsmen in comparison to that of the landed proprietors. Hence, when the cycle of medieval urban development drew to a close in England in the fifteenth century, a general uniformity prevailed. Everywhere were to be found towns, small in size, local in importance, often dependents of some local territorial grandee. Their richer inhabitants, masters of civic society, stood within the privileged classes of society but at the lower end of the scale.

From about 1500 many of the older towns began to decline in importance. New industry, particularly textiles, tended to take advantage of the freer opportunities of the countryside where neither guild nor municipal restrictions bound. New economic possibilities abounded, but they were developed through new types of business organization. On the one hand, individual entrepreneurs, such as the clothiers, and on the other, great combines like the Merchant Adventurers, took over the leadership in English economic life. In most of the towns the local oligarchies successively lost commercial importance and were relegated to minor status in the national economy.

The sixteenth century also saw many parliamentary boroughs becoming the political instruments of the aristocracy. Professor Neale has described the process by which the increasingly valuable parliamentary representation of the boroughs became the preserve of interested gentry, seeking secure family seats. The legal structure of the borough was to remain intact until the reforms of the 1830's, but the majority of the chartered towns had lost real economic or political consequence. Their vitality had vanished; only a dry husk of outward forms remained.

There were a number of important exceptions to this trend. Leaving apart London, always a special case, there was a group of boroughs which continued to thrive and to play a notable role in English economic life. The bases of their fortunes varied. Some, like Newcastle, exploited a new industry; others, like Norwich, adapted an old one; still others, Bristol for example, found opportunities in new markets beyond the seas. Among these Exeter holds a modest but noteworthy place.

Throughout the Middle Ages, Exeter had followed for the most part the general path of English urban growth.[16] A bishop's seat under the Confessor, it had already appeared as a fortified royal town under the earlier Old English kings. Exeter Domesday records a community holding land collectively and governed by two reeves. In the next century this community received its first royal charters from Henry II. In the early thirteenth century a mayor appears, assisted by four officers known as stewards, two of whom seem to have been the older reeves.

A marked change came with the development of the council, a process which occupied most of the fourteenth and fifteenth centuries. Probably the council emerged jointly from two earlier bodies, one a jury of presentment, the other an electoral group, which annually chose the city officers. Its membership was stabilized in 1450 at twenty-four councillors, who were in turn annually elected by another group of thirty-six.

The civic community had never been a democratic one, and the councillors of the fourteenth century are probably only a more formal grouping of the *probi homines* of the twelfth century. An examination of personnel reveals that both the twenty-four and the thirty-six were chosen from a very select circle indeed. What had happened was a formalization of the control which a small group of leaders had always exercised in the civic community. A final step in this process took place about 1500 when the Twenty-Four ceased

[16] For the history of medieval Exeter see E. A. Freeman, *Exeter* (London and New York, 1890), a very general but not very illuminating survey; George Oliver, *The History of the City of Exeter* (Exeter and London, 1861), a solid antiquarian account; and the able monograph of B. Wilkinson and R. C. Easterling, *The Medieval Council of Exeter*, History of Exeter Research Group Monograph No. 4 (Manchester, 1931).

to be elected annually and became a self co-opting body. In 1509 a privy seal writ of Henry VIII confirmed this arrangement and prescribed that the members of the Twenty-Four should sit for life unless removed for specified causes by their own brethren, and that the replacement of dead or discharged members should be made by the Twenty-Four themselves. In the choice of the mayor, the freemen of Exeter were to be allowed to choose between two candidates nominated by the Twenty-Four. These two candidates were to be members of that body who had held the office of receiver. With this act of 1509 the municipal constitution assumed a form it would retain for the next three hundred years.

The borough was not the only jurisdiction enclosed within the walls of Exeter, for side by side with it existed two ecclesiastical communities with their particular immunities. The greater of these was the Cathedral of St. Peter,[17] including in its precincts not only the Close with the adjoining streets (the so-called fee of St. Stephen) but also the parish of St. Sidwell, outside the walls to the east. The lesser ecclesiastical enclave was that of St. Nicholas Priory, commonly called Harold's Fee, to which was attached land in St. David's Down, north of the city. Into neither of these did the power of the civic officials extend, and the cathedral quarter, behind its walls, formed a city within a city. Friction was frequent, for the Bishop's Fee was often a resort of those who sought to escape the municipal officers, while the tenants of the bishop were unwilling to share the common burdens of the citizens. The most notable dispute of medieval times is preserved to us in the papers of Mayor John Shillingford[18] one of the most famous figures in Exeter in the fifteenth century. In this suit the city failed to vindicate its right to exercise jurisdiction within the Close walls, and the bishop continued to hold his own leet court.[19]

[17] See M. E. Curtis, *Some Disputes between the City and the Cathedral Authorities of Exeter*, History of Exeter Research Group Monograph No. 5 (Manchester, 1932), 11.

[18] *Letters and Papers of John Shillingford, Mayor of Exeter, 1445–1450*, ed. Stuart A. Moore (Camden Society, 1871). See also Curtis, *Some Disputes, passim*.

[19] The civic attitude toward the cathedral establishment is well summed up by Hooker in the short account of the city cited above in note 7. "It was verie

Exeter varied from the usual English civic pattern simply in the very uneventfulness of its civic history. Free from any dependence on a mediate lord, lay or ecclesiastical, it had developed its borough constitution without interference. Nor had it suffered the bitter internecine struggles, often marked by violence, which had occurred elsewhere. There were no common lands to excite the cupidity of the oligarchy or the jealous regard of the commonalty. The development of guilds which had been a major feature of urban life in England had made but little impression at Exeter. The origins of the local guilds may have been respectably ancient; certainly they abounded in the fifteenth century, usually holding charters from the city. But none of them attained to great power or wealth in the city except that of the tailors. For a few years in the middle of the fifteenth century this guild rivaled the civic corporation in power, but the latter was victorious at law and the tailors soon sank into obscurity.[20] In short, the city reached the opening of the sixteenth century with a tradition of moderation and of order, which had damped the fires both of class and of craft struggle and of friction between Church and city, keeping their disputes within the bounds of the courts and reducing to a minimum the social bitterness afloat in the society.

The early sixteenth century brought sweeping change in many areas of English life. In Exeter a sequence of important events unfolded quickly. On the very eve of the new century the city withstood the siege of the Cornish rebels and proved its loyalty to established order. Shortly afterward came the final adjustments in the borough constitution mentioned above. The eventful decade of the thirties brought with it the subversion of the old ecclesiastical order, and in 1536 the Priory of St. Nicholas was suppressed along with the friars' houses and St. John's Hospital.

---

ryche and endowed with ample large and greate possessions and ryches whereof by means of the ambytion and pryde of the bisshopps and prelates of the same no smale porcon hath ben consumed in usurpinge the lyberties and ffranncheses of and from the citie whose travells have ben allwaies to reduce the citie under there subiection."

[20] See Mrs. J. R. Green, *Town Life in the Fifteenth Century* (New York, and London, 1895), II, 172–181, and Youings, *Tuckers Hall* (chapter 4, note 5).

Coincident with the fall of the old religious order was that of the great house of Courtenay, the most powerful lords of the West. Their vast holdings in the country round about Exeter had made them influential neighbors. Most important of all, they controlled the manors along the river below the city, and in the fourteenth century installed weirs which effectively stopped shipping from coming up to Exeter. At the same time, as lords of the manor of Topsham they controlled the cranage of the port, the head of navigation in the Exe estuary. They were also owners of the little manor of Exe Island, close under the west walls of the city. It is impossible to know whether there is more than a coincidental connection between their fall in 1538 and the passage in 1540 of the Act of Parliament which authorized the removal of obstructions to navigation in the Exe.[21] At any rate the Courtenays were no longer proprietors of the weirs in question, and the way was open for reopening navigation between the city and the sea.

In 1535 and 1537 important changes in the city's status took place. In the former year,[22] the mayor, recorder, and those ex-mayors who ranked as aldermen were made justices of the peace with power to hear and determine felonies, trespasses, and misdemeanors. Two years later Exeter joined that select group of the greater cities, dignified by the title of counties in themselves.[23] The County of the City of Exeter now came into being; the mayor, recorder, and aldermen became justices of gaol delivery, while a sheriff of Exeter was added to the list of local dignitaries. The privilege not only conferred dignity but provided very practical advantages, for it gave the civic officials authority as justices within the episcopal fee.

Scarcely more than a decade later came the most dramatic and long-remembered event in Exeter's history—the Prayer Book Rebellion or, as it was locally called, the "Commotion" of 1549. There is no need to recount here the circumstances and events of that

---

[21] *Statutes of the Realm*, 31 Henry VIII, c. 4.

[22] No. XXXIII in the city charters calendared in the Historical Manuscripts Commission, *Report on the Record of the City of Exeter* (London, 1916), 5.

[23] *Ibid.*

rebellion.[24] From the point of view of Exeter's history its importance lies not so much in the dramatic events of the siege as in the firmness and courage of the city magistrates in the face of this emergency. The county gentry, led by the prestigious Carewes, had failed utterly in their efforts to stem the tide of insurrection. The feelings of the insurgents were reciprocated by a considerable group within the city, and the magistrates themselves—so Hooker tells us—were Catholic rather than Reformed in sympathy. The new Prayer Book was the instrument, not of a popular and puissant king, but of a divided regency, commanding none of the traditional loyalties of the people. Yet in the face of all these facts the magistrates stood firm, placing their abstract loyalty to the royal government and their own regard for social order ahead of personal sympathies. The Prayer Book Rebellion reveals the profound identification of the merchant magistrates with the cause of order, whatever its ideological dress, and illustrates the administrative ability of these men, backed by little of the traditional prestige of the gentry and almost solely dependent on their own talents and their own self-confidence. It is fair to suppose that this success was a psychological stimulus of some force to the governing class of the city, and an additional spur to the schemes of ambition and aggrandizement which already agitated them. Their loyalty won a very material reward, for in 1550 the royal government granted to the city the former Courtenay manor of Exe Island, the coveted lands lying just west of the city, partly on the mainland and partly on the river island.[25]

The sixteenth century also offered new and extensive opportunities to the businessmen of Exeter. In the past they had depended upon overseas trade and upon the city's position as a regional and ecclesiastical capital. Now they were presented with new possibilities. First of all, there was the increasing agricultural prosperity of Devonshire. This county was one of the last to feel the full effects of the great internal colonization of the Middle Ages. Only in the fifteenth century did the agricultural possibilities of its soil come to be fully

[24] See Frances Rose-Troup, *The Western Rebellion of 1549* (London, 1913). See also A. L. Rowse, *Tudor Cornwall* (London, 1941).

[25] No. XXVI in the city charters calendared in the Historical Manuscripts Commission, *Report*, 5.

exploited. No less important was the growing surplus of cloth for export pouring out of the villages and countryside of Devon.

The policy of the Tudors brought problems as well as opportunities. The religious conservatism behind the revolt of 1549 was part of the great pattern of religious and political revolution which shook the fabric of society, both nationally and locally. The decades of unrest and religio-political intrigue from 1530 onwards produced continuing vexations for the apprehensive magistrates of Exeter. Indeed, the increased scope of government under the Tudor monarchs and the ever-growing demands of the Crown laid a heavy load on the civic community. A stricter control over almost every aspect of life was to be enforced by order of the Crown through its local representatives, the mayor and Twenty-Four. And even though the local leaders heartily concurred in these policies, they often found them burdensome. Towards the end of the century war with Spain bore with special weight on Exeter. The exactions of ship money and other wartime levies 'as well as the burden of Parliamentary taxation had to be borne just when war had ruptured all the main trade routes of the Exeter merchants.

And, although the changes of the sixteenth century swept away one old enemy and weakened another, they also created new rivals. In place of the Courtenays stood the Russells, against whom the city fought a long legal battle over Topsham port. Nor were the bishops entirely to be despised, especially those prelates who had the ear of the Stuart kings. A problem of a different nature but of great importance, if Exeter were to share in the benefits of expanding trade, was the need for improved port facilities. And, at the same time, means had to be devised to funnel Devon's new cloth output into the hands of Exeter exporters.

The responsibility for facing this range of serious problems lay with the civic corporation. Well before 1500 the council of Twenty-Four, from among whom the mayor was annually chosen, had solidified their power. A self-perpetuating oligarchy, the council normally included the wealthiest and most influential citizens. Bound together by family and business ties, they were without rivals not only in the government of the city but in social and economic domination of the community. Most striking, throughout the century, is the unity of effort of this circle. Religious differences were openly acknowledged but never allowed to impair civic solidarity. Personal antipathies flared up from time to time, but there is no perceptible breach of the unvarying coöperation among the civic magnates.

This striking unity enabled the Exeter leaders to forge the right weapons for success in their struggle. Given identity of purpose, their position had many strengths. In itself, a chartered borough had a privileged position in English society, set apart by its rights of self-government specially granted by the Crown. This situation potentially offered at least three advantages: membership in the privileged orders of society; local control of local affairs; and protection from aristocratic interference. In addition there were the economic opportunities arising from the monopoly within the Exeter market enforced by the oligarchy. But all these favorable conditions needed careful handling. The bold, skillful, and successful exploitation of every vantage point and the creation of new ones by the Exeter magnates is the central theme of this book. Throughout the century, in one area after another, the city leaders secured new positions of strength for themselves and for the tight little circle of power of which they were the center.

Their advance began early in the century. In 1509 the Twenty-Four became by special royal grant a self-perpetuating body. Their political powers were augmented when Exeter became a county in itself in 1537. Later charter amendments served only to round off the legal and political position of the borough corporation. Closer to the heart of political realities was the city's relation to the monarch and Privy Council. Obviously important, it became doubly so under the comprehensive paternalism of the Tudors. The magistrates of Exeter became the recipients of a stream of orders flowing down from the Lords of Council giving direction on matters varying from tax collection to the administration of the sacraments.

For the most part obedience to these commands was a routine matter. But on occasion there was protest or grievance at the Exeter end of the line, or, more important, a grant of favor to be sought from the court. Then it was necessary to have friends in high places. In these circumstances the civic leaders developed to a fine art the political skills by which the weak manipulate the strong. In more than one instance they not only obtained what they sought but parried such dangerously influential rivals as the bishop. Here, as elsewhere, success begot a new self-confidence, a more assured stance in the difficult game of high politics.

The favors sought from royal hands were not solely political. With equal zeal the Exeter magnates pushed hard for economic vantage points. Their goals were always essentially the same, either to secure new market monopolies or to strengthen old ones. An instance is the building erected about 1538 to house the new weekly markets in yarn and cloth. This cost a suit before the Privy Council before the market was firmly established. But it served to channel a most important trade into the merchants' control. They complemented their new-won gains in domestic markets by a great step forward in foreign trade—the creation by royal charter of the Merchant Adventurers of Exeter in 1560. For once the lesser townsmen revolted against the will of the oligarchy, but a hasty regrouping of ranks gave decisive victory to the new company. This gain could only be exploited, however, by drastic improvement of Exeter's shipping facilities.

Since the thirteenth century the Exe below the city had been closed to shipping by a weir belonging to the Courtenay Earls of Devon. The Courtenays vanished in 1539 but more than mere destruction of the weir was needed to open the river to navigation. After long and costly experiment the city fathers boldly set out to build a canal from Exeter to the sea in 1563. It required many years and some thousands of pounds to overcome both natural and man-made obstacles. Expensive trial and error eventually solved the engineering problems; an almost equally costly lawsuit staved off the Earl of Bedford's bid for control of Topsham port on the Exe estuary. It took determined and long-sustained effort to achieve these successes but the corporation never showed signs of faltering, heavy as the costs were.

The sacrifices demanded by economic expansion were assumed

voluntarily; the onerous tasks of social regulation were imposed by the royal government. The Crown's determination to shore up the foundations of an hierarchic social order was based fundamentally on a deep-rooted world view, shared with fervent conviction by the Exeter oligarchs. This policy, lofty in purpose, amounted in execution to a very thorough policing of society. Religious or political heterodoxy was struck down ruthlessly. Vagrancy, idleness (whether voluntary or not), and sexual immorality were sternly suppressed by vigilant supervision and rigorous punishment. The Exeter magistrates were forever busy searching out and expelling unwanted immigrants from outside the city or punishing the misdoings of the disorderly within the city precincts. It was a time-consuming task but it was done willingly by magistrates who regarded this discipline as necessary for the maintenance of their own privileged position.

But their views of social responsibility were not solely negative. The Exeter merchants, particularly after the turn of the century, gave generously in gift and legacy to promote the welfare of the unfortunate, particularly the aged, and to encourage the young. Traditional endowments for outright relief in food, clothing, or shelter in an almshouse benefited the former. For the latter there were provided the possibilities of education and the means to launch a career once it was acquired. While some gave to endow the new schools of the 1630's, others established revolving loan funds to stake young merchants or artisans in their first ventures in earning a living. The common proviso in these philanthropic undertakings was that they should be controlled by the civic corporation. Government of the schools was wrested from ecclesiastical hands after a struggle which went up to the Privy Council; the various self-aid funds were carefully established under civic control.

Yet, aggressive and driving as their ambition was, the Exeter merchants were never revolutionaries, seldom reformers. In their maneuvers for advantage, they showed a genius for manipulating existing institutions to meet new needs. Indeed, in many ways the medieval civic structure was measurably strengthened and extended. Market control was widely expanded and tightened. The authoritarian and collectivist character of the community was re-affirmed and fortified. Not until the very end of our century do tokens of a new individualism begin to appear. And, in a larger sense, the masters of Exeter remained traditionalists, reverential of the existing order, anxious to identify themselves with it, and suspicious of any possible heterodoxy. In religion alone there was major change, accepted in Exeter because it bore the sacrosanct seal of royal authority. Only very late in our period does the yeast of Puritan enthusiasm begin to ferment in Exeter.

In brief, a tight oligarchy acting through the agency of the civic corporation controlled the little world of Exeter for its own ends. Its members showed their vigor and enterprise in many different ways during our century. Always their action was characterized by firm internal union and by the utmost use of their legal and political weapons to accumulate additional controls to their own advantage. They were generally rather successful, and only in the 1630's does their tough unity show signs of cracking. Their rewards were found in steadily increasing wealth, and in rising social prestige, accompanied by a marked gain in self-confidence. The details of this development are spelled out in the chapters of this book.

Chapter Two

The Framework of Government: Legal and Political

Every freeman of Exeter was aware that any exercise of his material rights and privileges rested on a complex legal fiction—the royally chartered corporation. The proper style "Mayor, Bailiffs and Commonalty of Exeter" gave legal title to a structure of power, complex in organization but supple in everyday operation. From a legal standpoint, the borough officers exercised authority by delegation from the Crown, a delegation that was in part a confirmation of immemorial custom and in part grants of specific privilege. It was customary to renew these grants at the beginning of each reign, an expensive and inconvenient procedure and a reminder that delegated powers were revocable. More vexing still were the uncertainties arising out of the complex accumulation of grants to which the city officers owed their authority and upon which the civic corporation based its whole existence.

A glance at the calendar of city charters will reveal something of this complexity.[1] The first of them dates from Henry II's reign, and by the death of Queen Elizabeth they numbered forty-two. The earliest ones dealt with freedom from custom in other boroughs; these were followed by the grant of fee-farm in the fourteenth century. Edward I granted the custody of the seal for the recognition of debts; his son allowed all pleas concerning lands, tenements, etc.,

[1] There is a printed calendar of these charters in the Historical Manuscripts Commission *Report on the Records of the City of Exeter*, Cd. 7640 (London, 1916), 1–8.

to be pleaded before the mayor and bailiffs. Edward IV conceded the goods and chattels of felons to the mayor and bailiffs. Grants of fairs also appear in the list of charters. Finally, in 1509 there was the writ of privy seal regulating electoral procedure.

Something like regularity was given this disorderly array in a series of important charters issued by Henry VIII and his son. First there was the grant of 1535, establishing the powers of the mayor and aldermen as justices of the peace within the city. Two years later followed the all-important concession of county status by which the mayor, recorder, and eight aldermen became justices of the peace and justices of gaol delivery within the new county. In 1549 the county obtained from Edward VI confirmation of its rights, including those granted by his father, and it was this document which Hooker called the "Grande Charter"[2] and which, apparently, he and his contemporaries regarded as the fullest and most authoritative statement of their county privileges. These grants accorded to the elected city officers the full extent of jurisdiction and breadth of power that the county justices of the peace, the principal agents of royal authority throughout the kingdom, held. They thus became full-fledged members of that body of officials, at once Crown appointees and local magnates, on which the Tudor monarchy principally depended.

From a legal point of view there now existed two entities, the County of the City of Exeter, with its jurisdictions carefully spelled out in the charters, and the Mayor, Bailiffs, and Commonalty of the borough of Exeter. The latter body depended primarily on custom; the functions and jurisdictions of its constituent elements were ill-defined. This situation, with its latent inconveniences and even dangers, was also remedied under Edward VI. In the charter of 1550 which granted the manor of Exe Island to the city as a reward for its proven loyalty in the preceding year, the Crown also bestowed formal incorporation on the Mayor, Bailiffs, and Commonalty.

[2] Printed in full in John Hooker (alias Vowel), *Description of the Citie of Excester*, ed. by W. J. Harte, J. W. Schopp, and H. Tapley-Soper, Devon and Cornwall Record Society (Exeter, 1919), II, 327–71. This confirmation rehearses in full the terms of the 1537 grant. Henceforth this work is referred to as Hooker, *History*.

Under that style they now became "one body perpetual and incorporate and one commonalty in matter and name." They were explicitly assured the rights of holding property and of suing and being sued. These two charters completed the long process by which the borough community gradually acquired full legal status as a chartered liberty within the realm of England. It was the end of a stage in the city's history; henceforth, the citizens could turn aside from the struggle to obtain maximum political and legal autonomy, hitherto a dominant theme in their history, for they had now attained their constitutional majority.

Sources of uncertainty about the city's legal position naturally continued to exist in a society so respectful of law and yet so untidy in its legal habits. Doubts troubled the city fathers from time to time, but not until the era of Charles I was anything more than a formal confirmation sought. In 1627, at a cost of £201, the city obtained a new and more comprehensive charter which remained the basis of its corporate existence until the act of 1835.[3] The defects of the older charters that had worried the Chamber were summed up in a petition to the King.[4] They were anxious that the election decree of 1509 should be incorporated in the charter, that additional powers delegated to justices of the peace by statutes passed since 1537 should be assured to the Exeter justices, and that "no other Justices of the Peace by association or otherwise intermeddle in the said city in that which to the office of Justice appertaineth." They sought also license to hold lands for charitable uses, and to purchase more land up to £100 per annum in value. The Chamber's petitions were favorably answered in the terms of the new charter.

Legal analysis, however, tells us little of the actual operation of the city's government. By the sixteenth century the original court with its two reeves had grown into an imposing array of officials.

---

[3] See ECM, RR 3–4 Charles I. It had cost £160 to secure confirmation by the new king only two years before (RR 2–3 Charles I). The new charter is printed in full in George Oliver, *History of Exeter* (Exeter and London, 1861), 296f. The Chamber was particularly anxious to prevent the bishop's being appointed a justice within the city as Bishop Cary had sought to be in 1623. For the full story of this, see below, pp. 254 seq.

[4] PRO, SP 16/84/39, 8 November 1627.

Foremost among them stood the mayor and the Twenty-Four, in the contemporary phrase, "the Mayor and his Brethren." (A synonymous term, often used, was the "Chamber of Exeter.")

This single house comprehended the select group of aldermen (*ex officio* justices of the peace) as well as the common councillors. From among their number were chosen the mayor, sheriff, and the receiver of the city. Chief among the executive officers were the recorder (*ex officio* an alderman and justice), the town clerk, and the chamberlain. A little lower in the scale were the three stewards of the city, the sword bearer, the stewards of the city manors of Awliscombe and Exe Island, the warden of Exe bridge, the warden of the Magdalen, and the lawyers of common counsel. There was also a body of town servants, the most dignified of whom were the four sergeants and the constables, but this group included also such humbler employees as the warden of the shambles, the market men, the gate porters, the waits, the bullring man, the scavengers, the common plumber, and the bellman. During times of military danger the city added a gunner and sometimes a muster master to its staff. In a somewhat different category was the mayor's chaplain, who drew livery and stipend from the city while usually holding the city living of St. Edmund on Exe bridge.

Later in the century the deputy lieutenants of the county of the city, invariably some three or four of the justices, were added to the top level of city officialdom. The social legislation of Elizabeth led to the appointment of an overseer of the poor, a warden of the house of correction (bridewell), and a keeper of the gaol. The commercial ambitions of the city brought about the establishment of the cloth hall and the appointment of a keeper for it. The building of a canal created the need for a supervisor there as well.

The choice of almost all these officers lay with the mayor and Twenty-Four, while they themselves, together with the bailiffs and the sergeants, were chosen under the provisions of the privy seal writ of 1509.[5] The details of this writ are clear enough. The King

[5] Printed as Appendix XI in B. Wilkinson and R. C. Easterling, *The Medieval Council of Exeter*, History of Exeter Research Group Monograph No. 4 (Manchester, 1931), 95.

appointed the present members of the Twenty-four to hold office for the balance of their lives. This group was empowered to remove a member for reason of poverty, disease, great age, or other reasonable cause, and upon such removal or upon the death of any member, to make replacement. The Twenty-Four thus became a self-perpetuating body, free to determine their membership as they chose and independent of any outside interference.

The election of the mayor was ordered thus. The council, on the Monday following Michaelmas, met and elected by written and private scrutiny two men, members of their own body, who had served either as mayor or as receiver. This being done, the two men so chosen were presented to the body of franchised citizens assembled in the Guildhall and they chose by acclamation one of the two. On the same day the new mayor and Twenty-Four also chose the four bailiffs (one of whom was receiver),[6] and three of the sergeants for the coming year.[7] By a separate process, provided for in the county charter of 1537, they elected the sheriff at the same time. Among the other officers, only the wardens of Magdalen almshouses and of Exe bridge served annual terms.

The formal structure of the city government is easily described; to analyze the daily round of politics and of administration is a more lengthy task. Clearly, the pivot of control was the Twenty-Four. First, it virtually selected the mayor from among its own number. Second, all the chief offices of power—the aldermancies, the justiceships, the lieutenancies, the receivership—were reserved to its members, while all the other officers were dependent upon the council for their appointment, for the direction of their duties, and for continuance in office. It had no rival. Between the Twenty-Four and the mayor there could be, as Professor Wilkinson points out,[8] no jealousy, for each of the Twenty-Four could in his turn fill the mayoral office. However, he goes on to suggest, this very absence of friction between the two chief powers in the government

[6] The Receiver was always a member of the Twenty-Four. The other bailiffs were usually not members, but appointment to this office was frequently the preliminary to entry into the Twenty-Four.

[7] The fourth sergeant was appointed by the new mayor.

[8] Wilkinson and Easterling, *The Medieval Council*, 51.

diminished the authority and activity of the council in favor of the mayor. Now that the Twenty-Four were securely established by royal authority as a part of the structure of government, they were content to leave the chief magistrate greater freedom of action. Professor Wilkinson goes so far as to assert: "The principle of monarchy seems to have triumphed in the sixteenth century in Exeter as it was triumphing in the country at large."[9] Hooker, too, seems to confirm this impression. In a rather obscure passage he declares that in times past the council had acted without the mayor and, indeed, this seems to have been the case in the alteration of electoral arrangements in 1496. But "this authority of theirs was in time of King Henry VII and VIII restrayned and by their orders under the privie Seal it was ordered that the Mayor should be always one of the Twenty-Four and then he with them and they with him and by his assent might do and procede to do all such things as should be thought good and expedient for the common wealth and good government of the same."[10] What evidence he had for these statements is not clear. The only writ preserved to us is that of 1509, which, although it provided for harmony of action between mayor and council, can hardly be said to have subordinated the latter body to the mayor.

Other evidence which might be helpful in determining the exact relation of mayor and Twenty-Four is denied to us. For earlier centuries, Professor Wilkinson was able to use the form of authorization for expenditure recorded in the receivers' rolls as an index of power, but the sixteenth-century rolls did not retain any authorization form. Likewise, now that councillors were no longer annually elected there was no election formula to afford a clue. Hooker does describe the general importance and functions of the council although his statements are rather vague. In writing of the ceremonies that attended the inauguration of a new mayor, he adds that the mayor had "twoo speciall places apointed unto him. . . ."[11] The first was the Guildhall where he sat to hear cases, both civil and criminal. The second was the council chamber "where he and his

[9] *Ibid.*, 49.
[11] *Ibid.*, 801.
[10] Hooker, *History*, III, 813–814.

brethren of xxiiii Do upon warninge to theym geven assemble and meete together for Matters concerninge the lands The Revenewes and profitts and all other things meet and necessarye for the salffitie and preservation of the whole Citie where the Mayor sytteth with his whole Company rounde aboute him." Then later, under the heading "What thinges the Mayor Maye Do and not Do"[12] the Exeter historian adds, "Also he cannot do any thinge Concerninge the causes of the Bodye of the Citie or for makenge of any Lawes or statutes for the good orderinge of the Citie without the Consent and presents of the xxiiiith or the more parte of theym," and again, "in all matters of importance Concerninge the prince and the state of the Comon welthe of this Citie to cause to be called and sommoned the Comon Counsell of the xxiiii and theirby their advise all things to be ordered and determyned." The final item in this list concludes, "Also without him nothinge Cann be Determyned in Comon Counsell neither cann they make any assembley of the xxiiii without his authoritie and Comaundement."

Besides the testimony of the Exeter antiquarian, there is little other evidence which remains to us for estimating the relative positions of mayor and councillors. The act books offer some help since they contain both the formula of enactment and the substance of business transacted in council. At each meeting of the council recorded in the act book there was, on the left-hand side of the page, a list of the councillors present, headed by the mayor. The minutes began with the invariable phrase, "which do wholly agree—" followed by the specific enactment. The antecedent of this phrase was, of course, the list of those present at the meeting. In this nothing distinguished the authority of the mayor from that of the council.

A more positive piece of evidence is afforded by an ordinance of March 1640, entitled "An act for matters for the public good even though the mayor will not consent."[13] This ordinance was passed by the Chamber. The gist of it was that henceforth business brought

[12] *Ibid.*, 804f.

[13] ECM, AB viii, 202. We employ modern pagination in all references to the Act Books.

up by the aldermen or councilmen was to be debated if a majority of the council approved, regardless of the mayor's vote. A penalty of £5 was to be levied on any mayor who failed to bring up such business within fifteen days. It is clear from the phrasing of the order that the mayor usually set the agenda for the council's meetings. How long he had exercised this right we cannot say. Obviously, it was a worthwhile advantage, but not so deeply rooted that the council could not wrest it from him.

As for the content of council business, it was of impressively wide range. Besides such internal problems as the election of new members (or the occasional expulsion of incumbents), the council was concerned with financial matters, with the management of the city property, with economic regulation, with ordinances for public order, provision for military obligations, purchase of grain against shortages, management of charities entrusted to the city, the building of the canal, and the appointment of city officers.

Financial problems consistently occupied a major portion of the council's time. Particularly important were the leases of city property and the farming of the various city customs, both of which were principal means for augmenting the city income as expenditures steadily rose. It is probably fair to say, considering the number of entries of this kind, that no lease of city property failed to come before the council. Likewise, the elaborate financial maneuvering which the city's mounting debts necessitated was subject to council control. It even considered such routine matters as the authorization for plumbing repairs to the water system or repairs on the walls. Here it was not a matter of specific allotments of funds, but of general permission to proceed which was customary. Again, specific authorizations of expense accounts for various city officials riding to London were made in council, and burgesses of Parliament were allowed their wages here. On the other hand, the often large sums disbursed yearly for legal purposes were authorized outside the council, for this kind of business was rarely noted in the act book and then with the briefest notices. Similarly, although general authorizations concerning the canal appeared in the act books, specific payments did not. The appointment of frequent committees of the council to survey and supervise the canal suggests that direct expenditure was in their hands. In short, most of the business concerning augmentation of income was transacted in the council, while a less thorough but quite extensive control was exercised over disbursement.

Economic regulations were also a regular item on the council agenda. The elaborate codes and tariffs of the market system were laid down item by item; and specific enforcement cases—particularly the offenses of "foreign bought and sold" and of nonpayment of custom—were judged. Petitions for the incorporation of guilds were deliberated on, and questions concerning the granting or revoking of franchise were settled in the council chamber.

Ordinances concerning public order were much less frequent, but when they appeared were usually lengthy and detailed instructions. The normal enforcement of police matters did not, of course, come before the council, especially after the establishment of the justice court. It is clear, though, that general policy in this regard was laid down in the council. Here also the related problems of social policy were settled in major outline. The building of the bridewell occupied the council's attention through all its stages, and they appointed the keeper and drew up the book of rules for the inmates. The administration of the city charities—even the admission of individuals to the almshouses—was within the council's jurisdiction. In times of shortage it authorized the purchase of grain. Lastly, there is no doubt that the appointment of city officials, of which we have already spoken briefly, always came before the council. Similarly, it approved the granting of pensions, such as those paid to the Cecils or the Carewes.

To sum up, the council gave extensive and detailed attention to most matters relating to finance, to the management of city property, and to problems of economic regulation. They gave less detailed supervision to problems of public order and social policy, but major decisions remained in their hands. Appointments were exclusively their business. Legal affairs or the details of negotiation which often accompanied them, all matters of justice, and the extensive investigative activity carried on by the magistrates at the behest of the Privy Council were matters seldom discussed in the council chamber.

This does not, of course, mean that all extraconciliar business was conducted by the mayor. Much of it passed through his hands and that of his fellow aldermen acting as justices or royal commissioners. Other, more strictly civic, affairs were conducted by committees appointed by the council from its own members, a device which became increasingly frequent as the century wore on. Regular committees audited the city accounts and those of the city manors and the city charities; others supervised canal construction or the management of the timber at Duryard Wood; still others carried on delicate legal negotiations such as those surrounding the suits over the canal. These committees certainly added to the efficiency of the council although they may, upon certain occasions, have concentrated important business in their own hands, thus shifting authority from the whole body of the council to themselves.

In summarizing the question of the balance of power between mayor and council, it would be incautious to push the parallel with the monarchy, suggested by Wilkinson, too far. The Exeter council certainly did not stand to the mayor as the Privy Council to the Queen. Aside from the fact that nothing in the formulae of the act books suggests this, we cannot suppose that the mayor was in a position to dominate the council in a manner analogous to that of a sovereign. An annually elected chief magistrate, chosen out of a small body of men who were his business, social, and (often) family intimates, could hardly assume airs of state during his brief term of office. The role of such a powerful figure as William Hurst, five times mayor, or the three Periams cannot be ignored, but their dominance in civic affairs arose not from official position but from wealth and, we may suppose, from force of personality. It was certainly true that the Twenty-Four no longer acted without the mayor, and probably the new dignities of the city gave its chief officer more extensive powers, wider duties, and loftier prestige than his predecessors had enjoyed. Nevertheless, it seems reasonable to say that, within the wide area of conciliar control, council and mayor acted as one body, a kind of grand committee, from which a few members were yearly delegated to the particular executive tasks of mayor, receiver, and sheriff, while the seniors in experience exercised the offices of justices and aldermen.

During the years from 1536 to 1603, some 163 men sat in the council for terms ranging from a few months to forty years. Or, in other words, the council renewed itself more than four, and nearly five, times. The bare figures do not give a complete picture, for they do not show the recurrence of office holding within a small group of families. In the total list no fewer than twenty-three families were represented by at least two members, and three families—the Smyths, the Martins, the Spicers—boasted four, five, and six members respectively. Thus, it will be seen that the charmed circle of office-holding families was more restricted than the figure of 163 suggests. On the other hand, admission of new members was not by any means difficult. There was a fair circulation of the available honours. Eighty-eight of the 163 held the mayoralty; one hundred and one rose to the somewhat lesser dignity of sheriff.

The attainment of these high civic dignities had been systematized by the sixteenth century. There existed a kind of *cursus honorum* through which each aspirant moved in his climb to the mayoral chair. The first step was almost always the office of steward (or bailiff) for which he did not even need to be a member of the Twenty-Four. There seems to have been no rule about the holding of this office. Sometimes, it preceded council membership by ten years or more; a few times it actually followed election to the Twenty-Four. After the stewardship the next step in the ascent was the shrievalty. Following that came the most burdensome and costly of the public offices, the receivership. This formidable obstacle cleared, the way was open for the mayoralty, and usually the highest magistracy followed two years after the receivership and six to seven years after the shrievalty. This pattern of promotion was a very regular one, and deviations were rare. Not by any means all completed it. We have seen that about half the council members of this period reached the mayoralty. Of those who went as far as the receivership, over two thirds passed on to the highest office. But in general the council, though an oligarchical and self-coöpting body, did possess a degree of flexibility which probably satisfied most of the inhabitants whose financial standing permitted them to aspire to membership, or beyond that, to office.

Entry into the council, though a coveted honor, brought with it tedious and sometimes weighty responsibilities. Membership in the council and, more particularly, a term in one of the executive offices, meant heavy burdens. Aside from the time-consuming tasks of attendance at council meetings[14] or service on one of the committees, there were financial obligations.[15] For instance, when it was necessary to purchase grain for the city's use, members usually had to advance the purchase money; the repair of one of the city weirs was financed in like manner. As we shall see in discussing city finances, the councillors had frequently to dig into their own pockets to meet crises in the treasury. Even though they were paid back, the councilors must have found these demands on their stock of ready cash burdensome, especially as money laid out for the city was usually earning nothing for them while it was in the city's hands. Consequently, members elected to the council were not always eager to serve, and those already serving occasionally sought release from office. Such release was not easily obtained. John Dyer, elected to the council in 1556, sought dismissal in 1563,[16] having previously been absent. The Chamber let him go with a five-mark fine.[17] In 1565, a senior member of the council, Hugh Pope, who had already held the offices of sheriff and receiver, refused to take the office of mayor and was released only under the penalties of a £20 fine and dismissal from the Twenty-Four.[18] In 1574, William Way, elected to the Twenty-Four in 1565, was about due to hold the receivership

[14] In the 1580's a meeting of the Chamber was held rather more frequently than once a month (thirteen meetings in a year).

[15] In 1579 a kind of entrance fine was imposed. Each member upon election had to provide a silver spoon worth 10s. for the common chest. More onerous was the custom that he should loan the city £20 for one year upon entrance to the Twenty-Four. See Chapter III.

[16] ECM, AB iii, 117.

[17] In the same year one of the eminent Prestwood family, the younger Thomas, declined to be sworn, but a fine of £6 13s. 4d. persuaded him to change his mind, and in 1564 he took office (AB iii, 148).

[18] AB iii, 162.

(although he had not been sheriff). Already he had been delinquent in attendance at the council, as a previous summons to attend indicates. In desperation he sought dismissal from the liberties of the city, claiming that he was unable to bear the burden of the receivership.[19] He was disfranchised and fined £10.[20]

The Chamber were not always so harsh in their attitude toward "decayed" or infirm members. In 1579, Richard Hellier was allowed to retire because of his infirmities without fine.[21] Similarly, in 1584, Hugh Wylsdome was allowed to resign and even to retain the councilman's perquisite of canon bread.[22] John Sampford, who had served as overseer of the canal, was evidently considered a special case, for he was not only discharged without fine but was even allowed a certain amount of annual free carriage on the canal.[23] Nevertheless, it apparently became customary for a retiring member to pay some kind of fine when leaving the Twenty-Four.[24] Retirement was not always voluntary; occasionally an inactive member was dismissed.[25] Altogether about fifteen of the 163 were either dismissed or resigned.

There is one case worth recording in full, not because of the importance of the issues but because it illustrates so neatly the kind of clash of personalities that could form the stuff of civic politics.[26] John Levermore was the member of a family that had already contributed one mayor; he himself was elected to the Twenty-Four in

---

[19] AB iii, 283 and 314.

[20] The story repeated itself with Henry Ellacott, sheriff in 1578–79, who sought dismissal from the Twenty-Four because of sickness. Apparently he was richer than Way, for this time the Chamber demanded £60 (AB iii, 431). In 1583 the Chamber readmitted Ellacott on the payment of £24 (AB iv, 426).

[21] AB iii, 431.

[22] AB iv, 446. "Canon bread" was baked at Christmas and Easter and distributed among the Twenty-Four with portions of wine. *OED*: "Canon," a "Pension, or Customary payment upon some religious Account," a "quit-rent."

[23] AB v, 341.

[24] This is assumed in an enactment of 1634 in which a member is allowed to resign without paying the customary fine. See AB viii, 19.

[25] See for instance the dismissal of aged aldermen Thomas Brewerton and George Perryman in 1590. AB v, 176 and 179.

[26] There is a full account of this affair in ECM, Book 55, which is not paginated. The account will be found under date 2–3 James I.

1574. As early as 1581 there was a note in the act book[27] that he had been disfranchised and imprisoned for abusing the mayor, but the penalty had been remitted. The real quarrel began when Levermore failed to obtain a lease of certain city property. He sued the successful bidder for the lease despite the mayor's efforts to arbitrate the issue. His suit was unsuccessful. Then, apparently out of anger at what he considered hard dealing, Levermore refused to attend Chamber meetings. Several successive mayors attempted to reconcile him but without success. Moreover, he took every opportunity to vent his spleen against the authorities. He brawled with private citizens in the streets, drove the chamberlain and a body of workmen from the city gravel pits at Northexe, claiming they were infringing on his property, and refused to pay the collector of the tenth and fifteenth, Nicholas Martin. Two law suits—one over the gravel pit, the other over the disputed tax payment—were instituted and lost by him.

Summoned by an outraged Chamber to appear before them in December 1589, he did so[28] only to declare that they were oppressors and then "departed contemptuously." In April 1590, the case was still pending, and Levermore was affirming his earlier charge against the house. Finally the Chamber struck at him with a rather futile display of wounded dignity, dismissing and disfranchising him "because he has broken sundry laudable acts of this house and has not well demeaned himself in this house."[29] In spite of his disfranchisement he continued trading, and when his goods were seized, appealed to Lord Chief Justice Popham. In the informal fashion so typical of Elizabethan government, the Chief Justice heard the case not in his official capacity, but as a private arbitrator, while a guest of Sir William Periam, the Lord Chief Baron (and member of a great Exeter family) at Fulford near Exeter. After hearing both Levermore and the civic officials, the Chief Justice held the disfranchisement to be good, but arranged for the former to be sworn again as a freeman and to have a reversion on the lease which had originally caused the quarrel. The reconciliation was

[27] AB iii, 28.　　　　　[28] AB v, 145.
[29] AB v, 169.

lasting, for in 1594 Levermore re-entered the Twenty-Four[30] and two years later attained the mayoral dignity. This little history measures the limits of the council's coercive power over one of its own members, although, in this case, it must be admitted they had to deal with a man of extraordinarily high and irritable temper.

Membership in the Chamber was not only a privilege but a responsibility not lightly to be cast aside. Exemption or dismissal was made a dearly bought privilege. Office was for most an eagerly sought goal, but it could become an irksome obligation. Certainly it required continued financial prosperity. Business ruin meant a corresponding loss of civic honors.

Besides these problems of recruiting and maintaining membership, the Chamber faced others of internal discipline. They lacked the machinery of parliamentary procedure necessary to ensure smooth handling of business—or perhaps, more accurately, they lacked the habitual attitudes that underlie the smooth enforcement of parliamentary order. At any rate, tempers flared and angry words passed. We may be amused by the spectacle of the staid elders of the Guildhall portraits calling each other "boy" or sometimes something stronger, but in that age it must have been a more serious problem. Social decorum was one of the hallmarks of degree, and, hence, all the more imperative for a class of parvenus. With this in mind the council had as early as 1518 passed a standing order[31] imposing a fine of 40s. on any member calling another "otherwise than by his proper name or brother or such other like honest name." Fines under this order were not infrequent[32] and in one case a councilman was imprisoned for forty days.[33] After being reprimanded for name-calling in the council chamber and fined the usual 40s., he had defied the sheriff, the constable and even the mayor's direct command.

It was also necessary to provide for some elementary order in

[30] AB v, 290.
[31] Printed in Hooker, *History*, III, 931.
[32] See for examples AB ii, 89, 306, 315; AB iii, 28; and AB v, 348.
[33] AB ii, 366.

council business, so in 1557 it was decreed that everyone should have his right to speak.[34] If "any of the Twenty-Four do interrupt him of his speaking or talk until such time as he shall end his full declaration of his mind which he shall then take in hand to declare" the interrupter was to be fine 12d. by the mayor.[35] Decorum had to be maintained in public, too, especially in the feast-day processions to St. Peter's Cathedral. In 1541 a schedule for processions was published: the mayor and ex-mayors in order of "auntientie" of office, then the sheriff and ex-sheriffs, and so the rest, each according to his seniority of election.[36] Even the wives of the council were assigned their places by an act of 1543, for the good ladies had been at "variance and strife" in the matter.[37] Orders were published also for the proper apparel of the civic dignitaries, crimson and scarlet for the receivers and sheriffs or those who had held those offices, violet for the stewards.[38] This requirement seems not to have been popular, for later there were frequent repetitions of the injunction.[39]

It was also thought necessary to take strong measures to protect secrecy of council business. Although under an order of Henry VII's time disclosure of council secrets was made punishable,[40] it was not until 1558 that an official oath of secrecy was demanded from each member of the council as well as from the clerk, recorder, and chamberlain.[41] Provision for a quorum was not made until 1630 when it was provided that no important act was to be repealed, altered, or renewed without the affirmative vote of thirteen members actually present.[42]

During this whole period no serious efforts were made to challenge the exclusiveness of the oligarchy. Almost the only indication of open discontent is a trivial one. An entry in the act book for

[34] AB ii, 315.
[35] Tardiness at meetings was also punishable by a small fine. See AB viii, 59.
[36] AB ii, 95.
[37] Printed in Hooker, *History*, III, 907.
[38] Printed in Hooker, *History*, III, 869.
[39] In AB v, 292, there is recorded a 40s. fine for failure to obey this injunction.
[40] Hooker, *History*, III, 890.
[41] AB ii, 341. Printed in Hooker, *History*, 890.
[42] AB vii, 767.

1 March 1560 records a conversation which Henry Ellacott had overheard about twelve months past.[43] A certain William Pynnefold, goldsmith, thought himself much aggrieved of the Chamber and talked of a time when the citizens on election day had chosen, not one of the two men put forward by the masters of the Twenty-Four, but a third, a poor man, whose expenses they offered to pay from their own pockets "and so the same man continued in spite of them all in office for that year." He added, he was afraid that when the masters came to electing a new mayor they would be so served. We hear nothing further of the matter, and doubtless it was no more than the muttering of a disgruntled man, but it was typical of the age and of the men, that the aldermen concerned themselves with finding out all possible details in the matter.[44]

The history of the Chamber during this period is very uneventful indeed compared to the struggle that had raged around its claims to power in the fifteenth century. The changes of the sixteenth century were less dramatic and less important but not without significance. There is evidence of a serious effort to increase both the prestige and the efficiency of the body. The very expansion of records—and the appointment of a special guardian for them in the person of the chamberlain—bears witness to a desire to rationalize and to systematize administration. Very practical evidences of this are seen in the frequent use of committees, both the standing committees of audit and the *ad hoc* ones, to which members with special interests or talent were appointed. By the end of the sixteenth century the Chamber of Exeter was an effective legislative and executive body, handling a wide range of different kinds of business with expedition and skill. We shall see more of this as we examine community life in detail. This skill in administration reflects the added experience in government that the Chamber acquired through the sixteenth century as well as the confidence that arose from their status as a chartered liberty, now cleared of ambiguity and secured beyond question. For the Chamber this was a period when their

----

[43] AB iv, 14.

[44] It may have had something to do with the struggle over the Merchant Adventurer charter which was then under way.

new position was consolidated and the opportunities it provided initially were exploited.

Next to the Twenty-Four in constitutional importance stood the mayor. In discussing his relationship with the council we have already indicated much of the character of his office. The official style of the mayoral proclamations, in which he always called himself the "King's Lieutenant in this city," suggests the dignity and the legal prestige of the office. The mayor was the executor of the royal will as made known to him in proclamations or royal letters, which he proclaimed publicly with all his panoply of sword and hat of estate, sergeants, and maces. His duties were wide[45] since he was *ex officio* a justice of the peace and of gaol delivery, clerk of the market, escheator of the city, general warden of orphans, and general overseer of the poor.

His judicial functions must have consumed a considerable portion of his time. Each Monday he sat in the Guildhall to hear civil and criminal pleas. Besides this purely municipal court, he also presided over the justices' court in their quarter sessions.[46] Likewise he directed their hearings when they sat as an investigating commission of Crown officers in such matters as taking evidence on the Carewe conspiracy, questioning sailors landed from Spanish waters, or hearing arguments on the proposed Merchant Adventurer charter. In addition his duties in regulating the economic life of the city, which bulk so large in Hooker's catalogue, also consumed much time even though he had various subordinates who handled the day to day routine of the markets.

But in one area the mayor bore a significantly heavier burden than his colleagues for, as chief magistrate, he stood responsible before the Privy Council in London and before the Lord Lieutenant locally. His duties increased especially in time of war. The type of situation which often confronted him is illustrated by an incident

[45] Hooker, *History*, III, 804–806. This is a catalogue of "what things the Mayor Maye Do and not Do."

[46] There was evidently no clear distinction between the kinds of cases heard in each of these courts. Criminal cases of all types seem to have been heard in the mayor's court, but possibly there was a gradual shift to the justice court as time went on.

of 1592. A captured galleon had been brought into Plymouth and Robert Cecil, then a young man on his first commission, was sent down to take care of the Queen's share of the booty. He found, as in other similar cases, that most of it had already disappeared. In a letter[47] that gives the impression of an officious and rather bumptious youngster showing off his authority among the provincials, he declared that he left an impression at Exeter by his rough dealing with the mayor and by stopping all travelers to and from the west. One can imagine the feelings of the distraught mayor, caught between the stripling Cecil and the impossibilities of the latter's demands. Another mayor, Simon Knight,[48] found himself in trouble when he was accused of being accessory to the escape of a notorious pirate from Exeter Gaol. There will be more to say about the mayor as royal agent in discussing the incidence of royal authority in Exeter. But we cannot doubt that his functions in this role had become the most important of his office by the late sixteenth century.

The tendency for a few families to monopolize power was even more marked in the case of the mayoralty than in the council.[49] During one hundred and one yearly terms (from 1540 to 1640, inclusive), in three of which a death in office occurred, only seventy-four men actually held the mayoral office. A second term was common enough. Nineteen returned at least once to office, and in 1564 second terms became the subject of a Chamber order.[50] It was decreed that because of the heavy burden of the office, no one should hold it within eight years of his last service. Consequently the years of service usually fell about a decade apart. Two terms was not the limit of service by any means. Besides the elder Hurst, who served

[47] *Calendar of State Papers Domestic, Elizabeth*, III, 272.

[48] PRO, SP 12/144/7.

[49] For the lists of mayors and sheriffs I have relied on Oliver, *History of Exeter*, 226-235 and 237-241 respectively. For the receivers I have used the manuscript list in Moore's catalogue of the city muniments in the Exeter City Library, supplemented by the steward's (bailiff's) lists in Samuel Izacke, *Remarkable Antiquities of the City of Exeter*, 3d. ed. (London, 1734).

[50] AB iii, 150. In 1586 (AB iv, 495), this was clarified by a further order to the effect that no man was to be re-elected mayor within nine years after the day he was chosen.

no fewer than five terms,[51] there were seven who served three terms. It is evident that the mayoralty was a dearer prize than the lower offices and attainable for a considerably smaller number.

One reason was the heavy financial burden of the mayoralty. We have already seen the eagerness of the poorer members of the council to escape this duty, even at a heavy fine. The mayor received a yearly stipend which at the beginning of our period was £26 13s. 4d. per annum.[52] Successive increases raised it to £133 6s. 8d. in 1590 but it was abated to £120 in 1596.[53] These increases reflected in part the heavy burdens of the mayor's office in the war years, in part the swelling consequence of the chief magistracy of a prospering city.

The weight of the mayor's social burdens is apparent from various entries in the act books. The entertainment of distinguished guests was the chief item.[54] In 1585, for instance, no less a personage than the Pretender of Portugal, Don Antonio, had to be lodged in the mayor's house,[55] and in 1588 three great Lords of the Council,[56] the Earls of Huntingdon and Essex and Sir Francis Knollys, were similarly entertained. The Earl of Bedford was in the habit of recommending friends or connections of his, such as a servant of the Prince of Piedmont[57] or a Spanish marquis,[58] to the city's hospitality. The city fathers probably breathed a sigh of relief when the winds carried Philip of Spain eastward to Southampton in 1554, for they had received a letter from Bedford[59] desiring them to prepare for the reception of that Prince with a train of some 400 or 500. But besides these great personages there was a steady flow of lesser dignitaries who had to be received and entertained by the mayor. There were the twice yearly visits of the justices of assize

[51] Two of these terms fell before 1540. He served in 1524, 1535, 1545, 1551, and 1561.
[52] ECM, RR 3–4 Edward VI.
[53] See AB v, 173, and AB v, 354.
[54] The mayor was provided with a cook paid by the Chamber.
[55] AB iv, 478.
[56] AB v, 122.
[57] HMC Rep, 34, Letter 33, 17 May 1553.
[58] HMC Rep, 38, Letter 44, 4 August 1558.
[59] HMC Rep, 35, Letter 34, 26 June 1554.

as well as the occasional appearances of the Lord Lieutenant— an office held first by the Bedfords and later by the Earl of Bath —which usually meant gifts of sugar loaves to the ladies, wine to the gentleman himself, and a mayoral festivity of some sort. There were the county magnates to be suitably entertained, Carewes and Champernouns, Chichesters and Raleighs, as well as commissioners from London, like young Cecil in 1592. In an age that placed high value on the pomp and circumstance of social life, an ambitious civic corporation had to be prepared to spend liberally to maintain its prestige. The city might piously regret but secretly rejoice that it had not to face the ruinous distinction of a royal visit from Gloriana herself.

There were other expenses for the mayor to bear, those of business, of journeys to London, of messengers sent there, the costs of tours of inspection of city property, and, of course, clerical charges. The mayor, even more than his brethren of the council board, was liable to be called upon for loans to the city in moments of financial straitness. Nor can we forget the indirect burden imposed upon a busy merchant by a year's distraction from his own affairs.

Of the mayoral election we know little more than the formal procedure. The ballot papers of the election were required to be burned as soon as the two council candidates were chosen,[60] but in one case, the election of Michaelmas, 1553, someone wrote into the act book the names of the several candidates and the votes which each had received.[61] Five men had obtained votes, but only two any sizable number, so that there was no question as to who should be presented to the freemen. We can only guess at the possible struggles over this choice within the oligarchy. They were softened though, we may suppose, by the remembrance that the office would be vacant again within a twelvemonth.[62]

[60] Hooker, *History*, III, 796.
[61] AB ii, 70.
[62] Not everyone was covetous of the mayoral office. John Periam had to be persuaded to return from London in 1587 to accept the mayoralty (AB iv, 520). A more serious case was that of Thomas Walker, elected mayor at Michaelmas, 1625. He had served twice previously. He alleged as grounds of

The completion of his term of office did not end the responsibilities of a mayor, for he remained an alderman and justice of the county.[63] The origins and history of the aldermanic office in Exeter during the Middle Ages are not clear. But in 1535 they were named justices of the peace within the city, and in 1537 were mentioned at length in the charter of the county of the city. The eight of them (the recorder ranked as ninth *ex officio*) were elected by the Twenty-Four from the ex-mayors for an indefinite term. They were granted the same privileges and powers as the aldermen of London by the charter and like them were to be justices of gaol delivery.

Within the borough government the aldermen also had important functions. Each of them was assigned to a quarter of the city and made responsible for the maintenance of order and punishment of misdoing in that district.[64] As Hooker observed, "Their Jurisditions ar rather inquisitive than judiciall";[65] they were really supervisors of police, meant to keep strict watch over any possible disturbance of the peace and to oversee the maintenance of clean and unobstructed streets, the observance of price and weight regulations, and the other details of everyday life in their respective quarters.[66] Particularly, they were charged with that problem which so haunted Tudor public authorities, the arrival of strangers. All strangers coming to Exeter had to be examined by the aldermen as to their past dwelling place, trade and prospects, before being

---

refusal that he was no longer a property owner in the city. Eventually the Privy Council compelled him to return; in the interval Ignatius Jurdaine, a former mayor, served in his place.

[63] In 1579 provision was made for the incoming mayor in case there were already eight aldermen. The least senior was to step down and not be an alderman that year (AB iii, 479).

[64] In September 1549, doubtless in the aftermath of rebellion, it was directed that each alderman should have a deputy, since he could not be in every part of his quarter when disorder occurred. Thus the two aldermen in each quarter appointed two deputies from the members of the Twenty-Four. See AB ii, 208, and the renewal of the order in AB iii, 122.

[65] Hooker, *History*, III, 812.

[66] They were also to see that each man had on hand his required weapons for the view of armor and also the ladder and leathern buckets required in each household in case of fire.

allowed to rent any lodging in the city. As we shall see, this duty was taken very seriously.[67] They were, in short, the police officers of a society deeply concerned with the regulation of its social and economic life. They bore immediate and direct responsibility for the preservation of that regulated structure.

Next in formal dignity to the mayor and aldermen stood the four stewards of the city. Elected for a year's term at the same time as the mayor, they were chosen by the council, but were not necessarily members of that body. It was required only that they be "franchised men and of good name and fame."[68] Their role in the city government seems not to have been so eminent as their dignity. Their principal function was the holding of the provosts' court, although they also attended the mayor in his own court.[69] In this court they heard civil cases: debts, trespasses, etc. They were also clerks of the market and responsible for such matters as the lighting of candles at doorsteps in the evening. They do not appear prominently in the records of the city, outside the rolls of their own court, but we may assume that they went on performing their ancient routines of office throughout this era, contributing their share to the complicated task of maintaining public order.

Of the individual officers of the city the one next in importance to the mayor was the receiver-general. His duties were onerous, for the receiver was charged with the collection of all the city revenues. Moreover—and this is the more important consideration—he was liable for all expenditures. In other words he undertook during his year of office to be personally responsible for appropriations authorized by the Chamber or required by permanent city obligations, whether or not the revenues provided sufficient funds to meet these requirements. Hence he was often compelled to pay large sums out of his own pocket in order to meet current city expenses. Very frequently, at the end of the fiscal year, he was the creditor of the city for a considerable sum. Repayment might be several years forthcoming. His yearly fee was but 39s. The receivership was, in

[67] The aldermen were required to hold twice each year wardmoots with a jury to inquire into misdemeanors.

[68] Hooker, *History*, III, 791.

[69] *Ibid.*, 807.

short, the most burdensome of the city offices, and the mayoralty, which usually followed it within a year or two, might legitimately be regarded as a reward for service in the borough treasury. Fortunately it was held but once.

Three other major officials of the city remain to be mentioned. Of one, the town clerk, not a great deal need be said. Hooker summed up his duties, declaring them to be "Like a skillful mariner to prick the card and to set the compass and to advertise and instruct the master how and in what order he is to keep his course and make his way."[70] His term was for life[71] and in the whole period from 1538 to 1620 two men, father and son, Richard and Edward Hert, filled the office. Along with the newly instituted chamberlain, the town clerk formed the city's permanent civil service, to use a modern term. The important although not conspicuous role which these two officers played in the city government by virtue of long service and experience, is evidenced by frequent appearances on the various *ad hoc* committees.

The chamberlain's office was created by an act of the Chamber of September 1555,[72] and its first holder was the most famous of Exeter's antiquaries, whose work is the source of most of our information about the city during his long lifetime, John Hooker. The new office was created in part to provide for the care of the orphan wards of the city and their affairs, and partly to assist in the adminis-

[70] *Ibid.*, 816.
[71] ECM, Book 55 contains an account of the Town Clerk's fees, under the entries for 1575. They are as follows:

	s.	d.		s.	d.
Pension	40		"For the rentall"	5	
Liveries (Summer & Winter)	32		Duryard	14	4
			St. Nicholas	4	8
Parchment for Guildhall courts	10		Exe bridge	10	
For enrolling same	13	4	Exe Island	6	8
For making city's accounts	20		Town Customs	6	8
			Awliscombe	5	8
			Magdalen	6	8

The total is £8 14s. 0d. By 1637 his pension was £4 15s. per annum. Additional rewards sometimes fell his way. For exceptional labors the Town Clerk received £40 in 1638 (AB viii, 151).
[72] Hooker, *History*, II, 285.

tration of the city's recently augmented properties. Along with his
chamberlainship, Hooker held the bailiwick of St. Nicholas Fee[73]
and shortly afterwards that of Exe Island as well as the custody of
Duryard Wood, with fees totaling more than nine pounds per
annum. Fortunately his duties included custody of the records of
the city, and thanks to his patient care and civic pride the vast store
of Exeter documents was put in order and catalogued for the uses
of posterity. We can hardly overestimate the influence of a civil
servant with so many offices in his hand, assured by his birth of
entry into the civic aristocracy, and by his learning and experience
of a respected place there. He was destined to fill this place and to
appear in all important civic affairs for nearly half a century, until
his death in 1600. His successors were not so distinguished personally but equally important as civic officers. The casual fees of the
office had become so valuable that they were revoked when a new
chamberlain was appointed in 1636 and replaced by a yearly salary
of £20.[74]

The third of the great appointive offices of the city was that of
recorder. This officer's duties were, of course, largely legal and he
was always a common lawyer. Much of the business he transacted
for the city was carried on in the law courts at Westminster, but he
could travel down at the necessary times for quarter sessions, or send
a deputy. Moreover, he was usually assisted by several additional
lawyers appointed counsel to the city at a yearly fee. His legal learning gave him a commanding place on the justices' bench while his
London connections made him a useful link with the great world
there. The office was always granted to a lawyer with some local
connections, either in the city or in Devon. The prominent county
family of Dennys held it for a good part of the sixteenth century. In
the early seventeenth century it was held by one of the Martins, a
very eminent civic family. The recorder's salary was £10 per annum
at the end of our period, but he received frequent gifts for particular
services besides the legal fees which might come to him as represen-

[73] AB ii, 336.
[74] AB viii, 86.

tative of the city in particular cases.[75] The Chamber was anxious here as in other matters to avoid dealing with a complete stranger. From the point of view of a rising young West country lawyer in the capital, the connection must have been a good one. In several cases it provided him with a Parliamentary seat.

Of the host of lesser city servants who carried out the orders of the council and the principal officers, little need be said here. Some, such as the market men, will be mentioned in other connections. The duties of the common sergeants, of the constable, of the gate porters, of the scavengers, or the plumber hardly require explanation.

By the close of the sixteenth century the specialists who formed the nucleus of the city's officialdom had added much to the tradition of administrative practice which had already been built up by the medieval generations. Under them the act books steadily expanded in volume and detail while the receivers' rolls were supplemented by account books listing very item of expenditure or receipt. Neither the continuity of this practice nor the continuity of a permanent civil service would be broken in the future. These developments are another aspect of the maturing process by which the civic government gained in strength and effectiveness in this century.

Last, and in the political scheme quite the least, came the freemen. How small a part they played in the political life of the city has been made evident. Their only power of control over the government was their meager share in the mayoral election. True, freedom of the city was necessary for office holding (or for qualifying a burgess in Parliament from Exeter), but, as we have seen, this did not open the city offices to any but a small minority of the freemen. Probably this was not a serious deprivation for the freemen. As Professor Wilkinson has pointed out, there had been no time in the past when they had enjoyed political power in the city, and, indeed, the rights of the freemen were primarily economic. What really distinguished them from the nonfreemen was their right to trade

[75] For instance, in 1635 the recorder for his great pains at the Council board (before the Privy Council) was given £20 (AB viii, 51). In 1637 for his work on a suit he was granted as a gift £15 (AB viii, 115).

and deal freely in the city markets without payment of a fine or of city duties. The nonfreeman was in Hooker's eyes a "foryner," one outside the economic privileges of the city.

There were three ways in which one could become a freeman.[76] First, the eldest sons of freemen, provided they dwelt in the city, became free after the death of the father. Second, there was freedom by apprenticeship. After the usual seven years and upon payment of a small fee, the apprentice could receive citizenship by the testimony of his master. Last, there was the method of purchase. For a payment of not less than 20s. an artificer could buy his freedom, but for the merchant the fine might be whatever the magistrates set. Several instances of such fines occur in the act books. Thomas Brewerton, afterwards magistrate and mayor, paid for his citizenship in 1563 the sum of £20;[77] two years later John Pope paid £10.[78] Sometimes, a trader of some consequence lived and traded in the city without being a citizen, for in 1546 we have an instance[79] of an alternative being presented to one William Reynolds, who was to pay £4 for his freedom or else 6s. a quarter as a shop fine. In this same year a general order was passed requiring any person selling wares within the city to become a freeman within fourteen days or else pay a shop fine.[80] These regulations lead one to believe that control over the trading community in the city was not so strict as custom demanded that it be. Of quite another nature was the free admission of outsiders in order to allow them to hold office in the city. Sir Robert Denys, recorder, and Sir Peter Carewe, burgess in Parliament, are examples of this type of admission.

The general impression left us is that the privileges of freemen of Exeter were not so highly valued or strictly enforced as they had been at an earlier era. Nevertheless, the freemen continued to form a privileged group within the city, and most of the economic regulation of the city's life was designed for their benefit.

The administrative, like the constitutional, structure of the city had attained all its major characteristics by the sixteenth century.

[76] Hooker, *History*, III, 788.
[77] AB iii, 125.
[78] AB iii, 161.
[79] AB ii, 147.
[80] AB ii, 146.

It was staffed by a group of professional civil servants, guided by long established routines. Under their guidance a perceptible process of rationalization was carried on in the handling of accounts and records, while at the same time the legislative body of the city undertook a similar task in its procedures, by clarifying its rules and by the development of the committee system. Both legislative and administrative branches were to prove competent to deal with the additional burden of government imposed during the Elizabethan era. Our survey of the city government would not be complete, however, without a discussion of fiscal methods and policy.

Chapter Three

The Framework of Government: Fiscal

At best, the fiscal history of an English borough is likely to be prosaic. Neither the sums expended nor the purposes for which they were employed engage the imagination. Accounts, totaling in all a few hundred pounds annually, and filled with such items as the repair of the gaol or the beadles' wages, have not even the redeeming quality of quaintness. Nevertheless, they demand serious attention, for nowhere else are the purposes of the civic oligarchy more succinctly summed up than in the dry columns of pounds, shillings, and pence of the receivers' rolls. Nothing else so clearly reflects the expansive drive and the bold self-confidence of the Exeter merchants as the risky maneuvers by which they eked out a relatively inflexible income to meet the ever-increasing costs, not only of ordinary civic expenses, but also of their own ambitious and sometimes extravagant schemes.

The facts of their fiscal history are plain. (See Table I.) In the century 1540–1640, expenditure was increased more than fourfold. Average annual expenditure in the decade of the 1540's was £227; in the last decade of Elizabeth's reign, £847; in the decade ending in 1640, it amounted to £1,082, almost a five-fold increase. A high proportion of this increase was due to the steady rise of prices, but the Chamber's own enterprises accounted for a great deal. Their most ambitious project (and most costly) was the canal between Exeter city and the estuary. But this was only the largest item of extraordinary outlay in the period; to it the Chamber added a long

TABLE I.—*Revenues (pounds) of the City of Exeter, 1540–1640*[a]

Fiscal year	Total income	Total expenditure	Surplus	Deficit
31–32 Hen. VIII	258	269		11
32–33 Hen. VIII	Missing			
33–34 Hen. VIII	220	187	33	
34–35 Hen. VIII	217	180	37	
35–36 Hen. VIII	213	162	51	
36–37 Hen. VIII	302	235	67	
37–38 Hen. VIII	229	180	49	
38 Hen. VIII–1 Ed. VI	368	263	105	
1–2 Ed. VI	327	252	75	
2–3 Ed. VI	238	212	26	
3–4 Ed. VI	285	363		78
4–5 Ed. VI	327	358		31
5–6 Ed. VI	256	272		16
5–6 Ed. VI–1 Mary	Missing			
1 Mary–1 & 2 P.&M.	379	394		25
1 & 2–2 & 3 P.&M.	409	321	88	
2 & 3–3 & 4 P.&M.	Missing			
3 & 4–4 & 5 P.&M.	440	406	34	
4 & 5–5 & 6 P.&M.	Missing			
5 & 6 P.&M.–1 Eliz.	378	355	23	
1–2 Eliz.	431	385	46	
2–3 Eliz.	420	380	40	
3–4 Eliz.	384	371	13	
4–5 Eliz.	734	739		5
5–6 Eliz.	442	367	75	
6–7 Eliz.	531	482	49	
7–8 Eliz.	419	487		78
8–9 Eliz.	453	547		106
9–10 Eliz.	548	519	29	
10–11 Eliz.	774	820		46
11–12 Eliz.	361	462		101
12–13 Eliz.	542	614		72
13–14 Eliz.	444	749		305
14–15 Eliz.	380	453		73
15–16 Eliz.	528	589		61
16–17 Eliz.	602	657		55
17–18 Eliz.	512	516		4
18–19 Eliz.	474	568		94
19–20 Eliz.	472	508		36
20–21 Eliz.	759	690	69	
21–22 Eliz.	627	614	13	
22–23 Eliz.	755	885		130

TABLE I.—*continued*

Fiscal year	Total income	Total expenditure	Surplus	Deficit
23–24 Eliz.	503	799		296
24–25 Eliz.	495	674		179
25–26 Eliz.	1,024	1,027		3
26–27 Eliz.	760	667	93	
27–28 Eliz.	626	635		9
28–29 Eliz.	676	688		12
29–30 Eliz.	512	463	49	
30–31 Eliz.	929	981		52
31–32 Eliz.	644	702		58
32–33 Eliz.	581	697		116
33–34 Eliz.	564	536	28	
34–35 Eliz.	836	837	1	
35–36 Eliz.	787	895		108
36–37 Eliz.	904	1,044		140
37–38 Eliz.	745	796		51
38–39 Eliz.	750	791		41
39–40 Eliz.	994	1,106		112
40–41 Eliz.	600	634		34
41–42 Eliz.	736	770		34
42–43 Eliz.	842	788	54	
43–44 Eliz.	1,114	1,057	57	
44 Eliz.–1 James I	681	811		130
1–2 James I	759	793		34
2–3 James I	820	756	64	
3–4 James I	1,031	1,105		74
4–5 James I	872	840	32	
5–6 James I	1,304	1,417		113
6–7 James I	1,306	1,228	78	
7–8 James I	1,052	1,032	20	
8–9 James I	993	930	63	
9–10 James I	1,407	1,275	132	
10–11 James I	Missing			
11–12 James I	1,082	906	176	
12–13 James I	1,287	1,214	73	
13–14 James I	957	1,042		85
14–15 James I	1,145	1,249		76
15–16 James I	1,528	1,476	52	
16–17 James I	901	845	56	
17–18 James I	840	837	3	
18–19 James I	807	834		27
19–20 James I	1,014	1,010	4	
20–21 James I	864	777	87	

TABLE I.—*continued*

Fiscal year	Total income	Total expenditure	Surplus	Deficit
21–22 James I	782	776	6	
22 James I–1 Charles I	1,015	905	110	
1–2 Charles I	631	678		47
2–3 Charles I	1,222	1,189	33	
3–4 Charles I	1,353	1,365		12
4–5 Charles I	918	913	5	
5–6 Charles I	1,774	1,679	95	
6–7 Charles I	893	947		54
7–8 Charles I	823	772	51	
8–9 Charles I	729	657	72	
9–10 Charles I	1,135	1,100	35	
10–11 Charles I	787	964		177
11–12 Charles I	828	814	14	
12–13 Charles I	1,524	1,391	133	
13–14 Charles I	2,219	1,566	653	
14–15 Charles I	976	1,266		290
15–16 Charles I	1,280	1,202	78	
16–17 Charles I	961	1,086		125

* The receiver was charged on the income side with all moneys due the city, but he was allowed on the expenditure side for due rents not paid. Hence, the expenditure figure represents total expenditure plus this allowance.

list of smaller ones, ranging from the sheer vainglory of the new Guildhall to the sober necessities of a workhouse and a new gaol. There were, of course, also the ordinary running expenses of government to be met. The city's property, most of all its elaborate network of weirs controlling the flow of Exe, required constant maintenance and repair. The tasks of government, too, demanded an ever larger staff of civic officials and servants, whose wages mounted steadily. Lastly, no corporate body in that litigious age, least of all the busy governors of Exeter, could avoid frequent and costly lawsuits. And we must remember that the civic budget did not exhaust the sum of public financial burdens, for the heavy costs of war at the end of the century and the permanent obligation of poor relief were not included on the receiver's rolls.

There follows an analysis of the city's fiscal condition in the century under study. Both income and outgo are examined in some detail, but particular attention is given to the new sources of revenue exploited in order to meet the added costs of government. We can begin by looking at revenue. Basic income figures roughly paralleled those for outgo. In the decade 1540–50, receipts averaged about £265 a year; in the last decade of Elizabeth this figure had risen to £815; between 1630 and 1640 the annual average was £1,126. (We may note by comparison that in 1633 the Chamber of London had an income of £98,000 and spent £70,000. Bath spent about £162 in the 1570's and Leicester had about £180 to spend after 1589; Newcastle had £5200 in the 1640's.[1])

The city's sources of income were, in type, not unlike those of the Crown. Three main classes may be distinguished: (1) rents from civic property, both lands and buildings; (2) the farmed customs and dues; (3) a large but fluctuating income from various "extra-ordinary" sources which will be described below. Over and above these the city had certain miscellaneous types of income, such as the profits of courts or fairs, or fines levied on entering freemen, but these latter seldom amounted to a significant proportion of the total.[2]

Civic property fell under several heads. First of all came the tenements within the walls, possessions of the civic corporation for immemorial generations. They consisted of houses, gardens, and shops, scattered through the city and divided into approximately 137 parcels.[3] Of these 137 parcels of property, 74 were let on lease

---

[1] Cf. *Econ. Hist. Rev.*, 2nd ser., I (1948), 46–53: Melvin Wren, "The Chamber of London in 1633"; W. G. Hoskins, "An Elizabethan Provincial Town: Leicester," in *Studies in Social History*, ed. J. H. Plumb (London, 1955), 34–67; Roger Howell, *Newcastle upon Tyne in the Puritan Revolution* (Oxford, 1966), 293–297 and App., Table VII.

[2] Profits of courts brought in a sum varying from £13 to £15 in the mid-sixteenth century, slowly declining to a somewhat smaller total until merged with other issues of the city on the receivers' rolls. Fees for admission to civic freedom were more unpredictable, but often the total ran above £20 a year. Another ancient form of income, fees from city fairs and from the city guilds, amounted to a few shillings at the most.

[3] See Hooker, *History*, III, 673–763, "The generall Liger or Rentall booke of all the Lordshipps Mannors Landes Rentes and Revenewes appertayninge to the Citie of Excester according to a booke and survey thereof made in the xxviith yere of the Raigne of our most Soueraigne Ladye Elisabeth Queene of England &c."

for terms of years or lives in 1580, most frequently the latter. The usual formula was three lives or 99 years "if any of them shall live so long." It was not expected that such a term would be fulfilled; significantly, most of the leases recorded in the 1580 survey had been made since the accession of the Queen.[4] Rents on these properties were generally customary ones; the sole exception to this rule was in the case of shops. Here a true economic rent was charged, and it is the increase in the number of shops that accounts for the doubling of income from the city tenements, from £66 in 1540 to £124 in 1640.

Outside the walls Exeter owned two manors, Duryard, closely adjoining the city on the north, and Awliscombe, lying near Honiton. The former had belonged to the city immemorially; the latter was a gift to the city from an ex-mayor in 1496. Consisting largely of agricultural land, the two manors produced about the same amount of income across the whole century under consideration. Duryard's value was increased somewhat by the lease of mills on the Exe, but from 1550 on it usually brought in about £90 per annum.[5] Awliscombe, much less valuable, produced about £6 annually.

During the sixteenth century, substantial additions were made to the civic properties by the acquisition of Exe Island and the former monastic lands within the city. The island came as a reward for the city's loyalty in 1549. Its income in years when heavy repairs to the weirs were not necessary, averaged a little above £30. The monastic lands (St. Nicholas Fee) brought in about £12. Altogether, the city enjoyed in 1640 stable annual receipts of about £270 from real estate, roughly a third of total income. This contrasts with the circumstances of 1540 when rents from property provided well over half of a year's revenue.

[4] In many cases the three lives were the lessee's, his wife's, and his son's or daughter's.
[5] Duryard manor also contained Duryard Wood, which was retained under direct city control and which afforded valuable timber and other supplies for the building activities of the borough. The city also possessed a quarry from which came the vast quantities of rock and earth necessary for the canal and for the weir system.

The next principal source of income was the various customs of the city, all of which were farmed for yearly payments. Besides the petty customs collected on goods brought into the city by sea,[6] there were the market dues. These included the fees on sales in the fish market, the ancient customs of bacgavell, chepgavell, and brew gavell,[7] and the monopoly of barrel bearing. The last gave the farmers the franchise for transporting all commodities contained in barrels within the city. There were other small fees farmed out, such as those on the sale of apples, honey, and oil. In 1540 the total of all these farms, including the petty customs, was about £33.[8] The city fostered and extended this type of income carefully; new types were added with the establishment of wholesale markets in wool, yarn, and cloth, and other commodities. At the same time increased volume of trade brought a natural expansion of returns from dues. By 1581[9] the old farms, the petty customs, and the new farms on sealing of leather, weighing of wool, and weighing of yarn brought in a total of £100. By 1600 the farm of the canal added another £100 a year. At the end of our period the addition of dues from the cloth hall and an increase in the canal rent produced a revenue of £332 from farmed dues.[10] This accounted for roughly another third of total annual receipts.

[6] Exeter petty customs were paid only by merchants coming from towns that did not enjoy a reciprocal arrangement with Exeter exempting their citizens from payment of petty custom. For the most part this meant the small West Country towns like Taunton or Collumpton just now rising in importance as wool centers. Town customs produced a steady £20 per annum during much of our period, rising to £30 at the end. They were collected at all landing places within the port. See RR, 8–9 Elizabeth.

[7] See J. W. Schopp and R. C. Easterling, *The Anglo-Norman Custumal of Exeter*, History of Exeter Research Group, Monograph No. 2 (Oxford, 1925), 20–21. According to these authors "chepgavell" was the ancient payment for the exercise of retail trade in the city. It is not to be confused with entrance fines or shop fines charged nonfreemen. "Bacgavell" was the baking-toll and "brewgavell" the brewing-toll, paid by the bakers and brewers respectively. See also Hooker, *History*, III, 552.

[8] RR, 31–32 Henry VIII.

[9] RR, 23–24 Elizabeth.

[10] See RR, 12–13 Charles I

Fish custom with other ancient customs	£20		
Sealing of leather	13	6s.	8d.

Increases in these reasonably stable sources of ordinary revenue, although very substantial, were not sufficient to match the even greater increases in outgo; the city fathers had to seek additional funds elsewhere. This need first became acute about 1570 and resulted in a series of expedients, varying in detail but all essentially short-term loans. Borrowing money was hardly a novel expedient, but the character of this extraordinary revenue is of interest.

There were few sources to which the city could look for loans. The most obvious alternative was some wealthy merchant or landowner who might be willing to loan on interest. The Chamber was always loath to adopt this practice and only resorted to it in times of real emergency. The most serious of such emergencies were the dismayingly frequent breakdowns in the system of weirs which controlled not only the flow to the canal but also to the fulling and grist mills. Such a catastrophe had to be remedied immediately and the large sums of cash needed could only be raised by borrowing.[11] In 1608, for instance, £400 had to be borrowed for such a purpose.[12] On some occasions the Chamber had to go cap in hand to some neighbouring gentleman, but these occasions were very rare. Usually the loan could be raised from some member of the Twenty-

Weighing of yarn	24
Weighing cloth and wool	45
Haven (Canal)	160
Profits of cloth hall	20
Farmers of coal	20
Town custom (petty customs)	30

Total £332 6s. 8d.

The separate item, "profits of cloth hall," probably refers to fees on goods other than cloth. The farmers of coal had a monopoly on the sale of coal in the city, but had to sell at specified prices.

[11] When Callabeer weir broke in 1568, £55 was borrowed from William Hawkins of Plymouth who was repaid in 1570 (AB iii, 228). A similar catastrophe in 1596 occasioned a loan of £100 from Mr. Edmond Parker (AB v, 351).

[12] AB vi, 310 for £100 from Mr. Parker; AB vi, 317 for the same amount from Sir John Acland; AB vii, 327 for the same amount from John Tuckfield at 8 per cent; AB vi, 334 for the same sum from Nicholas Duck. These gentlemen were neighboring landowners except for Tuckfield, whom I cannot identify.

Four or at least from a citizen. The money cost from six to eight per cent in the early seventeenth century. The Chamber never liked this kind of loan and paid it off as rapidly as possible, usually after one year. A more tempting arrangement was to borrow from one of the civic charities. Since these were capital endowments, the Chamber could undertake to perform whatever benefaction was intended out of its funds, until repayment was made to the charity.[13] It was certainly not a happy fiscal practice, but one that became increasingly common as time went on, and increasingly tempting as the endowments grew.

But if sources of loans were few, civic ingenuity devised a new and very promising one. Following the model of London, Exeter in 1560 obtained a royal charter for a municipal court to handle the estates of all orphans within the city.[14] "Orphans" meant all minor heirs of a townsman regardless of whether or not the mother was still alive. The stated intention of the charter was to provide protection for the property of these minors, of whom the corporation became the guardian. This creditable end was secured, but at the same time a deposit and loan bank was in effect created. The funds of the estates were deposited with the court, which was free to handle them as it saw fit. In practice the money was placed out at interest with specified trustees, who had free use of it until the majority of the heir or heiress concerned.[15] Most of these moneys were loaned out to private individuals, but when necessary the Chamber itself became a borrower. The first time a loan from this

[13] There was a case in the early 1560's when the legacies of Mrs. Tuckfield, William Bucknam, and Parson Herne, totaling £345, were borrowed to finance the canal. See Herne in RR, 4–5 Elizabeth, others in RR, 6–7 Elizabeth. This loan was repaid. Or note the list of debts AB viii, 169, 12 February 1639, which includes £300 owed to the hospital of St. John (£100 from Lady Prideaux' gift, £100 from Mr. Borough's, £100 from Mrs. Jurdaine's) as well as £100 from Borough's gift to the poor and £300 from the Atwill benefaction.

[14] Hooker, *History*, II, 447–461.

[15] The estate trustee of the sixteenth century faced a real problem in the absence of banks or forms of investment where money could safely be laid by. Hence a municipally controled system of loans was a sensible solution to a real problem.

source appeared on the accounts was in 1571.[16] Thenceforward they became a steady and important item in the city's finances. At any one moment the city probably owed several hundred pounds to various orphans. They do not seem to have suffered, for they were provided an allowance during minority and payment at majority seems to have been prompt.[17] Nearly two hundred estates passed through the city's hands between 1570 and 1640 including some of the first fortunes of the city, so that there were constantly available very adequate sums not only for civic but for private borrowing.

Equally important to the civic fiscal system were the disguised loans from the receivers, the annually elected treasurers of the city. Each year the receiver was made personally responsible for all charges against the city during his term of office. Consequently, when city expenditures exceeded income in any year, the receiver had to pay the difference out of his own pocket and wait for repayment. Thus a deficit at the end of the fiscal year was owed to the ex-receiver, always a member of the Chamber. These deficits were frequent (no less than 49 out of the hundred years under consideration) and often large. In the fiscal year 1581–82 John Periam, Receiver, was creditor to the city for £317 at the end of his term,[18] and it was not until 1586 that he was repaid in full. This was the largest annual deficit of the century, but sums above £100 were quite common. It was a most convenient method of borrowing; there were no interest charges,[19] the debt was owed to a member of

[16] RR, 12–13 Elizabeth.

[17] There is no clear indication that interest was paid by the city on such loans earlier than 1609 although provision had always been made for the maintenance of orphans by yearly allowances. See AB vi, 348 for first clear order to pay interest on a loan from the Parr estate (interest at 6⅔ per cent). Other instances occur in AB vii, 300 (Moggridge money) and AB viii, 6 (Anthony money).

[18] RR, 23–24 Elizabeth and AB iv, 444 and 494.

[19] This was true until the stringent period early in James' reign. In 1609 it was ordered that the receiver, on quitting office, should receive 8 per cent on all money owing him above £50. Later (see AB vii, 329 and AB viii, 6) interest was allowed on the whole deficit. Some effort to pay off the recorder in a reasonable time was made; an order of 1604 (AB vi, 162) provided that anything above £50 was to be paid off by All Saints' Day of the new term and another of 1615 (AB vii, 176) ordered payment before the auditing was closed. These probably remained pious hopes.

the city oligarchy; and there was no hurry for repayment. These forced loans without interest had simply become part of the burden of civic office, and the unlucky receiver could be thankful that the term of office lasted but a year and came but once in his career.[20]

The third major source of extraordinary income was an innovation of the late sixteenth century. Returns from the city's lands were mostly quite inelastic, governed, as they were, by the conditions of customary tenure. But there remained one possibility for expanding income from the city's landed estate; relief fines could be increased. The inadequacy of records makes it impossible to trace out the increase in relief fines on individual parcels of property, but it is clear that during the last quarter of the sixteenth century the amounts of single fines grew astonishingly large as compared with those of the previous generation. A second, and equally profitable, novelty of the same epoch was the sale of reversionary leases.

Up to about 1575 no relief fine exceeding £20 occurs in the records, and reversionary leases are uncommon. In 1574 Thomas Martin paid £100 fine for the lease of 160 acres of land in Duryard manor,[21] and a year later William Trevet paid £72, made up of various fines, all of them reversionary. It was the beginning of a practice that grew rapidly. The sums raised in this fashion were very substantial:[22] in at least one year £1,000, and in many others over £500.

Frequently the Chamber ordered competitive bidding for leases to raise more money. The order of 8 May 1602[23] expresses the spirit of many such orders. "And [the Chamber] further agree where by consent of this house divers lands and tenements of this city have been offered to be set for further estates ... for that the city is sundry ways indebted and hath many occasions to undergo, many burdens,

---

[20] There was also a regular system of loans from new members of the Twenty-Four. Each incoming member was required to loan the Chamber £20 for one year. See AB vi, 273, which in 1607 refers to this custom as already established. There is an explicit order in AB vii, 40.

[21] RR, 15–16 Elizabeth; AB iii, 326. For Trevet see AB iii, 349.

[22] RR, 5–6 Charles I.

[23] AB vi, 29.

and great charges more than they can well discharge without making of fines for such lands as will yield the same." Active competition for desirable plots drove up bids correspondingly.[24] There developed also a considerable trade in reversions, an indication of the real value of much of the city property, particularly in Duryard manor and in Exe Island manor.[25] This trade and the general bidding for leases was a game at which only the wealthy could afford to play, and most of the money raised by this device came from the inner circle of oligarchs.

These various types of borrowing led to a complex system of fiscal juggling in which a loan from Peter was frequently necessary to pay Paul. A draft on the orphans' funds used to pay off a personal loan would in turn be paid by a fine. It may be useful to observe the actual functioning of the fiscal system over a short period of time. A fair sample is the term of years at the very end of Elizabeth's reign. In March 1596, the Chamber, after several deficits, borrowed £100 from Mr. Edmond Parker, the money to be paid back at Michaelmas.[26] In September a reversion of Duryard mills was sold to Christopher Spicer, a member of the Twenty-Four, for £170, out of which £100 went to pay Parker.[27] But immediately after, in order to pay off the deficit due Hull, Receiver for 1593-94, a second loan of the same size had to be negotiated from the same source.[28] Again, when this debt fell due in March 1598, yet another loan had to be made, this time from two Chamber members, Bevis and Seldon, and the £50 raised from each of them served to pay off Parker's second loan.[29] Hard upon these loans the Chamber had to resort again to the orphans' court, and in March 1599 borrowed £200 from the orphans of Jasper Horsey.[30] The

[24] There was such an instance in 1583 (AB v, 269). The Shillay meadow outside the West Gate was up for bid. The mayor, Thomas Spicer, offered £35 against the tenant, Richard Martin's £30. The Chamber countered by offering it to Martin for £40; otherwise it was to go to Spicer at his bid.

[25] In 1624 (AB vii, 602) the Bonhay mills were let in reversion for a fine of £700 to George Pyle. This was the largest fine recorded, but there were frequent fines of several hundred pounds.

[26] AB v, 351.
[27] AB v, 362.
[28] AB v, 371.
[29] AB v, 380.
[30] AB v, 414.

widow was granted £6 13s. 4d. a year for the four orphans, but this was voided later with the proviso that the city should not have the money for more than three years. In 1600 the sum owed Dorchester, the ex-receiver, was borrowed, again from Parker, and to reimburse the latter the city was driven to desperation. An effort to sell the reversion of a tenement in Awliscombe apparently failed, and eventually additional loans had to be made, £20 from Walter Borough, £10 from Alexander Germyn, and £10 from John Periam (all Chamber members).[31] Finally, in March 1601 Parker was paid off. By summer an offer of John Periam to lend £50 for six months had to be accepted[32] and to repay him £50 had to be borrowed in two £25 installments from two more Chamber members, Crossing and Newcomb.[33] A fine on land in Duryard paid them off in October 1601,[34] but the city's finances remained embarrassed.

A herculean effort to clean the slate was made with the order for sale of leases quoted above. No less than £431 of reversions[35] was sold and the returns allocated to pay immediate debts totaling £311, while another £83 was to be paid off at stated dates during the next twelve months. The nature of the debts is of some interest. £200 was due to orphans; £21 was due on charities administered by the city; £80 on ex-receivers' accounts. This little exercise in fiscal gymnastics is a perfectly typical one and illustrates the hand-to-mouth character of municipal finance during much of our period. The Chamber had to perform a constant series of juggling feats to keep the city reasonably solvent. But even more impressive than the Chamber's ingenuity is the real skill with which scant resources were exploited and care taken to keep the city's obligations within the family circle of civic magnates.

Additional funds from a tax levy on the townspeople was a possible but hardly practicable alternative. The city, like the Crown, was expected to live on its own, and levies were rare, justified only by a general emergency touching all. Repair of the water system,[36]

---

[31] AB v, 487–488.
[33] AB v, 540.
[35] AB vi, 21, 58.

[32] AB v, 503.
[34] AB vi, 5.
[36] AB v, 509.

militia training,[37] or provision of royal post horses[38] were such occasions. The largest collection taken, about £90,[39] was for the building of the house of correction in 1579–80. Sometimes a levy might be made within a particular parish for some local need. Collections of money which was later repaid were also common particularly in times of famine or of some general calamity such as the collapse of Callabeer weir in 1569.[40]

Up to this point we have considered only income, but clearly the real dynamic in the situation was ever increasing outgo. What was the nature of the growing expenses which drove the Chamber from one doubtful financial expedient to another? The answer falls under several heads. The cost of living was, of course, steadily rising during a considerable part of our century. How this affected the municipal budget can be demonstrated in several ways. For instance, there was the salaries and wages bill of the corporation. Salaries and perquisites (principally liveries) amounted to £90 in 1549–50; in the last year of Elizabeth they stood at £274;[41] the average for 1632–42 was £310. A few key items demonstrate the point. The city paid for its liveries in 1550 a total of £8; in 1637 they cost £36. The mayor's cook was paid £3 a year in 1571;[42] in 1637 he had £8. The fees of standing legal counsel, fixed at about £6 per annum in 1550, had risen to £21 by the end of our period. The most highly paid civic officer, the mayor, enjoyed £120 a year by 1640 as against the £26 13s. 4d. of his predecessors during Edward VI's reign. In short, the municipal salary bill had increased more than threefold in the century and now totaled more than the entire budget of 1550.

Another aspect of rising costs can be seen in the city's wage bills. The constant repair of walls, buildings, and weirs required a good deal of casual labor, and the wages of workmen constituted a high proportion of the general expense account, probably not much under

[37] AB ii, 137.
[38] AB v, 427, 522, 547–548.
[39] RR, 21–22 Elizabeth.
[40] AB iii, 249. See also AB iii, 2.
[41] See RR, 3–4 Edward VI and 16–17 Charles I.
[42] AB iii, 269.

fifty per cent.[43] In 1540, common labor for picking ivy from the walls could be had at 5d. per diem;[44] demolition workers at St. Nicholas Priory got 6d. By 1572, men hewing stones for the weirs had either 11d. or 12d. per diem.[45] In 1615, wages had risen to as much as 1s. 2d. per diem for workmen.[46] They remained at this level in the 1630's. In short, the city was paying more than double the wages of 1540.

Obviously, much of the increase in expenditure must be charged to the rising cost of living, but a second important element was the Chamber's own ambitious mood. With little hesitation they repeatedly embarked upon programs of lavish spending well beyond their ordinary resources. The most notable item was, of course, the building of the canal. Expenses connected with this project included not only the actual cost of building but also the very high maintenance and repair charges that were the price of inadequate engineering knowledge. To these must be added the charges of litigation with the engineer Trew and with landowners along its course. From the incomplete records available, total expenditure for the canal over the eighty year period beginning in 1563 appears to have been about £6,950. To offset this the city received in rent from 1597 on something over £5,500.[47] This means that after 1600 the canal was paying its way, at least in most years, but in the thirty years after 1563 the city had to find about £2,000 before any revenue began to appear.

A more immediately profitable investment was the modest expenditure put out for the establishment and maintenance of markets

[43] For instance, in 1637–38 £133 was spent on the repairs of Trew's weir. About £60 went for labor costs. See RR, 12–13 Charles I.

[44] RR, 31–32 Henry VIII.

[45] RR, 23–24 Elizabeth.

[46] RR, 12–13 James I.

[47] This figure is based on a total of items in the Receivers' Rolls headed "haven" plus the costs of litigation with Trew. It is very approximate because of the casual nature of the expense accounts in which there is no consistency of classification. Probably it should be larger. It does not include such items as high rents on land crossed by the canal or the wages of the permanent staff. The income figure is based on receipts of rent from the haven from 1598 on and does not allow for occasional lapses in rent payments.

for wool, yarn, and cloth. From 1555 on, the city rented the New Inn from the dean and chapter for £5 a year; there were occasional renewal fines and repairs,[48] but the income averaged £20 per annum. In 1612 the New Inn was remodeled so as to provide stalls for London dealers and thenceforward another £70 in shop rents came in each year. The yarn market built between 1569 and 1571 at the cost of £289 brought in an annual average of £17 during the next seventy years.

Other expenditures of the Chamber during this period were of less profitable character. Nowhere is the expansive, even extravagant, mood of the Chamber better reflected than in the baroque splendors of the Guildhall which was elaborately rebuilt between 1593 and 1596. These extensive alterations which gave the building very nearly its present exterior, cost £789. A more prosaic addition to the civic buildings was the house of correction which cost £96 in 1580. The prison was rebuilt in 1629–30 at a cost of £200.[49]

In addition to these nonrecurrent expenses deliberately assumed by the Chamber, there were others of a more or less fixed nature. The modest fee farm of £45 due the Crown was a minor burden as were the rents of Topsham cranage and the fishing of the Exe so long as they lasted. The real bulk of expenditures was usually summed up in the receivers' rolls under the heading "Repairs and other expenses." It is impossible to break down this item very closely, for it included a multitude of small expenses. The largest general heading was the repair of city property, buildings, streets, walls, and gates, the water system, and most costly of all, the elaborate system of weirs, embankments, and ditches by which the Exe was diverted to serve the grist and tucking mills of the city. The last was often the largest item. For instance, between 1552 and 1570, weirs, mill leats, and banks cost the city £1,134 in money and

---

[48] There were expenses for repairs, as for example in 1637–38, and the renewal fine in 1633 was another £80. See RR, 11–12 and 12–13 Charles I; see also AB vii, 857.

[49] RR, 21–22 Elizabeth and RR, 23–24 Elizabeth. For the prison see RR, 3–4 and 4–5 Charles I.

more than £190 worth of timber out of the city woods.[50] Again, in the single year 1608 major repairs to the weirs cost £926,[51] and there were almost always smaller annual outlays for the same purpose.

The Chamber of Exeter shared the prevailing taste for litigation. During the twenty-one years of the seventeenth century when legal costs were itemized separately, the average comes to £62 per annum. And if law came dear, so did Parliamentary representation; the nine sessions between 1603 and 1629 that are itemized, averaged £53 each. An annually recurrent cost was the donation for the poor at Easter and Christmas, which in the 1630's cost about £20. At the same time, interest charges on the floating debt were running to about £50 each year. Thus, leaving aside the costs of the weirs, we find annually recurrent charges totaled almost £500.[52]

The fiscal position of the city of Exeter resembled in some measure that of the Crown. In both cases customary revenues, above all those derived from land and from customs duties, were proving inadequate despite efforts to make them produce as much as possible. Borrowing presented serious difficulties because of the lack of an organized money market. The city solved its problems somewhat more satisfactorily than the royal government. Short-term loans, often without interest, from the principal merchants of the city were supplemented by drafts on the orphans' funds, by relief fines, and by the sale of reversions in leases. This enabled the city to avoid an external debt, and shrewd albeit sometimes risky maneuvers kept the city solvent. But there was always a floating debt owing the

[50] See ECM, Book 55, special account for mills, leats, etc. This does not of course include the cost of maintaining the canal and its weir.
[51] RR, 5–6 James I.
[52] This total is made up as follows:

Salaries	£300
Fee-farm	46
Rents	7
Poor	20
Law	62
Interest	50
	£485

orphans' court, the charitable funds, or individuals, with accompanying interest charges. At the end of the 1630's this debt totaled about £1,500.[53] Exeter's public finance at the end of our period remained on doubtful foundations. Yet the merchant governors of the city had managed to avoid absolute bankruptcy, and they had a list of genuine public benefits to show for their policy of deliberate extravagance.

[53] See AB viii, 169, 12 February 1639, for a statement of the city's fiscal condition at that time. The Chamber owed a total of £1,560:

to new English school	£300	
to orphans	400	
to Atwill's fund	600	
to Borough's benefaction	150	
to three members of Twenty-Four	60	(£20 each)
to the gunpowder fund	50	
	£1,560	

The last item was a fund raised by a rate to keep sufficient supplies of gunpowder on hand. The loan from the school was, of course, from its capital endowment, and represented a form of investment for the school trustees.

Chapter Four

The Structure of Social Control

Exeter in the sixteenth century was an authoritarian society. Tight control was exercised over many aspects of the individual citizen's life. His economic activity was checked at every turn by the watchful guidance of a patriarchal civic government. At the same time, the magistrates were ever on the alert to check the slightest threat to social order. The most careful precautions were taken not only to prevent ordinary outbreaks of violence or of crime (constant fears in a society without adequate police), but also to suppress any criticism of the established social, political, and religious order. This paternalism had its benevolent side, and during the period under study serious efforts were made to cope with the difficult problem of the desperately poor and the unemployed.

PART 1: ECONOMIC CONTROL

The Exeter merchant community showed a willingness to undertake ambitious and even speculative enterprises in search of new wealth, but it also retained a strong degree of conservatism and adhered firmly to an economic policy hallowed by centuries of custom. We have marked the desire which it showed for as much political self-control as possible. In economic matters the same sentiment prevailed, in this case reinforced by a set of institutions that allowed a higher degree of autonomy than was possible in political affairs. Exeter remained at the end of the sixteenth century an economic unit unto itself, not as yet submerged in the larger economic entity of England. It retained a body of economic rights that served to secure to its freemen in their own area a monopoly of trading advantage not possessed by the rest of the Queen's subjects. The latter remained, in economic terms, "foreigners" and were systematically excluded, as far as possible, from the enjoyment of commercial advantage in the town trading area. These trading privileges were not equally enjoyed by all the freemen of Exeter. The greatest benefit was derived, as one might expect, by the great merchant class. These men, as individual traders, were in competition with one another, but, as mutual beneficiaries of a chartered monopoly, they were linked together against the rest of the economic world, English or alien. Thus in one sense they remained a medieval economic entity, preserving their economic identity and self-consciousness in the face of the national state.

Let us examine in detail the institutional structure of this community. The primary distinction was that between freeman and nonfreeman, whether the latter was a resident of Exeter or not. This select group of franchised citizens, a minority of the local population,[1] enjoyed a monopoly of all economic opportunity within the city. All wholesale and retail trade was reserved to them. In every way the conditions of the market were weighted as heavily as possible in favor of the Exeter freeman. Local producers coming to Exeter with their goods could sell only to him; and from him alone could they make their purchases. Traders from more distant points, seeking either a market for their commodities or supplies of West Country products, must go to him. All consumers within the city had to purchase their needs from him. At the nexus of every transaction, wherever gain was to be made, the Exeter freeman had a privileged position. So far as trade could be corralled within the city's bounds, its benefits were assured to the franchised citizen. No offense was more sternly regarded by the Chamber than a violation of this monopoly; the act books are full of judgments against such offenders.

[1] It is impossible to state precisely what proportion were freemen, but it may have been 10 per cent. Between 1620 and 1640 about 26 were admitted annually. In 1674, there were about 1,000 freemen in a population of 11,000–12,000 (W. B. Stephens, "Merchant Companies and Commercial Policies in Exeter, 1625–88," TDA 86 (1954), 139).

For the artificer the franchise of the city was not absolutely necessary. By consent of the mayor and the Twenty-Four, he might, upon payment of a quarterly shop fine, be allowed to pursue his calling without becoming franchised. There is some evidence of a change of policy in this matter during the sixteenth century. In Henry VIII's time there were several instances in which an alternative was presented. Either the individual was to become a freeman or else he was to pay a quarterly shop fine.[2] The fine was probably deliberately set high enough to discourage the choice of this alternative. In 1549, John Strobridge, who had married the widow of a freeman, was given the alternative of a £6 13s. 4d. franchisement fine or else a quarterly fine of 13s. 4d. "until he be made free."[3] But in 1563, Thomas Brewerton, afterwards mayor, but then not a freeman, was absolutely forbidden to sell in the city unless he became a freeman at a £20 fine. Although he refused to pay at that time, he did later become franchised.[4] In 1562 there was the case of a tailor who was presented the usual alternative. In the following year, however, George Evans, haberdasher, formerly of London, was forbidden to exercise his craft of pressing caps and felts upon pain of imprisonment.[5] After this, shop-fine entries disappear from the act book. Evidence from the tuckers' records suggests that efforts to enroll artificers as freemen were spasmodic and lax. About a third of the weavers, tuckers, and shearmen admitted to the guild between 1560 and 1600 also became freemen, indicating that most of them were producers or processors rather than buyers and sellers; none was an exporter.[5]

The number of cases of fines for "foreign bought and sold" coming before the Chamber was very high. This offense involved the sale of goods purchased by a nonfreeman to another nonfreeman. In other words it invaded the monopoly of trading that was the very essence of the freeman's privilege. The penalty was confiscation of the goods involved, but usually the procedure was to compound

[2] AB ii, 146 and 147, February 1546, where the alternative of a £4 entrance fine or else 6s. a quarter was offered.

[3] AB ii, 202.

[4] AB ii, 126–127.

[5] AB ii, 128; and see Joyce Youings, *Tuckers Hall, Exeter* (Exeter, 1968), 42.

for a small fine of from twenty to forty shillings. Very probably not all such cases were detected but a determined effort was made to protect the freeman's privilege.

In the mid-sixteenth century new strength was given to this system of commercial control by the establishment of new markets directly under city governance.[6] Violations of the trading regulations were becoming troublesome at this period. A regulation of 1542 reaffirmed that no person who was "foreign" should sell wares by retail in the city except at fair time.[7] The decision as to what wares were included in this order was left to the mayor. In April 1549 and again in January of the following year, there were cases in which citizens let their houses to be used by strangers for illegal sales.[8] The second case resulted in two disfranchisements and a regulation for stricter enforcement of confiscation. But in 1552 there was another case of the same nature.[9] This type of case doubtless influenced the Chamber in its efforts to establish a better system of regulation. But at least as important, if not more so, was the desire to secure to the city, and particularly to its merchants, an additional share in the prospering cloth and wool trade of the West.

Already in 1533 an order of the Chamber had provided a place in the Guildhall, kept at the charge of the city, where foreigners bringing linen and woollen cloth were to carry on their business.[10] But it was the initiative of Henry Hamlyn, mayor in 1538, that obtained the establishment by the city of a weekly market for wool, yarn, and kersies. He met with opposition in the Chamber itself, and he and his friends had to undertake the construction of the market building themselves, providing stone out of St. Nicholas cloister and money from their own pockets. Trade was small at first, but it began to grow once the yarn house was completed. The most serious opposition came from the town of Crediton, then the only wool market town in the county, and its citizens commenced a suit

---

[6] There already existed, of course, the usual food markets for grain, meat, etc.

[7] AB ii, 106.

[8] AB ii, 201 and 216.

[9] AB ii, 242.

[10] Hooker, *History*, III, 884, and AB i, 107.

to the Privy Council, Bishop Veysey being engaged to intercede for the smaller town. However, the suit was decided in favor of Exeter.[11] An act of the Chamber of 1542 records the details of the new establishment.[12] All raw cloths and yarn brought to the city on market days (Wednesday and Friday) were to be taken for sale to the new building over against St. George's Church, and sale elsewhere in the city was made punishable by fine.

This policy was extended in 1555 when the city leased the New Inn, a property of the dean and chapter, and converted it into a "common hall for all maner of clothe lynnen or wollyn and for all other merchandises and which shalbe called the merchauntes hall."[13] They also appointed a keeper to supervise the hall. In 1569 a separate yarn market was built in St. Mary Major parish. By the seventeenth century the old quarters of the wool and cloth market were too narrow. After long preliminary discussions, new quarters were found for the wool market in the lower hall of the old St. Johns Hospital buildings.[14] Regulations and fees were announced in April 1636.[15] The usual restrictions about place and time of sale were set up for foreigners, but freemen were allowed to sell wool bought here or outside the city at any time or place regardless of the ordinance. At the same time, extensive alterations were made at the New Inn to provide a larger market place for cloth.[16] Thus by 1640 the city maintained three separate official establishments for the sale of wool, of yarn, and of cloth.

The regulations for the merchant hall appear in two different forms in the act book, 16 August 1555 and 14 December 1556.[17] The second version, more detailed in its provisions, is probably the draft of the proclamation issued at the opening of each fair. All merchants coming from outside with wares and merchandise were

[11] See ECM, Book 51 (Commonplace Book of John Hooker), fol. 345 and 346 for all these details. They are copied in substance in Isacke, *Antiquities*, 120.

[12] AB ii, 98.

[13] AB ii, 276, printed in Hooker, *History*, III, 884.

[14] AB viii, 56.

[15] AB viii, 72.

[16] RR, 11–12 and 12–13 Charles I.

[17] AB ii, 284 and 297–298.

to do their business in the merchant hall and in no other place, paying there the dues provided in the schedules. These amounted to a few pence on each sale, the charge varying with the commodity involved.

Outside merchants were divided into several categories. First came the Londoners. To them was extended the right to sell their goods freely "to all manner and kind of people," freemen or foreigners, in gross or in retail, during the days of the four principal Exeter fairs, St. Nicholas, St. Thomas, Ash Wednesday, and Whit-monday, and for three days before and four days after (eight days in all) within the hall. But they could not sell to anyone, free or foreign, at any other time. To the other merchant strangers—not Londoners—few concessions were made. They were not allowed to sell to foreigners at any time except actual fair days. On ordinary market days they were allowed to sell only to freemen of Exeter, and, of course, in gross only. They secured constant access to the Exeter market, but always as wholesale sellers to the limited clientele of freemen. The Londoners enjoyed less frequent access to the Exeter market, but with the major concession of full trading rights. Subsidiary provisions were included. The Londoners had to obtain the mayor's license to sell, and they had to make delivery during the eight days of the fair, a procedure which prevented sale with promise of future delivery. But during the intervals between fairs they were allowed to store goods in Exeter. One other group of merchants is mentioned, the northerners, whose great commodity was linen. They were given somewhat larger concessions than most since they could sell to freemen on any day of the week, instead of being limited to market days. (These market days were Wednesday, Friday, and Saturday between seven and eleven, and between one and four.)

The schedule of rates issued in 1583[18] slightly amended the earlier regulations. The lengthy schedule of fees included indicates the range of wares dealt in at the merchant hall. Besides all kinds of cloths and wool itself, there were woad, raisins and figs, various kinds of metal, glass, pitch, sugar, spices, paper, soap, honey, hops,

[18] AB iv, 414.

mather, leather, French canvas, and tin. In this code the trade of the northern merchants is described more precisely. Those bringing "byttes styrropes or any other harde ware or anye woolen clothes or any other Northeren wares" were permitted to sell to freemen on any day in the week.[19]

Strict enactments were made to prevent the violation of these rules by inhabitants of the city, franchised or otherwise. If any freeman made illegal purchases, he was disfranchised; other inhabitants were to suffer fine for the same offense. That the regulations were not strictly kept is evident from the number of fines levied for foreign goods bought and sold. In 1592, for example, there was a complaint that disorders had arisen among those not free of the city, and that men who were foreign sold wares as freemen.[20] One of the Twenty-Four was appointed to seek out such cases with the aid of two assistants and with the promise of a share of forfeitures.

The reissue of the schedules of rates in 1602 reflected the same objectives.[21] But, significantly, the regulations attached dealt with possible violations by citizens rather than by outsiders. There was a clause against receiving foreigners' goods into private houses without signifying this to the keeper of the merchant hall and paying hallage. A related enactment provided penalties for those who denied having foreigners' goods in their houses but against whom the allegation was proved. Also, no merchant or other citizen was to repair to any inn to buy merchandise, and innkeepers were threatened with punishment if they permitted such sales to take place. In all these cases penalties were provided for first, second, and third offenses, an indication of the frequency of the offense and the pessimism of the officials as to the possibilities of enforcement. Regulation was harder to enforce, and there must have been much evasion, yet the rising returns from the farmed fees at the merchant hall are an indication of relative success in confining trade to official markets.

---

[19] One slight concession was made to nonfreemen. Goods imported from overseas by them could pass on without further ado after a payment of hallage. This was no doubt for the benefit of merchants from the smaller Western towns who did not enjoy reciprocal trading privileges in Exeter.

[20] AB v, 221.

[21] ECM, Miscellaneous Roll 31.

There were other minor alterations in 1602 of which the most significant was the addition of a fee of 6d. per pack on kersies fulled in the city for a foreigner and sold to a freeman. Sale to anyone else was, of course, forbidden.

Fairs were the only occasions when this elaborate code was suspended. They numbered seven throughout the year, all of ancient origin. The fairs of Whitsuntide and St. Nicholas (6 December) were the most important; the others were held on St. Thomas Day (21 December), Ash Wednesday, Shere Thursday, St. Mary Magdalen Day, and Lammastide. On fair days it was required by mayoral proclamation that all shops in the city be closed and that no merchandise be sold except within the limits of the fair. The city still received a small fee from the fairs, but the yearly total from all did not exceed £4.

The fairs represented the one great breach in the walls so carefully erected to guard the Exeter freeman's monopoly of the market. We have seen above that the privileges of the Londoners at fair times amounted to a suspension of the monopoly. For eight days the Exeter market was given over to London dealers. For the latter it provided the opportunity to conduct their extensive distributory trade in the West. Here (and at Bristol and Chester fairs)[22] the chapmen of the smaller western places came to buy and to settle up accounts. The intrusion of the Londoners into the market area of Exeter was, of course, not popular, but the merchants of the capital were too powerful to be gainsaid. Quarrels flared up from time to time, but fortunately the expanding economy of the West Country provided ample opportunities for all.

Relations with the metropolitan merchants were harmonious for a long period during the early sixteenth century, but in 1563 an acrimonious dispute broke out. The issue seems to have been the payment of coverage fees by the Londoners. It soon became serious, for in November 1563 the Chamber revoked all the special privileges of the Londoners, limiting them to trade on fair days only,

[22] See *APC*, PC 2/47, v. 13, fol. 366, 3 May 1637. This is a complaint by certain London traders who alleged they were being excluded from the Exeter fairs for private reasons rather than the stated reason, plague in London.

like other subjects of the Queen not free of the city.[23] At the Ash Wednesday fair of 1564 their goods were distrained for nonpayment of coverage dues.[24] The Londoners resorted to selling their goods in an inn outside the Eastgate and were for this arrested and fined.[25] In the meantime, as an act of retaliation, the goods of the Exeter merchants, Hurst and Periam, had been arrested in London under a clause of London's charter of Henry III.[26] Not until 1571 was judgment given in favor of the Exeter merchants. In the interval cooler counsels prevailed, and accommodations were made.

Permanent arrangements with the London merchants dealing at Exeter were made early in the seventeenth century. They had always been permitted to store goods in Exeter between fairs; now a part of the New Inn (the merchant hall) was given to shops for their use during fair time. Fourteen Londoners took leases for a term of twenty-one years, paying altogether £70 annual rent.[27] Thus the corporation drew some revenue at least from the privileged outsiders. The quite legitimate prohibitions against Londoners entering Exeter during plague outbreaks in the capital occasionally produced bursts of irritation, but on the whole friction with the metropolitan dealers never struck off more than a few sparks.

Hitherto we have traced the policy by which older measures of control over the wholesale trade within the city were strengthened while new devices for widening the monopoly area were introduced. But there was another side to the story. All the while there continued the immemorial routine of retail market regulation, following paths hewn out centuries before and changing but little during the sixteenth century. The regulation of food markets, which was concerned largely with the provision of victuals to the inhabitants of the city, was controlled not from the trader's point of view but rather from the consumer's. A good summary of this policy is contained in the annual proclamation of the mayor, made upon his

[23] AB iii, 123.
[24] AB iii, 138.
[25] AB iii, 151 and 159.
[26] Hooker, *History*, III, 617–627.
[27] AB v, 551. See renewals of leases in AB vii, 8, and vii, 859.

entry into office.[28] Along with general and specific regulations on a great number of subjects, he proclaimed that fish were to be sold only in the open market set aside for that purpose, and by retail only; that apples, pears, and other fruits, butter, eggs, cheese, poultry, such as "hennes capas cheekens cockes geyse duckes ganacockes pecockes" should all be sold in their assigned markets; that bread and beer should be "good and wholesome for mannes body" and sold according to the assize; and that butchers should have no more gain than one penny in every shilling, "besides the hedd the feete and the Inwardes." In short, regulation of the retail markets proceeded on familiar medieval principles. Plentiful supply, cheap price, and assured quality were the aims pursued. Selling conditions were strictly set so as to assure first access to local buyers. Producers, such as bakers and brewers, came under a very strict surveillance both as to the quality of their goods and the prices at which they were sold. The specific characteristics of this policy are recalled by the following items from Hooker's list of mayoral duties: [29]

> Also he is to attende the markets and see vyctualls to
> be sold at pryces reasonable
> He is to see to be punyshed all ingrossers forestallers
>
> He is to see all waights and Measures to be yerely
> viewed sured and measured
> He is to geve weekly to the Bakers their assise and to
> the Brewers a reasonable pryce for their beere and Ale
> and their vessels to be viewed.

The act books bear abundant witness that these principles were carried out with consistent care throughout the sixteenth century. First of all, the markets themselves were carefully maintained. For each commodity there was a specified place of sale, and only the Chamber could move any of these sites. Hours and conditions of sale were rigidly specified. A good example was the corn market,

[28] Hooker, *History*, III, 847.
[29] *Ibid.*, 805.

kept each Wednesday and Friday in the High Street.[30] No sale could take place before the ringing of the bell and then only free citizens and inhabitants could buy in order "to have the preferment of the market." At the second ringing of the bell all were allowed to buy, but no farmer could make a purchase of corn unless he had some of his own to sell. Market men were appointed by the city to see that no engrossing, forestalling, or regrating took place. They were also to report to the mayor the highest, lowest, and middle prices of corn sold, and he would base the bakers' assize on the last of these.[31]

The execution of these policies was a reasonably frequent concern of the Chamber, although a certain amount of this routine business passed through the mayor's and provost's courts. An assize of bread was recorded in the act book only once, in 1565.[32] Assizes of ale are found more frequently in the act book. Hooker lists nine between 1560 and 1576.[33] Wine selling, too, was closely controlled; licenses were granted by the justices, and prices were set.[34] The most serious scandal involving the brewers occurred in 1549.[35] Nicholas Rowe, brewer and member of the Chamber, was accused of having been "a great hinderer of the common wealth of the city as well in disobeying several commandments of the mayor as also in comforting and consulting with other brewers of the city to hold their victual

[30] Hooker, *History*, III, 819. See also AB iv, 141, 25 October 1561, in which the justices of the peace ordered that the mayor should view the corn market weekly and allow no foreign bakers to come into the same until the last bell was rung and then they were to buy only with the consent of the officers and not to have more than necessary for their needs at that time.

[31] Hooker, *History*, III, 819. See the Mayor's Court Rolls where a weekly notation of these prices is to be found.

[32] AB iv, 235.

[33] Similarly there were frequent measures to secure the use of lawful measures and weights. See, for instance, the proclamation of the mayor of 12 July 1557, AB ii, 309, and the act book entry later that year (AB ii, 316) in which the seven brewers of the city are noted as agreeing to obey this regulation.

[34] In 1583 the act book states that licenses for wine selling are to be issued by justices of the peace to freemen only, who are to be nominated by the recorder. See AB v, 237.

[35] AB ii, 209.

as beer and ale at high and excess prices, causing dearth among the citizens and others resorting to the city." He was severely punished by dismissal from the Chamber and by a fine of twenty marks.

On other occasions the brewers gave offense. In 1563–64 the mayor was ordered to find out how many of them brewed and at what times.[36] They were to brew less often or else a common brewhouse would be established. Later in the century sale of beer by brewers not members of the brewers' corporation occasioned penalties against anyone buying such beer.[37] Another dispute with the brewers went to the Privy Council in 1633 and had to be settled by the justices of assize.[38]

Other problems vexed the Chamber in its regulation of the victual (meat) markets. As early as 1571 standings in the yarn market were let to foreign victualers (butchers) who could sell there on Wednesdays and Saturdays during certain hours: to 2 P.M. on Wednesday, to 3 P.M on Saturday.[39] We may presume that the motive behind this move was to provide more abundant supplies of meat than the city victualers could make available. For some years no more was heard on the subject, until an angry entry in 1591 appears.[40] It seems that the city victualers had obtained a charter from the Lord Chancellor, allowing them to restrain any foreign victualer from selling food in the city. Under its authority they had seized food sold by foreigners, defying the mayor's orders until bound over. The Chamber indignantly declared such a victualers' corporation to be harmful to the city and pledged city funds to procure its defeat. It was two years before the issue was settled, but in 1593 the Chamber seems to have won the victory.[41] The local victualers submitted, promising not to offend against the foreign victualers. They were to redeliver their grant of corporation from the Lord Chancellor and to have a new one as the mayor and justices

---

[36] AB iv, 242.   [37] AB v, 90–91.
[38] APC, PC 2/43, v. 9, fol. 467 and fol. 539.
[39] AB iii, 277.
[40] AB v, 193.   [41] AB v, 236.

thought fit. Shortly thereafter the old conditions for the foreign victualers were restored.[42]

Another economic control of typically medieval nature was supervision of the local producers' quality of output. Most prominent in the act books is the searching of leather. The searchers of leather were minor officers of the city.[43] The usual procedure, upon a seizure of suspected goods by them, was to appoint a committee of experts to examine and judge the quality of hides or manufactured leather goods. The penalty was forfeiture, but as in the case of goods not paying custom, it was usually remitted for a fine.

Although these regulations of quality were largely carried out for local purposes, they had behind them the authority of proclamation or statute. In the case of woollen goods this was more specifically adduced. There is a list of the tailors of the city[44] for 1563 who were obliged to give recognizances to obey the specifications of the new proclamation regarding material. Raw cloth also came under supervision. The penalty for selling falsely made kersey in the market was severe, as the pillorying of such an offender in 1564 indicates.[45] Later, in 1582, under the terms of a proclamation, two men were appointed to view the new kersies each market day, and over them were placed two members of the Chamber.[46] Finally, after the act of Parliament for the weighing, marking, and searching of Devon kersies in each market town, three searchers were appointed,[47] and were required to give sureties.[48]

[42] AB v, 262.
[43] Hooker, *History*, III, 845.
[44] AB iv, 178. [45] AB iv, 268.
[46] AB v, 213. [47] AB v, 251.
[48] Other routine matters of control were varied. Fines for forestalling, regrating, and engrossing fish are recorded in AB iv, 301, 327, 328. Victualers' offenses against regulations also appear, such as those of selling outside permitted hours and killing calves against the law (AB iv, 420). There were also victualers, licensed to sell flesh in Lent to those with faculties, who made great profit by engrossing "to the hurt of the common wealth" (AB v, 245). To provide against this the mayor henceforth was to license not more than two for such purposes, and they were to sell only to those licensed to eat flesh lawfully under the mayor's hand. The whole body of victualers were to enjoy this privilege, turn by turn.

Besides these routine regulations the Chamber faced a continuing problem in its care for the provision of victuals to the city. The corn supply on the Exeter market was not always sufficient for the needs of the city. Consequently the Chamber had to find additional supplies. The usual practice was to raise a loan or a subscription for the purchase of a bulk supply which was then sold at cost to the poorer inhabitants. Sometimes members of the Chamber provided the money; on other occasions a general subscription from the whole community was taken. In 1555, for instance, there was a serious dearth and the Privy Council sanctioned the stopping of ships bound for Portugal at Plymouth and the compulsory purchase of their cargoes.[49] Exeter raised £500 for the purchase and transport of 604 quarters of rye. In 1597, it was the Merchant Adventurers Company which stepped into the breach and put up money for purchases of grain from Danzig.[50] The problem was not one of general famine, but rather of local dearth, and could be remedied by buying at a lower price in some convenient market.

Closely related to the problem of the supply of grain was that of grinding it. According to the ancient order of the city the bakers and brewers were to grind in the city mills only, that is, in the mills of the city manors. This was a regulation that was increasingly hard to enforce and it seems to have become a dead letter by the end of our period.[51]

The controls over economic life had their profitable side for the city, for they provided an important source of income. The various city customs—port duties, the ancient market tolls, and the tolls for weighing of yarn and wool—were farmed out. As we have seen in Chapter III, this revenue was appreciably increased during the period under consideration. The most jealously guarded, though not the most profitable, of these tolls was the town custom levied on goods landed in Exeter port. The act books are full of entries concerning nonpayment of town custom. It was particularly irksome to

[49] See ECM, Book 55 under this date and AB ii, 288. In 1589 a single wealthy citizen, John Periam, lent the required sum (AB v, 114).

[50] AB v, 377. See also Chapter VI.

[51] There was a petty conflict with the Earl of Bedford over this matter. See Chapter IX for an account of the squabble over the Exwick mills.

merchants of the smaller West Country market towns who lacked the exemptions which the great ports conceded one another in this regard. For example, there was the case of four merchants of Taunton, Tiverton, and Collumpton, importers of raisins, whose goods were confiscated in 1576. They were let off with a fine of £4, and one of them was allowed to compound with the city by making a yearly payment of 10s. for town custom on any goods he might enter.[52] Entries in the act books concerning nonpayment of these duties remained extremely common, and it is apparent that they were a source of great irritation to foreign merchants. Nevertheless, the collection of this duty was rigorously insisted on throughout the period, and income from this source slowly rose.

An important part of this whole system of control was the guild structure of the city. As we have indicated above, there was no great medieval flowering of the guild order in Exeter, as there had been elsewhere in England. Only in one instance had a guild challenged the Chamber's monopoly of power. In the middle of the fifteenth century the tailors had obtained a special charter from the Crown which enabled them to recruit membership from other trades and to exercise authority of very wide scope. The mayor and corporation, threatened by this rival jurisdiction, fought back valiantly and secured a legal victory that restored their monopoly of authority and destroyed the threat of possible guild influence in the city.[53]

It is difficult to describe the condition of most of the city guilds during the sixteenth century. Both the confusion in all the sources as to the dates of the granting of charters and the actual fact of frequent charter renewals suggest the unstable and even ephemeral character of several of these guilds. There is some evidence that the Chamber pursued a deliberate policy of incorporating or reincorporating the various city trades in order to establish a structure of control through which the various economic regulations of the city as well as the economic legislation of the Crown could be carried out. This is borne out by the frequent grants and regrants of com-

[52] AB iv, 486.
[53] See Mrs. J. R. Green, *Town Life in the Fifteenth Century* (New York & London, 1895), II, 172–181, for an account of this affair.

pany charters during the Elizabethan period. In the act for the summoning of the Midsummer watch—the annual review of the city militia—in 1561, there is a list of the companies in existence.[54] They numbered eight: butchers, smiths and cutlers, glovers and skinners, bakers, shoemakers, tuckers and weavers, tailors, and lastly the newly formed merchant adventurers. These represented the older companies of the city, for all of them except the butchers, the smiths, and the merchants had charters dating back to late Plantagenet or early Tudor times.[55] The smiths and cutlers were a new company, chartered in 1560. The butchers present a problem, for no charter is recorded for them earlier than 1566 although there is an undated entry, probably of 1562, to the effect that the butchers were to have a corporation.[56]

Within a very few years this array of companies was considerably increased. In 1563 the cappers and haberdashers were added.[57] Next to be incorporated—in 1565—were the helliers and coopers;[58] in 1579, the brewers;[59] in 1586 the painters, joiners, glaziers, and carpenters were made one company.[60] In the same period, moreover, the cordwainers[61] and the skinners[62] both received new charters, while the butchers and brewers[63] obtained regrants. It is reasonable

---

[54] AB iv, 117.

[55] There is the utmost confusion about the dates of incorporation of these companies. What seems probable is that, with the exception of the tailors and probably the weavers and tuckers, they did not have continuous existence, so that many of the incorporations are really re-incorporations. I have followed Hooker himself for the older companies (see Hooker, *History*, III, 826 and 892). The glovers and skinners were incorporated in 22 Edward IV; the bakers in 2 Edward IV and again in 3 Henry VII; the cordwainers in 20 Edward IV; the tuckers and weavers in 17 Edward IV and again in 5 and 6 P & M; while the tailors, according to Isacke, *Antiquities*, 63, received a charter from the King, Edward IV, in the sixth year of his reign.

[56] The incorporation of 1566 is in AB iii, 186; that of 1562 in AB iv, 172.

[57] Hooker, *History*, III, 892. There is an old charter of 8 Henry VII, according to the same source, which probably had lapsed.

[58] AB iii, 186, and Hooker, *History*, III, 892.

[59] AB iii, 411 and 424.

[60] AB iv, 488.

[61] Hooker, *History*, III, 825.

[62] *Ibid.*, 826.

[63] AB iii, 424.

to assume that this spate of new incorporation and reincorporation was not accidental, but part of a deliberate policy of tighter economic organization practiced by the Chamber. The foundation of the merchants' company and of the wool and cloth market were other aspects of this same policy.

The theory behind this was expressed by Hooker when he asserted that all the citizens, according to their arts and occupations, were reduced to several companies.[64] This, he added, was a "greate ease" for the mayor since he could leave all their causes to be dealt with by their own governors. The same purpose appeared in the instructions to the new brewers company in 1579, which directed the masters and wardens to bring in any members summoned by the mayor or justices, and required them to be responsible for the troublesome task of maintaining legal weights.[65] Similarly they were ordered to undertake the execution of the Statute of Apprentices.[66] If, however, the guilds were to provide established organizations upon which the responsibility for executing the borough's economic policy was to devolve, they were also to remain strictly subordinate to the civic authorities. In the butchers' charter of 1566 the right to revoke within one year was expressly reserved to the city,[67] and in their regrant of 1575 this right was extended for an indefinite period.[68] We have already seen the reaction of the city to the victualers' effort to win independence through a royal charter. The Chamber was clearly determined to keep guild charters within its grant so that it might limit their terms.

One company, at least—the weavers, fullers, and shearmen—was able to secure a measure of independence by obtaining a royal charter in 1621. This guild, the sole one to survive into modern times and the only one whose records remain, had built a chapel in 1471; it had acquired in the town a small endowment of properties which narrowly escaped confiscation, and its chapel was rebuilt into a meeting hall. But not until 1602 did the company acquire legal

[64] Hooker, *History*, III, 824.
[65] AB iii, 424.
[66] AB iv, 228.
[67] AB iii, 186.
[68] *Ibid.*, 357.

recognition through a city charter.[69]

Perhaps no other aspect of the Exeter community so clearly displays its medieval character as its economic organization. The maintenance of monopoly conditions in the wholesale markets, to the benefit of local merchants, and the rigorous protection in retail markets of the city consumers' interests, strengthened the traditional structure of economic life.[70] Although signs of strain became evident in the seventeenth century, Exeter remained, at least until the Civil War, a highly regulated and largely autonomous economic unit, in which almost every facet of commercial and industrial activity was effectively controlled by the borough government.

PART 2: THE PROTECTION OF THE SOCIAL ORDER

A rigidly ordered system of regulation secured the economic bases of the community. It was equally necessary to protect the whole social structure of the city by correspondingly elaborate controls. The public peace, never quite secure in this violent age, had to be preserved. Hand in hand with this task went the maintenance of the orthodoxies of politics and (what was almost the same thing) religion. And at a still more profound level, it was the obligation of the community to enforce the precepts of a morality resting upon immemorial tradition. In all these respects Exeter was deeply conventional, anxious to keep social disturbance at a minimum and to conform to standards laid down by an aristocratic and conservative national society.

[69] The charter reflects the conflict between the exporters, concerned to keep the quality high and the costs low, and the artisans, fearful of interlopers who pursued their craft outside the guild. In securing from the Crown a monopoly over their trades within the city and the power to maintain their rights without reference to the civic authorities, the artisans had successfully defied the merchant oligarchy within the city. See Youings, *Tuckers Hall*, ch. 3.

[70] See ECM, Deeds 1739 and 1739a, entitled "Exceptions to proposed articles of weavers, fullers, and sheermen." The city objected to the provision which would have allowed a man to be free of the company without being free of the city. They refused to exclude from the city workmen not free of the company. The Chamber also insisted on punishing faulty workmen itself rather than allowing the wardens to do this, and lastly the magistrates refused to allow the company officers to punish assaults on wardens or masters.

The first problem was the maintenance of the public peace. The concern of Tudor officialdom with this problem is an historical commonplace. To their minds the margin between a mere breach of the peace and the complete dissolution of society seemed a narrow one. The magistrates of Exeter shared in this general fear for local as well as for national reasons. The outbreak of 1549 was fresh in their memory, and the existence of religious and economic discontent, here as elsewhere, gave good grounds for concern.

The machinery of peace enforcement was simple. Nominally headed by the mayor, it was administered primarily by the aldermen. From 1537 they united in their persons the legal powers of aldermen and of justices. In their first capacity "rather inquisitive than judiciall," as Hooker says,[1] they were to see the peace be kept. A pair of aldermen was assigned each quarter of the city, wherein, following the custom of London, they were to hold their wardmoot.[2] By an act of the Chamber of 1549, renewed in 1563, they were assigned two assistants out of the number of the Twenty-Four.[3] Occasionally this office involved active intervention on the part of the aldermen to put down open riot. Such was the case when Blackaller and Hurst had to act at the time of the dissolution of St. Nicholas Priory. A more routine but most important duty was that imposed on them by an act of the Chamber in 1560.[4] By this it was ordered that no resident of the city was to let dwelling space to any newcomer without first bringing him before the alderman of the quarter. The alderman was to inquire from whence the stranger came and the cause of his departure from that place. The occasion for this new regulation was stated in the act. Various persons, banished from the city "for their lose & lewde lyffe," had returned and were being sheltered by certain citizens who were now threatened with heavy punishment for such action. Thus by a species of police registration the city authorities could keep a fairly strict watch over the movement of strangers and act promptly to oust undesir-

[1] Hooker, *History*, III, 812.
[2] *Ibid.*, 813.
[3] AB ii, 208, and AB iii, 122. See Chapter II, above.
[4] AB ii, 368, printed in Hooker, *History*, III, 941. See also AB iii, 43. These instructions were frequently reissued by the Chamber.

ables. The alderman had other inquisitorial duties as well, as the instructions of 1560 indicate.[5] He was to inquire in his ward after anyone "that lyveth suspiciously, any skolding brawling woman or drunkard in his warde, any stranger or suspecte person . . . any vagabonds, upright men, guyler byrdes, myghty beggars, bawdes, whores or any myslyving people." He was to look out also for that notoriously unruly element of sixteenth-century city life, the apprentices, to see that they spent every night in their masters' houses and refrained from unlawful games.

The aldermen, besides their councillor assistants, had at their command two constables for each quarter,[6] who were the paid officers of the city, the patrolmen of this police force. They had also in times of emergency the watchmen. The latter were summoned up out of the citizenry by the magistrates. This was usually done in any time of crisis, as during 1550 or after the Gunpowder Plot. Thirty-two men were on duty each night, eight per quarter.[7] They assembled at the Guildhall and thence went through the city two by two to see that the gates were fastened and fires and candlelight looked to. The watch was an institution proverbially ineffective, and a clause in the instructions that "they do watche and not sleepe all night" makes one suspect that the Exeter watch was no exception. Besides the watch the city regularly employed beadles,[8] whose duties were not only to supervise the poor but also to keep a watch for beggars and to arrest them.

The aldermen enjoyed a dual legal personality, for they also bore the Queen's commission as justices of the peace and of gaol delivery. In the latter capacity they judged many of the offenses which in their aldermanic capacity they were bound to search out. And it was

---

[5] *Ibid.*

[6] AB iv, 260.

[7] See Hooker, *History*, III, 820, and AB vii, 414. In the latter, order is taken for a watch from 8 P.M. to 5 A.M. from early November through Candlemas in February. The watchmen were to have 6d. a night. The levy to pay them fell on all subsidy-men on the last roll. Every three rated £1 in land and every two rated at £3 in goods were to find a watchman on pain of distress. Those assessed at higher rates paid proportionately.

[8] AB viii, 190, in which the beadles are given a reward of £1 for arresting beggars and encouraged to keep up their good work.

primarily as justices that they administered public order in Exeter. We are very fortunate in our knowledge of their activity, thanks to the ubiquitous Hooker. In the first part of Act Book iv there is a miscellaneous collection of entries, dating from 1559 to 1569 and mainly concerning cases heard before the justices of the peace during this period. These are not the formal court records, but mostly mere notations on the nature of the case and the punishment, interspersed with copies of depositions taken at these trials. Thus they give us a good idea of the activity of the justices of the city over a full decade, enabling us to see something of the particular problems of public order which engaged their attention.

Several general categories of offense sort themselves out of the miscellaneous mass of cases noted. There were, of course, many ordinary breaches of the peace, violence done to other persons, thievery, or general disorderly conduct. Two types of cases more peculiarly characteristic of the period stand out. The first of these comes under the general term of vagrancy, a word which to the Elizabethan magistrate denoted the mere condition of social displacement. The unemployed, masterless man, drifting from job to job and from place to place, was a subject of grave suspicion on the part of the Tudor justice, who felt that such men were almost certain to fall into active misbehavior. The second general type of case was that concerned with moral offenses. The frequent appearance of these cases in the court makes it clear that the justices considered them to be the concern of a secular court as matters affecting not only the religious well-being of the offenders, but also the health of civil society.

Let us look at some of these cases and at the action which the court took in each of them. There are, of course, many examples of the most common offenses. Stealing almost invariably was dealt with by a sentence of banishment from the city, sometimes accompanied by the pillory or a whipping.[9] Active violence usually meant being bound over to keep the peace, although if the offense were aggravated by resistance to the officers of law it might mean some time in gaol. A closely related offense was that of playing unlawful

[9] For such instances see AB iv, 101, 124, 127, 177, 268, 285, 301, and 302.

games, particularly that known as "nine holes." For this, too, the punishment was to be bound over by recognizance.[10] Gambling was punishable by like penalty.[11] The offense of name calling which so vexed the councillors and justices themselves in the council chamber was punishable severely. Thomas Marshall who called Mrs. Tothill and Grace Walker names in the street and also insulted Gilbert Saywell, one of the stewards of the city, was given forty days in the city gaol and bound over in £40.[12] A more severe punishment was visited upon Johan, daughter of John Twychen, who was whipped and banished for calling her father a thief and her mother a whore.[13] Other offenses of a more peculiarly sixteenth-century character were "scolding" and sumptuous dress. The common scold suffered for her particular offense by a particular kind of punishment. She was "cocked," that is, ducked in Exe. A local variation of this punishment was to be towed down the river behind a boat. One day in 1562[14] no fewer than four women were so punished.[15] Sumptuary regulations were emphasized in the instructions to the aldermen and evidently regarded seriously. Apprentices were thought to be peculiarly susceptible to this kind of temptation.[16] Apprentice Thomas Goodale, who in the Christmas season of 1561 made an unseemly display of great hose, great ruffs, and silk hat, paid 3s. 4d. for his presumption.[17]

The subject of vagrancy is a complex one. Behind it, as we have said above, lay deep fear of the idle and homeless man, wandering across the country, as a threat to the most elementary kind of social order. To the magistrates of Exeter the problem was a more imme-

[10] AB iv, 2 and 302.

[11] AB iv, 154, 189. One gambler, who had induced several scholars of the high school to play with him and had won, was ordered to repay the money and also to retrieve the schoolboys' books from pawn (AB iv, 156).

[12] AB iv, 176.

[13] AB iv, 136.

[14] AB iv, 187.

[15] The offense could involve banishment as in the case of the two scolds put in the "cage" until they gave surety for not returning to the city (AB iv, 197). On another occasion a husband was ordered to provide a place for his wife outside the city because of her unquiet behavior (AB iv, 199).

[16] HMC Rep, 315.

[17] AB iv, 153.

diate and local one. Their object was at once to get rid of the un-
desirable wanderer and to punish him severely enough to frighten
him from returning, thus giving the city a reputation among the
vagrant class which would discourage others; hence the repeated
punishment of whipping and banishment imposed on vagrants.[18]
Such a policy shifted the burden of responsibility from the Exeter
magistrates, but did little to solve the problem of the vagrant.

   We may look more closely into the action of the justices in individual cases. The list of cases is long, but not many of them specify
the circumstances. The usual situation is represented by two instances of December 1559.[19] In one of these two men were whipped
"for their runagate and vagrant life," given their letters, dismissed
and banished out of the city. In the other, John Smale of Holy
Trinity parish was taken for a loiterer and vagrant, imprisoned for
nine days, and then given until Shrovetide to leave with his wife
and children. These cases could be duplicated in substance many
times in the following years, and it is evident enough that the mere
fact of "runagate and vagrant life" was sufficient for condemnation.
Occasionally, however, we have a more specific account of the
activities of the vagrant. In February 1562, two vagrants, one of no
fixed residence, the other late of Windsor, were whipped for wandering about and pretending to be tooth drawers and surgeons.[20]
Mercy tempered judgment here, for one of them was pardoned and
allowed to remain becoming common servant to a barber of Exeter
for one year, with 40s., meat, drink, and the profits of tooth pulling.
On another occasion, four Irishmen were arrested and ordered to
be whipped severely, because they had gone about the country asking
alms, saying that they had lost by sea to the French sums of £1,200
or £1,600 or other sums. They were ordered sent to Padstow for
transportation to Ireland.[21]

   One rather pathetic account, that of a certain Alice Smythe, taken
in March 1560 with a vagrant whom she claimed was her husband,

[18] Hooker, *History*, III, 848.   [19] Both these are found in AB iv, 3.
[20] AB iv, 163.   [21] AB iv, 251.

may serve as a model for the adventures of many of these unfortunate beings.[22] She had been wandering for more than a year, having left Wales a twelvemonth ago Christmas. Alice had crossed the Bristol Channel to Ilfracombe, where she stayed until Lent before moving on to Barnstaple to work awhile at spinning. From there she had made her way to Padstow in Cornwall, back to Barnstaple, to Tiverton, to Bradninch, and finally terminated her wanderings at Exeter. With her as with so many others, it was a story of desperate search for livelihood in place after place. Most pathetic are stories of whole families in like plight, such as four vagrants coming from Brecknockshire, a man, woman, child, and the man's mother. The woman was carted, the man whipped, the mother released to go to a brother at Collumpton.[23] It is difficult to discern motive among this mass of drifting humanity, to distinguish between the unemployed laborer seeking honest employment and the habitual vagabond, living by whatever means he could.

Probably they could not have made such a distinction themselves: hard necessity blunted the most honest intentions. The Exeter magistrates on occasion made such allowances as the law permitted. In the case of a Worcestershire victualer, William Sparkman, in February 1565–66,[24] warning was given that he was to bring testimony for "good a-bearing" within one month or else be treated as a vagrant. Exception was made, too, for the licensed beggar. Such a one was Henry Burton of Yorkshire who was taken with £10 5s. 9d. on him. He was released with his begging letter, but the money was kept, and after inquiry made to the Lord Mayor of York turned over to the use of the poor.[25] From the cases mentioned above it will be obvious how wide an area these wanderers traversed. In one single group of vagrants seized in March 1565, there were found persons who were dismissed to their respective places of origin in Cornwall, Somerset, Worcestershire, Berkshire, Berwick, and London.[26] Most frequent were vagrants from other parts of

---

[22] AB iv, 16.
[24] AB iv, 289.
[26] AB iv, 271.

[23] AB iv, 262.
[25] AB iv, 300.

Devon, and from the adjoining counties of Cornwall, Somerset, and Dorset.

Part of the offense lay not in the vagrants themselves but in the inhabitants of Exeter who gave them reception. The law was explicit upon this subject, for in the annual proclamation of the new mayor it was charged that no person should receive into his house any stranger without first presenting him to the mayor and his officers.[27] That this regulation was widely evaded is evident from the number of cases involving illegal reception of lodgers. Typical of such cases was that of John and Joan Bott, who were peremptorily ordered not to keep lodgings any more,[28] or that of William Pinnefold, gold-smith, accused of keeping a tippling house and receiving suspicious persons to lodge without license.[29] He was put in ward until he should give sureties. More scandalous, however, was the case of Thomas Weare.[30] One of the beadles of the city assigned, among other things, to prevent any begging in the streets, he had made his house a center for vagrants. In punishment he lost his office and was deprived of the right to sell ale and to keep lodgings. One result of this complacency on the part of various Exonians of the lodging and alehouse keeper class, was the frequent return of banished vagrants to the city. Returned vagrants, if caught, were subject to a second punishment usually accompanied by whipping. The recurrence of such cases is testimony to the limited effectiveness of the magistrates' policy towards vagrancy.

The problem was not, however, entirely confined to wanderers from outside the city. Within the walls idleness presented itself not so much as an economic but as a social question, for idleness meant an aimless and disorderly way of life. In some instances it was a man who shirked the responsibilities and routine of family life. Edward Smythe promised to keep to his wife, master, and work, and not to run about the country.[31] Thomas Weare, who had been a vagabond and left his wife for other women, was warned to return

---

[27] Hooker, *History*, III, 848.
[28] AB iv, 93.
[29] AB iv, 151.
[30] AB iv, 271.
[31] AB iv, 210.

to good behavior or else he would be whipped.[32] Then there were apprentices who did not stick to their work, such as those brought before the justices in March 1560.[33] Their particular offense, besides idleness, was playing at the forbidden "nine holes." All were released on condition of taking a master again, the terms of service being specified by the justices. An even more direct concern with idleness—and here in a higher walk of life—was seen in the case of Henry Southron.[34] He followed no vocation, so was compelled to agree either to get himself to some man's service or to leave the city by the end of the next sessions and go to the Inns of Court for his study.

The second great concern of the Exeter justices was that of offenses against the moral law. In a city which had taken the seesaw of religious settlements from Henry to Elizabeth with remarkable equanimity, and where the characteristic symptoms of Puritanism were late in appearing,[35] one is a little surprised to see such a vigorous enforcement of sexual morality. It is probably necessary to look elsewhere for the roots of this policy. Significantly, in the mayoral proclamation the clause directed against women of evil life, ordering their immediate departure from the city, was grouped with the similar provisions against vagabonds and against receiving strangers to lodge.[36] In other words, in the eyes of the magistrates, moral offenders were a danger to civil society of the same kind as vagabonds. Of course, the immediate peril was not of such an obvious nature as in the latter case, and we must suppose that a strong infusion of a general religious sentiment strengthened the policy. Nevertheless, it remained primarily a matter of law enforcement rather than one of the moral direction of society.

There is no need to recite the long list of sordid little histories recorded in the act book; they are all of a likeness. A few general remarks may be made. Punishment fell much more frequently on the woman than on the man. It was usually she who was banished,

---

[32] AB iv, 173.
[34] AB iv, 168.
[36] Hooker, *History*, III, 848.

[33] AB iv, 18.
[35] See Chapter VIII

or, occasionally, carted and whipped. A striking example of this was the case of Richard Sweet.[37] He was convicted of begetting a child by an unmarried woman. Her punishment was banishment; his, forty days imprisonment (with bread and water on Wednesday and Friday), but he was released within two weeks, upon promise of amendment. The culprits were always of the lower classes, and very frequently the offenses of vagrancy and immorality were coupled. This doubtless strengthened the magistrates' conviction that the two were closely connected. Punishment for these offenses was the same: banishment, sometimes accompanied by whipping. A special clause appeared in the mayoral proclamation against the return of anyone banished for moral offenses. Here again, the problem of collusion between lodging keepers and the offenders appeared, and there were cases in which citizens guilty of this offense were severely punished.

Some question may be raised as to why these matters were not drawn into the bishop's consistory court. At least once this issue was raised by a citizen, who in his petition to the bishop protested his innocence of charges cast upon him, claimed the protection of the episcopal jurisdiction, and implied that his secular judges were themselves men of frail lives.[38] There is no evidence that his petition succeeded. The city was deeply jealous of episcopal jurisdiction, and in this case may have feared that the relatively milder punishments of the consistory court would not prove a severe enough deterrent to would-be offenders.[39] In any case, the borough justices continued to exercise a rigorous and determined policy in this matter.

Other, rather miscellaneous, matters which occupied the attention of the justices may be mentioned briefly. The most important of these was the examination of "reporters of slaunderous tayles and

[37] AB iv, 152.

[38] AB iv, 129.

[39] The Bishop did protest against this practice of the Chamber. See ECM, Miscellaneous Roll 103, Document 1, p. 30. "They intermeddle in many matters of ecclesiastical concern as punishing some for disorders in church, others for incontinency, examining some upon articles and otherwise for speaking against some preachers by them misliked either for their doctrine or discipline."

newes," largely of subjects who disapproved of the new establishment in religion. But civil matters also arose. In August 1560, for instance, one John Tucker was summoned before the justices[40] for having said there were three men of Exeter trading with London, whom he would meet between London and Exeter before Christmas and "make them in such case that they would not be able to trade the other nor help themselves to buy any one cloth." He added that he would meet them on the hills and make them crouch on their knees before he left them. Under examination he admitted he meant Richard Taylor, the master of the weavers and tuckers, Richard Maunsell, and Ambrose Howell. The justices contented themselves with a reprimand and a warning that if in the future he acted against any of the men mentioned he would be bound over to his "good abearing."

A similar case in the same year involved a citizen who had sheltered a discharged soldier from Berwick who was without a passport.[41] The citizen had stood surety for the appearance of this man in court, but the latter had absconded. In the course of his examination on this matter the man said "that it will come to pass as some have said that they hoped to see some of the tailors hung and that a report hath been that a new Underhill would rise up among them again." He refused to say who had said this, and was held in custody until the Earl of Bedford could be consulted. The latter thought the man should be pilloried, but in the end he made his submission and was let off because he had many children. Both of these episodes were probably connected with the current struggle between the newly incorporated merchants' company and the retailers, led by the tailors' company. Neither of them was a matter of any seriousness, but they afford us glimpses of smoldering resentments, often merely personal, but capable of being generalized into sentiments dangerous to the civil order. It is not difficult to understand the concern of the Exeter magistrates, rulers of a society potentially so rich in sources of general discontent.

This brief account of the problem of public order in the city

[40] AB iv, 44.   [41] AB iv, 35.

reveals a zealous and persistent magistracy. Their conception of public order was not entirely a narrowly legal one, the mere restraint of the unruly and vicious. It involved a view of society in its largest aspects as a static but functionally arranged entity, forever threatened by disarrangements of the constituent parts that might be fatal to the whole. Acting in this context, they were often ruthless towards the offender and blind to the circumstance of his offense. Hence the intractable problem of vagrancy, at least partially economic in its roots, was treated merely by the punishment of the vagrants. Moreover, even though the social view of the magistrates had a certain breadth, they seldom generalized it in terms larger than those of the local community. Perhaps, to do them justice, they were too hard pressed maintaining the social equilibrium within their own city walls to worry about the problem elsewhere. At any rate, action took a form calculated to relieve them of present, and to minimize the possibility of future, responsibility. By their ceaseless attempt to banish the offenders, the magistrates merely evaded their burden temporarily, for it encouraged a similar policy elsewhere and engaged them, as the cases evidence, in a vain game of battledore and shuttlecock with other local authorities in which the unfortunate vagrants were tossed back and forth. In general, one suspects, the vigorous efforts of authority resulted only in a kind of equilibrium in which neither order nor disorder gained perceptibly. Under the circumstances this might be accounted a real victory for the forces of order.

PART 3: THE CARE OF THE UNFORTUNATE

Strict supervision and rigorous punishment could hold the vicious and the morally unreliable in check, but another and perhaps more dangerous source of discontent was poverty. At the beginning of the sixteenth century this fact was but dimly recognized, and only slowly and reluctantly did English society at large come to understand it and to accept some measure of public responsibility for the problem. The religious obligation to care for the poor was, of course, of long standing, and at Exeter as elsewhere charitable foundations partly lay, partly ecclesiastical, had been reared by private individuals during the Middle Ages. These foundations were intended as works of individual piety acceptable in the sight of God, although a motive of civic pride, a desire to leave some monument of benefit to the community, was also visible. We can best begin by describing what private charity provided for the unfortunate of Exeter at the beginning of our period.

Of the monastic foundations within the city, one, St. Johns, was established as an eleemosynary as well as a conventual institution. Out of its income of £102, £29 went for the support of thirteen paupers living in the hospital and nine students of grammar.[1] St. Nicholas Priory, although primarily conventual, also provided certain charitable services. Hooker describes the institution of the "Poor Men's Parlor,"[2] a room in the monastery to which each day seven poor men came to receive their dinner. On Fridays the number of recipients was swelled to include all the poor among the tenants of St. Nicholas' Fee. Besides these two foundations, there were a few small endowments, parts of chantries or benefactions attached to parish churches. These were all very modest. One of those in the cathedral, Horsey's foundation of 1518, left a few pounds of income from lands, over and above the priests' stipends, to the poor and to the prisoners in Exeter.[3] At St. Mary Arches the income of £19 was shared between the priest and twelve poor men.[4] All these endowments vanished at the Dissolution with the exception of certain reserved rents at St. Johns Hospital. When the hospital passed to the Crown, this income was set aside for the use of the poor, and in 1562 the Queen granted to the city the nomination of the four paupers who now yearly received 21s. 8d. each, out of the reserved rents of St. Johns.[5] They no longer lived in the hospital.

In addition to the endowments managed by ecclesiastical hands, there were also several private foundations, controlled by lay feoffees

---

[1] *Valor Ecclesiasticus*, 6 vols. (London, 1810–34), II, 314.

[2] Hooker, quoted in R. J. E. Boggis, *History of the Diocese of Exeter* (Exeter, 1922), 355.

[3] George Oliver, *Monasticon Diocesis Exoniensis* (Exeter, 1846), 472.

[4] *Ibid.*

[5] Hooker, *History*, III, 607.

or by the Chamber. These included seven almshouses. The oldest
was that of St. Mary Magdalen, outside the South Gate, which had
come into the possession of the city as early as the time of
Henry III.[6] Originally founded as a leper hospital, by Tudor times
it housed the poor of any condition. Its warden was an officer chosen
yearly by the Chamber out of its own members to administer the
lands.[7] By the middle of Elizabeth's reign, these lands brought in a
yearly income of £18 6s. 7d., out of which each poor resident
received 6d. per week, while the chaplain received £2 a year.[8] At a
maximum, twelve people could be accommodated here.

The fifteenth century had seen the foundation of the other almshouses. In 1408, Lord Bonville, then one of the great magnates of
the West, had founded an establishment in St. Mary Major parish
which housed twelve poor and provided each with 7d. per week.[9]
The patronage of these houses passed through various private hands
until by the forfeiture of the Grays of Dorset and Suffolk it came to
the Crown in the first year of Mary.[10] In 1562 when Elizabeth
granted the nomination of the paupers at St. Johns to the city, she
also allowed it the right to nominate those of Bonville's houses, but
the income of the house remained in Crown possession and there
were no funds for upkeep available, for the Crown rents provided
only the pensions.[11]

In 1439 another foundation was established by William Wynard,
Recorder of Exeter.[12] Here twelve poor were accommodated along
with a priest, who served a little chapel commonly known as God's
House, and who lived on the premises. These paupers were in

[6] Isacke, *Antiquities*, 10–11.
[7] Hooker, *History*, III, 822.
[8] *Ibid.*, 686–694.
[9] Oliver, *Monasticon*, 404.
[10] *Accounts and Papers*, 1909, LXV, Endowed Charities of County Borough
of Exeter, 59. All references to *Accounts and Papers* are to volume LXV.
[11] *Ibid.*
[12] Richard Isacke, *An Alphabetical Register of Divers Persons, who by their
last wills, grants, feoffments, and other deeds, have given tenements, rents,
annuities, and moneys toward the relief of the poor of the County of Devon
and City and County of Exon; and likewise to many other cities and towns in
England* . . . (London, 1736), 165.

receipt of 8d. weekly. Here, at the Dissolution the priest's pension of eight marks passed to the Crown, but the administration of the lands and nomination of the inmates remained with the Speke family, descendants of the founder.

Of two other fifteenth-century foundations we know less. In 1406 a certain Simon Grendon (mayor in 1405)[13] founded ten houses, afterwards known as the Ten Cells, which he enfeoffed to the civic corporation. The income of this establishment was but £2 per annum. The other foundation was that of St. Katherine's almshouses, the donor being Dr. John Stevens, a doctor of physic and canon of the cathedral.[14] Thirteen poor nominated by the dean and chapter were provided with 4d. by the quarter. At the close of the century a baker of the city, John Palmer, built houses outside the South Gate for four poor women, with yearly pensions of 6s. 8d. each, and enfeoffed the endowment lands to the city.[15] Thus, in 1540 within the city and its precincts there were places for 63 poor in the various almshouses. Of these, 42 were in the nomination of the city. The Reformation and its attendant political convulsions had swept away the habitation of the poor at St. Johns, destroyed their endowment, and reduced them from thirteen to four. It had also swept away the lands of Bonville's foundation, but had left the pensions for the poor.[16]

Over and above the almshouses the city possessed certain other endowments. The most important of these was the foundation of St. Edmund upon Exe bridge, established in 1250 by Walter Gervis, a mayor. Out of an income of £18 15s. there came £2 10s. for a priest and other small payments made to the two friaries and for obits in the cathedral, while the balance went to the upkeep of the bridge itself.[17] The secular endowment of this establishment

[13] *Ibid.*, 65. See also Isacke, *Antiquities*, 207.

[14] *Ibid.*, 131. In 1630 in a Chancery judgment on a commission under the Statute of Charitable Uses, the Dean and Chapter of Exeter were ordered to pay 17s. 4d. annually to the poor in St. Katherine's Almshouse, a payment which apparently was in arrears.

[15] Isacke, *Antiquities*, 206.

[16] For a summary of the data on the almshouses see Table II.

[17] Oliver, *Monasticon*, 474. There may also have been some almshouses on Exe bridge of a separate foundation, but their history is very obscure.

remained to the city, and in Hooker's survey of 1585 was shown as bringing in £27 6s. 11d.[18] By that time it was incorporated into the regular city receipts and no longer reckoned as a separate item, although expenses for the upkeep of the bridge still had to be met out of it. Another endowment which had been incorporated into the regular city revenue was that of the manor of Awliscombe. Originally given by Thomas Calwodeley in 1497 for the relief of the poor from the burden of royal taxes, it was apparently early regarded as general income and appeared as such in the receivers' rolls.

We cannot know how effective a provision for the poor could be made from these resources, but about the middle of the sixteenth century considerable changes altered the whole picture. First came the fundamental shift in attitude by which public responsibility for the unfortunate was accepted. This new policy was inaugurated from above and found expression in ever more stringent acts of Parliament that exacted public contribution for the relief of the poor. At the same time came a renewed impulse of private generosity, which in the milieu of the Reformed religion took radically new forms of expression. All these changes were mirrored in the Exeter scene. It will be convenient to treat the two sides of the question separately, dealing first with private benefactions and later with publicly financed measures of relief.

The term "private benefaction" is somewhat misleading since in practice it usually meant private provision of funds but public management of the endowment. Very frequently the board of trustees set up by the donor would be a civic corporation; the advantages of an official and perpetual body are obvious, especially for smaller endowments. The corporation of Exeter thus became the manager of a considerable number of trusts (which became in effect civic property), and even where the benefactor had nominated a private board he usually selected individuals who were also members of the Chamber. Substantially the civic rulers managed both publicly and privately provided funds for poor relief.

The list of benefactions added to the existing structure of endow-

[18] Hooker, *History*, III, 695–704.

ment in Exeter is rather long and certainly complicated. It is most convenient to present it in tabular form (see Tables II and III). Two tables have been prepared; Table II lists the funds based on land endowments. Most, although not all of these, were bequeathed for more or less traditional charitable purposes. Table III includes the revolving loan funds, different in type and in purpose. (The whole question of educational endowments has been deliberately excluded here in order to give it separate treatment later.)

The traditional endowments followed an age-old pattern. Land, the only stable form of wealth, was set aside to provide perpetual income for some charitable purpose. With the Reformation the motive behind these gifts altered somewhat, but the fundamental impulse of Christian charity remained. The forms which they took had been more or less stereotyped during the Middle Ages. The most generous gifts of this sort made in Exeter during our period

TABLE II.—*Exeter Almshouses, 1640*

Almshouses	Date of foundation	Annual income	Number of inhabitants	Allowance per capita per week
Magdalen	temp. Henry III	£20 (av.)	12	6d.
Bonville's	1408	21	12	7d.
Wynard's	1439	20.16.0	12	8d.
Ten Cells (Grendon's)	1406	8.13.4	10	4d.
St. Katherine's	15th century	5.15.10	13	2d.
Palmer's	15th century	2.10.8	4	3d.
Hurst's	1567	20[a]	12	20s.[b]
Davy's	1600	20.16.0	6	2s. 4d.[c] 1s. 6d.[d]
Flaye's	1634	48.13.4	8	4s.[c] 2s.[e]

[a] Hurst left an income of £12 per annum; it was supplemented by a legacy of £8 per annum from John Lante in 1614.
[b] Per annum.
[c] Per couple.
[d] Per single man.
[e] Per widow.

TABLE III.—*Endowed Loan Funds*

Donor	Date	Amount
Revolving Funds		
Joan Tuckfield	1568	£300
Thomas Prestwood	1576	40
Alice Macey	1578	50
Thomas Chappell	1589	30
Hugh May	1592	60
Joan Cleveland	1599	200
Peter Blundell	1599	500
Christopher Spicer	1599	100
Hugh Atwill	1602	6.13.4
Philip Whitrow	1602	16
John Haydon	1602	200
Jane Hewett	1603	10
William Spicer	1604	60
William Martin	1609	20
John Berryman	1614	100
Ralph Hamer	1615	75
John Periam	1616	1,000
Augustine Drake and son	1641	60
	Total	2,827.13.4
Accumulating Funds		
Nicholas Spicer	1628	Net worth 1640–41 £751
Sir Thomas White	1583	Total 1640 300

were the three almshouse foundations.[19] The donors were all prominent civic figures; each had served as mayor. William Hurst's houses were built in 1567 with an endowment of £12 a year out of land near the city.[20] John Davy's were opened in 1600; their endowment of £20 16s. a year came out of the rectory of Mariansleigh,

[19] The Chamber also acquired in 1538 by the will of John Gilberd (or (Gilbert), an almshouse at Newton Bushel in Devon, with an income of £4 annually and three inmates, but these houses were not available to Exeter citizens.

[20] Isacke, *Register*, 69. See also RR 10–11 Elizabeth et seq. The twelve almsmen received £1 a year each.

Devon, of which the city became the proprietor.[21] The third foundation was that of Thomas Flaye,[22] made in 1634 and added to later by his wife, with a total income of £48 a year. Unlike the other two this was not directly enfeoffed to the Chamber, but remained under the control of private feoffees who were, however, members of the Chamber. Altogether, these almshouses provided places for twenty-six more aged poor. Hurst's houses later received an additional £8 a year by the gift of Alderman John Lante in 1621.[23]

Generous legacies were left for other purposes than the almshouses. With the dissolution of the monasteries and charities, there were no sources of direct poor relief funds except the poor rate. But almost immediately after 1560 legacies for the benefit of the poor began to accumulate. The initial gifts were not large; in 1588 they amounted to less than £10 a year, but shortly afterwards handsome additions were made. By 1640 the income from endowments for general poor relief amounted to about £86 a year (see Table IV). Most of them derived their income from land, but the big Periam and Walker charities drew their revenues from the interest on loans.[24] In many cases certain poorer parishes were specified as beneficiaries. Some donors provided for clothing or bread; others left their gifts unrestricted. It is worth comparing the £86 a year going to direct relief out of private funds with the only poor rates known

[21] Isacke, *Register*, 49f. Two married couples and two single men were provided for, the couples to have 2s. 4d. a week and the single men 18d. each a week. They were to have lived in the city for ten years and were forbidden to beg.

[22] See *Accounts and Papers*, p. 143. Under the indenture of 1667 made before the death of Mrs. Flaye, it was provided that four single women and two retired ministers with their wives should be provided for, the single women at 2s. a week, the married couples at 4s. Thomas Flaye had left £22 13s. 4d. in rents to which his wife added another £26.

[23] See ECM, Ten Cells, etc., RR 18–19 James I. Lante had left £100 which was let out on loan at 8 per cent.

[24] For the administration of these funds see ECM, Periam Charity Rolls, 1625–26 et seq. Lands left to the city for charity before 1588 along with the Davy lands were consolidated under one officer, whose accounts are preserved in the Ten Cells etc. RR. For the Acland, Seldon, Borough, and Bevis charities there are no contemporary rolls. See *Accounts and Papers* under those headings.

Table IV.—*Endowment Income for General Poor
Relief administered by City*

Net annual income before 1598	£9.7.2
Additions from 1598 (annual income)	
Seldon bequest (1598)	19.10.0
Bevis bequest (1602)	4.0.0
Acland bequest (1616)	11.14.0
Periam bequest (1616)	20.0.0 (av.)
Borough bequest (1625)	6.16.0
Walker bequest (1630)	15.0.0 (av.)
Total annual income[a]	£86.7.2

[a] Besides the bequests listed above, the endowment left by Lawrence Atwill in 1588 provided £11.7.5 annually for the specific purpose of buying materials to provide work for the poor.

to us, those of the 1560's, which varied between £120 and £140 per annum.[25]

Some individual parishes had endowments in lands for their own poor; the very incomplete records suggest that in most cases such income, if it existed, did not amount to more than a pound or two a year during our period. The one exception was the parish of St. Sidwell, the poorest and perhaps the most populous one. The dean and chapter had lands here and were obligated to pay £20 16s. a year for the poor. Their payments lapsed in 1604 but were restored by a Chancery judgment of 1633 along with a lump payment of arrears amounting to £420 on which £21 interest was annually paid by the Chamber.[26] An uncertain but sometimes handsome addition to these funds came from cash bequests of various Exeter citizens. It was a custom, although not a universal one, to leave a gift of money in one's will to be distributed among the poor. These gifts varied from £1 up to £20 or £30 depending upon the size of

[25] See p. 112.

[26] See *Accounts and Papers*, 235 and 259. See also ECM, Book 148 under date 13 May 1647, and AB viii, 14 and 89. See also a sheet folded with the Ten Cells rolls for 13–14 Charles I which is a receipt of £24 from the dean and chapter due for the poor of St. Sidwells and paid to the wardens and overseers of the parish.

the estate, but in some years they must have made a sizable addition to poor relief funds.[27]

In the first half of the seventeenth century far larger endowments were made by Exeter citizens than in any previous period, but only a part of them went to the traditional type of direct relief discussed above. The fount of charity played more generously than ever before but its streams were directed into new channels. There was a marked swing away from mere relief of suffering toward positive efforts to reduce poverty. Self-help was the motto of the new philanthropy. The recipient was to be offered aid in winning his economic independence. In its indirect form this meant schooling, in more immediate form loans to launch him in a calling.

The revolving loan fund was very popular in Exeter, where the fashion was set by Mrs. Joan Tuckfield, widow of an ex-mayor. In 1568 she left among other benefactions a fund of £300 which was to be loaned out in individual sums of £5 to £20 to artificers of the city as capital for starting in their crafts. They were to have the use of the money for two years. This device caught on quickly; between 1568 and 1617 about £2,800 was left to be used in a similar way (see Table III). The largest gifts came from Peter Blundell, the famous clothier of Tiverton, £500 for the benefit of artificers; and from John Periam, the great Exeter merchant, £1,000 to be loaned out in sums of £200 to young merchants of the city.[28] The most intelligently conceived of these funds was that founded by the ex-mayor Nicholas Spicer in 1610. The barton of Slowe, which he left to the city as feoffee, brought in £40 in rents yearly.[29] The accumulation of the rent with the addition of renewal fines increased the sum available to nearly £800 by the early 1640's. Exeter also

---

[27] This statement is based upon over 60 Exeter wills of this period, deposited in Somerset House. John Hurst, who died in 1552, left 200 marks (see copy of will in Exeter City Library). Thomas Mogridge left £20 to the poor of Exeter and £3 to those of Topsham (PCC 84 Weldon). The list could be expanded to great length.

[28] See ECM, Books 149 and 316B for accounts of these and the other loan funds. See also Youings, *Tuckers Hall*, 82.

[29] See ECM, Book 150A for the Nicholas Spicer charity.

benefited from the generosity of Sir Thomas White, and from that source £300 had accumulated by 1631.[30]

The administration of these funds always presented difficulties by the very nature of the endowments. Not only were defaults on loans possible but boards of feoffees were unlikely to spend their own money on expensive lawsuits to recover losses. Accounts of the Exeter charities are extant for only a few, and it is probable that some of the smaller endowments vanished within a generation of their establishment, but at least £2,500 of the £2,800 mentioned above (over and above the Spicer fund) can be traced down to 1647, and the larger funds were certainly intact at that date.[31]

The hopes of the donors seem to have been justified by the continued solvency of the funds over more than a generation. It is hard to overestimate the importance of this considerable fund of credit to the general economy of the city. Both the accumulation of these surplus funds and their successful management are testimony to the underlying prosperity of the era.

A rather different type of fund, but one equally representative of the new outlook, was that left by Lawrence Atwill, a Londoner but descended from an old Exeter family. In 1588 he left funds to be invested in lands by the Chamber.[32] From the rents they were to create a fund that might be used to buy materials to set the unemployed to work. The importance of this fund will be seen below.

The new philanthropy reflects a new temper altogether. There was, of course, a measure of utilitarianism in it, thriftily designed to reduce the poor rate. But there was in these sober and cautious, yet generous, benefactors an element of social calculation, an effort to remove causes of poverty, to make permanent improvements in the social structure which had been altogether lacking in the haphazard charity of the past. It strikes too a note of secular optimism which had not been heard before.

[30] The famous White charity was set up by the London merchant, Sir Thomas White. The income from the endowment was £100 a year. Twenty-four cities shared the benefits, one each year. The money went out on loan at 4 per cent interest; every 24 years it was augmented by another £100.

[31] This statement is based on ECM, Book 316B and Book 149.

[32] See *Accounts and Papers*, 66. The Chamber paid £600 for these lands.

But these private efforts to assist the poor had already, before the end of the sixteenth century, been powerfully supplemented by public action. The new policy was initiated by the royal government, but like so much else of Tudor policy, the burdens of execution were laid almost entirely on the shoulders of local authorities. The work of the central government lay largely in general direction of policy and in the provision of adequate legal powers. As early as 1536 statutory provision had been made for the voluntary collection of alms in church.[33] They were to be gathered weekly by the church-wardens (under the direction of mayors in the cities) and applied to the impotent poor. In 1552 this act was expanded[34] by a provision that ordered the nomination of two collectors of alms in each parish. These collectors were to make a register of the contributors as well as of the recipients of the weekly distributions. In this act it was also provided that persons reluctant to contribute should be hailed before the bishop and reasoned with. The act of 1563 introduced a new element of coercion,[35] for now persons declining to yield to the bishop's exhortations were to be bound over to appear before the justices of the peace and might be committed to prison for refusal to be bound. The justices had the power to commit these recalcitrants to prison if they did not agree to pay the sum assessed. In towns where poor parishes were unable to care for their own needy, the mayor was to persuade the wealthier parishes "charitably to contribute somewhat."

The first evidence provided by the Exeter records concerning the administration of these statutes is an act book entry of 1560.[36] On 14 April it was ordered that six men should be appointed to attend in the Guildhall each Monday to receive from the collectors of each parish the sum of money due for the poor, as well as all other money given for them. Four days later another order appointed[37] two beadles of the poor who were to make "continual search that none

---

[33] 27 Henry VIII, c. 25, printed in J. R. Tanner, *Tudor Constitutional Documents*, 2d. ed. (Cambridge, 1948), 479–481.

[34] 5 & 6 Edward VI, c. 2, printed in Tanner, *Documents*, 476.

[35] *Ibid.*, 471.

[36] AB iv, 22.

[37] AB iv, 25.

beg at any man's door within this city." The names of all the officers of collection and distribution were also included. Besides the six members of the Chamber who were to keep the book of collections and distributions, there were twenty-two collectors and eighteen distributors for the four quarters of the city. Virtually all of the Twenty-Four were included in the list. The sum to be distributed each week in each quarter was also listed. By far the largest went to the parishes of the North quarter, which included St. Sidwell, with an allotment of £1 9s. 8d. weekly; the South quarter received 9s. 7d.; the West 7s. 1d.; and the East 7s. In the same month a windfall, out of the balance left over after the recent revaluation of coin, was given to the poor. Casual contributions of this nature, such as fines, were frequently added.[38]

There are still extant the accounts of the poor from 1563 to 1572,[39] and they provide much information on the administration of poor relief in our period. As in 1560, the city was divided into four quarters, but the grouping of parishes was somewhat different, for St. Sidwell's was now included with St. David, Holy Trinity, and St. Martin to form (quite illogically) the East quarter. Each parish was assessed a given weekly sum, and within the parish an assessment among individuals was made, apparently by agreement between parishioners and churchwardens. In accordance with the statute, the assessments were measured by the parish's wealth rather than by the need of its poor inhabitants. Thus in 1565 the wealthy parish of St. Petrock was assessed at 10s. 11½d. per week, while the poor parishes of St. Lawrence, St. David, and St. Sidwell paid 10d., 17d., and 17d. respectively. But in terms of relief paid out, St. Lawrence was receiving 4s. 7d., St. David 5s. 2d., and St. Sidwell 10s. 8d., while St. Petrock expended but 1s. 8d. Altogether, eight of the eighteen parishes contributing were receiving more than they paid in. The five parishes assessed at more than 4s. paid £1 14s. out of a weekly total of £2 14s. In 1563 the total annual expenditure for relief was approximately £119; in 1564–65 it was about £140,

---

[38] For example, in 1561 fifteen dozen of bread forfeited for light weight was given to the poor (AB iv, 160).
[39] ECM, Book 157.

while in the latter year collections were about £144 14s. 2d., after allowing for assessments unpaid at the end of the fiscal year in July 1565.

The individual contributors to the poor relief funds during the same fiscal year 1564–65 numbered about 375. Individual assessments varied from the 3s. 4d. paid by Mr. William Hurst to the one farthing a week paid by residents in St. Sidwell and other poor parishes. The average assessment also varied from parish to parish according to the standard of wealth prevailing, but payments in excess of 4d. a week were rare anywhere. The recipients of poor relief numbered 176 in the year 1564–65 (in 1563–64, 101) counting nineteen in almshouses. Of these 110 were women. Individuals were receiving from 4d. to 8d. a week each; a fortunate few had as much as 12d. (The official schedule of wages in 1567 allowed a "meane servant" wages of 7d. a week.)[40]

The parish with the largest number of poor was St. Sidwell with thirty, although the relatively wealthy St. Mary Major had twenty-five. St. Petrock counted but three, and St. Olave one, while St. Pancras and St. Kerian do not appear at all on the roll of recipients. In the absence of comparative figures it is hard to make much out of these statistics. It may be pointed out, however, that the financial burden during these years was between a fourth and a fifth of the city's budget in those same years. The problem of meeting the costs was not serious during these two years, for besides the collection from the parishes there were other funds. Collections taken in the cathedral on the four principal feasts of the year brought in about £5 on each occasion, and even when the expense of the beadles' fees, totaling about £13 a year, were deducted, there were still adequate funds for the needy.[41] The number of defaulters at the end of the fiscal year seems reasonably small, since there were only twenty.

The administration of poor relief occupied more and more of the

[40] ECM, Miscellaneous Roll 35.

[41] AB v, 173. The expense of the beadles was transferred to the city budget (AB v, 173). One beadle was to be the bellman also, with £1 8s. over and above the latter's fees; the second was to have the profits of the market men and £1 6s. 8d.; the third, the profits of the bullring with £1 6s. 8d.

Chamber's attention as time passed. In 1573 the Chamber appointed a special officer to control all income for the poor in the city;[42] in the following year a special collector for the rents of almshouses was also appointed. In 1576 a statute directed the erection in each city of workhouses (also called houses of correction or bridewells).[43] Here not only the deserving poor but also the deliberately idle were to be put to work on materials purchased and sold by the magistrates. After some delays for want of money, Exeter's house of correction was opened by the summer of 1579.[44] In 1593 a permanent governor was appointed and a code of rules drawn up. He was to be provided with £200 (£100 in the first year, the balance in £11 annual sums) as well as £5 per annum for maintenance and a salary of £2 10s.[45]

The Chamber's intentions regarding the house of correction are made clear by the extant rule of the house drawn up in 1613.[46] All idle persons able to work but refusing to do so were to be committed along with all single persons without means of living or without service. Vagabonds, "night-walkers," drunkards, and quarrelers would be sent to join them. The inmates were to be provided meat, drink, lodging, and clothing on condition that they worked. The recalcitrant faced either the stocks or what was euphemistically called "thin diet." The governor of the workhouse was provided with £200 by the city while he put up another £100, and he had to promise to preserve this investment of £300, so that at least that much would always be circulating in the enterprise. The work done was weaving, spinning, and knitting. His respon-

---

[42] AB iii, 310. Presumably this was done in obedience to 14 Elizabeth, c. 5, requiring the appointment of such an officer. See Tanner, *Documents*, 472.

[43] 18 Elizabeth, c. 3, in Tanner, *Documents*, 481.

[44] See AB iii, 382, 405, 411, 414.

[45] AB v, 270.

[46] See ECM, Miscellaneous Deeds 1721. This code included provision that for any inmates over the number of fifteen the governor was to have 10d. per capita per diem. For the sick, unable to work for more than four days, he had 4d. There was an annual inspection by a committee of aldermen and a weekly one by appointed councilmen. Another article provided that any apprentice or child who was undutiful or incorrigible might be confined on complaint of his master or parent.

sibilities did not stop at the gate of the workhouse since he had to keep employed a total of sixty persons within and without the bridewell. Those outside received regular wages.

The Chamber plainly hoped that the workhouse could become a self-liquidating enterprise and that similar self-sustaining projects could be set up in the parishes with a little initial capital. Their attitude was the same as that of the benefactors who established the revolving loan funds. Atwill's lands, which had been given for the purpose of setting the poor on work, provided capital both for the workhouse and for similar schemes in individual parishes. From 1590 onwards the Atwill fund provided sums of from £20 to £50. In some instances it was entrusted to an individual;[47] in others to parish overseers;[48] always to provide stocks of material for the employment of the poor or their children. It is unlikely that these schemes were self-sustaining, although there are no accounts by which we can trace the fate of the money sunk in them. Some of them were patent failures, as the large debt owing the Atwill fund in 1638 clearly shows,[49] and the workhouse passed from one unsatisfactory manager to another. But even if the Chamber's hopes for self-sustaining poor relief were not realized, these schemes did provide substantial relief for the adult poor and training in a craft for their children.

The problem of the poor and the sick was a constant one, but trade depression, war, plague, or famine intensified suffering to such a degree that the Chamber was driven to supplement ordinary methods of relief as best they could. In 1587, in 1591, and again in 1598, £20 had to be provided by the mayor for those sick of the plague.[50] In 1591 and in 1605 special poor rates had to be levied for the sick.[51] Direct contributions from city funds to buy bread and beef at Easter and Christmas were made spasmodically from 1588 on, and after 1614 they became permanent. The annual average of

[47] AB v, 156.
[48] AB v, 455, and AB vi, 29.
[49] AB viii, 153 and 156. The city were debtors to the extent of £1,153 to the fund.
[50] AB iii, 245; A.B. iv, 505; and AB v, 183.
[51] AB v, 183, and AB vi, 129.

these subsidies by the 1630's was about £20.[52] Sometimes collections were taken from the inhabitants during times of special stress. On one occasion, as least, the city provided public works for the unemployed. In 1636 they were set to work filling up holes in the Southernhay common land outside the walls.[53] Work continued for some three months, but the experiment does not seem to have been repeated.

Other methods of relieving the poor were also devised during this epoch. Purchase of grain in times of shortage was a common feature, as we have noted above; there was now added the purchase of coal for the poor. By 1640 the Atwill fund had been charged with some £500 for this purpose.[54] All these measures were, of course, supplementary to the poor rate itself which was collected year in and year out.

In the absence of comparative studies, it is hard to draw many conclusions from the Exeter scene. We cannot say whether poverty was greater or less here than elsewhere, but the dimensions of the problem do clearly emerge. As a community dependent upon commerce, the city had to face the problem of unemployment and poverty produced by trade cycles and by the great uncertainties of market conditions. These were particularly grievous for Exeter in our century because of successive wars in its principal foreign trading areas. Added to that were visitations of the plague with all its accompanying misery. But behind all these assaults of circumstance lay the basic conditions of the community's economic life. A great part of the community lacked any private reserve funds and, indeed, had little hope of accumulating them. The possibility of saving was beyond the hopes of the majority of the community. At any emergency of unemployment, sickness, or injury, they had to turn to their richer neighbors for help. And in the final helplessness of old age they had to seek the same assistance. The fatal inability to save also hindered the chances of the younger generation to make a start in the world. Learning a craft or purchasing the most elementary tools of a trade were impossibilities for the children of the poor.

[52] See RR *passim* for these.
[53] AB viii, 82 and 90.
[54] AB viii, 153 and 191.

The structure of private endowment was an intelligent effort to make up for this deficiency of savings by providing funds to launch the young in their careers, to care for the unavoidable emergencies of everyday life, and to provide some security for helpless old age. The private effort was not sufficient to cope with the problem, and public aid had to supplement it, but what is important for the history of the community is not the relative failure but the quality of the effort made. We shall see in the chapter on education the same resolute and serious spirit at work, the same deep consciousness of social responsibility resting on religious sanctions.

Chapter Five

Education

The story of the foundation of the two schools in 1633 and 1636 follows logically from the previous topic, for it represents a very important aspect of the new philanthropic drive. From this new point of view, self-help could be encouraged in several ways. The revolving loan funds were a direct and useful means. But strong faith was also placed in the more indirect means of education. The boy with some education, even if he had mastered only reading, writing, and ciphering, was in a far better position to push his own career than the unlettered lad. If he had ability, the highest places in the learned professions were open to him, and in any case some learning was now a *sine qua non* for all but the very lowest strata of the population. Moreover, the Reformed religion was based on a literate laity, and so both religious and secular ends were served by educational endowment.

In Exeter the two schools were not founded until the very close of our period, but the long preliminaries of the effort began much earlier. They became entangled with another project and we must begin with an account of the short-lived but instructive experiment at St. Johns Hospital. It illustrates rather neatly the mixed motives of Puritan philanthropy. This experiment was the "hospital" or orphanage for poor children at St. Johns. It was to be at once a home for these youngsters and a workhouse where they learned a trade under supervision. It would thus satisfy the benevolent impulse to help the unfortunate and the utilitarian purpose of training them to help themselves. The project had been bruited as early as 1605,[1]

[1] AB vi, 127 and 147.

but nothing was done until money was provided by the Crossing family in 1623.[2] Hugh Crossing (mayor in 1609 and in 1620) died intestate, but his widow and his son Francis (mayor in 1634) put his intention into effect by purchasing the buildings and grounds of the dissolved hospital of St. John for a house to keep children at work. After long deliberation, the Chamber decided in 1629 to establish there a hospital for poor children and to bring in a pin maker to teach the children his trade.[3] Contributions provided money for refurbishing the hospital;[4] the Atwill fund paid for the equipment;[5] and a governor was appointed to oversee the children.[6] Not until November 1630 were six boys actually installed at St. Johns, fully equipped with blue kersey gowns, blue caps, beds, sheets, and bolsters.[7] The money for these last purchases came from a gift made by Alderman Walter Borough.[8] The foundation so hopefully begun had a short history. In December 1632 the pin maker was in prison, the boys "unsettled and masterless," and the Chamber decided against employing another pin maker since that trade was not conceived to be so necessary as others for the education of boys.[9] For the time being the boys were still maintained in the hospital, but the experiment was at an end. Its failure paved the way for a more successful scheme for aiding the young. There followed the foundation of the Exeter free Latin school and the orphanage English school.[10]

The education of Exeter children was provided for in traditional ways. The very young, boys and girls, were sent to dames' schools, if their parents could afford the 10s. per annum which John Hayne paid for his daughter in 1642.[11] But for boys' more advanced education there was only one establishment in the sixteenth century.

[2] See *Accounts and Papers*, 1–4.
[3] AB vii, 717.   [4] AB vii, 676 and 680.
[5] AB vii, 743. The sum of £144 was provided from the fund.
[6] AB vii, 707.   [7] AB vii, 773.
[8] AB vii, 772.   [9] AB vii, 828.
[10] For the detailed history of the foundation see H. Lloyd Parry, *The Founding of Exeter School* (Exeter and London, 1913).
[11] See John Hayne's diary, TDA 33 (1901), 187–269, ed. J. N. Brushfield, "The Financial Diary of a Citizen of Exeter, 1631–43."

Exeter Latin high school was of very good repute. Its early history is obscure, but it was certainly flourishing in the early sixteenth century. Under clerical patronage, its schoolmaster was licensed by the bishop, and its site owned by the chapter. In Edward VI's time a legal injunction ordered the latter to provide £20 annually for the master (he being allowed to take other fees) while the master in turn was to pay £5 a year in rent to the chapter.[12] In 1561 under the joint urging of the master and of John Hooker, a public subscription was raised for the reconstruction of the school building.[13] In 1602 George Perryman, quite probably a native Exonian, was appointed master by the bishop with the cordial approval of the Chamber.[14] During the next few years the school building was much enlarged with funds privately given and supplemented by the master himself.[15] The new building of two floors boasted an upper room sixty feet by twenty feet with seven windows, and a lower room twenty-three feet long.[16] In 1630 the master and two ushers taught about 200 students; it could claim among its alumni seven fellows in one Oxford college (probably Exeter), six of them citizens' sons. In spite of these fair seeming circumstances, the schoolmaster was an unpopular and even hated figure in the city by the 1620's, and the movement for another school was in full swing.

The motives of the city fathers were very mixed in this instance. As early as 1618 the Chamber was petitioning the archbishop to license additional schoolmasters in the city.[17] Their argument, frequently repeated in the controversies of the next few years, was that

---

[12] ECM, Letter 340, Testimony of Dr. Robert Vilvaine. Dr. Vilvaine, a practising physician in the city in the 1620's, attended the school in the last decades of the sixteenth century. See also Parry, *Exeter School*, 10f.

[13] ECM, Book 51, fol. 354, sub anno 1561.

[14] AB vi, 30.

[15] See Letters 235 and 275 for the divergent accounts as to who provided the money, the master or private benefactors. In Letter 273 Lord Bedford mentions that the master secured a fortune by marriage.

[16] PRO, SP 16/169/74.

[17] AB vii, 289. There was another schoolmaster, named Spicer, teaching in the suburbs at this time with the bishop's consent. He died about 1624. See ECM, Letters 278, 340 and 348.

population increase demanded more facilities. Moreover, Exeter as the chief place in the West ought to be a center where not only citizens' but also gentlemen's sons could go to school, especially when such smaller places as Plymouth and Salisbury had two schools each. But philanthropy and civic pride were soon powerfully enforced by personal enmity towards schoolmaster Perryman.

The controversy began in 1622 and lasted over a decade; the questions in dispute seem to have been largely personal and petty. It is probable that the rather stiff-necked and aging master became unpopular with students and parents alike,[18] and that in turn his ill-temper and sense of injury increased. A riot in which some city youths had insulted the master and ushers was but halfheartedly punished by the magistrates.[19] This was followed by disputes over the master's liability to taxation.[20] The latter petitioned the Privy Council for redress of his grievances, and the city magistrates were rebuked for their prejudiced actions.[21] Personal relations thus became exceedingly venomous on both sides. The Chamber unquestionably showed personal spite towards the master, but his actions were certainly calculated to arouse their animosity. In any case, out of this personal rancor arose the Chamber's determination to have another school under their own control.

To achieve this they needed consent from the bishop, or failing that, the archbishop or Privy Council. All these authorities were approached, but without success. Bishop Cary listened politely to the civic emissaries but reported unfavorably to the Council, declaring that present facilities were adequate and imputing private prejudice rather than public zeal to the citizens.[22] The Chamber kept

[18] See Letter 281 where parents complain that there are too many scholars for the staff to handle, that children are whipped five or six times a day, and that as a consequence they go "a-meeching" half a year at a time. Some parents sent their children to country schools, others to the school of Thomas Spicer in the suburbs.

[19] See Letter 235 and Bishop Cary's report to the Privy Council, Letter 276.

[20] Letters 235, 273, 274.

[21] Letters 278 and 335.

[22] Letter 243, 27 April 1624, records an interview in London between the bishop and his chancellor on one side and the Recorder, John Prowze, and William Chappell on the other. The bishop's report to the Council is contained in PRO, SP 14/184/39.

stubbornly at it, and when Bishop Hall replaced Cary they besought his support.[23] Finally, in June 1630, orders were given to collect money for a new school and active preparations were made for its establishment.[24] Perryman had now retired from active teaching and leased the school to his former usher, but the battle was none the less a hot one.[25] The bishop, Hall, confirmed the judgment of his predecessor against another school, and in this the chapter joined him.[26] Perryman petitioned the Privy Council against the new school (and against being taxed for the subsidy).[27] The Council forbade the Chamber to proceed in the erection of the school.[28] This wrung an angry reply from the Chamber, which accused the chapter of selfish motives. Perryman's complaisance saved them the £20 they should be paying to the school, it was alleged. In fact, by now the Chamber was almost as bitterly aroused against the clerics as against Perryman, and determined to free itself from ecclesiastical intervention.

It took some months and a great deal of correspondence[29] before this tangle of angry disputants could be separated and tempers generally cooled. The Council's first proposal for a compromise would have endowed the existing school with the moneys collected for the new one, and would have placed the whole under a joint board of canons and aldermen, the bishop having a deciding vote. This the Chamber characterized as "the Chimaerian free Schoole to be erected on the Chapter's land and endowed with the citizens' largesses." The proposal for joint control was a "meer mousetrap" since the bishop would always give his casting vote to his clerical brethren. The final solution, made by agreement at Exeter and confirmed by the Council in May 1631, was more to the Chamber's liking since it provided for complete separation of the two schools.[30]

---

[23] Letter 306.   [24] AB vii, 758.
[25] Letter 349.
[26] Letter 276 and endorsement on SP 14/184/39.
[27] Letter 334.
[28] Letter 335 and PRO, PC 2/40, v. 6, fol. 55.
[29] See Letters 340 and 345–349.
[30] PRO, PC 2/40, v. 6, fol. 517. The schoolmaster of the old school was not to demand more than £1 a year for fees.

Neither was to have more than 150 students until the other had the same.

The battle was won, and the city was now free to establish its own educational foundation unhindered by clerical interference. The first steps had been taken even before the struggle began. In 1629 an indenture[31] was entered into by Alderman Walter Borough, Francis Crossing, the heirs of Alderman Thomas Walker, and the Chamber. The Walker estate provided £200, Walker's daughter another £50, and Alderman Borough £100 towards a free Latin and Greek school; the Crossings granted the lower part of the old church of St. Johns Hospital as premises for the school; while the city promised an income of £20 to the schoolmaster. Thus, when the orphanage for young pin makers came to its untimely end, the free school was already half-established on the same premises. For the time being the former project was set aside while the new one developed rapidly. In June 1633, William Noseworthy, M.A., was appointed master at £30 per annum, to be paid by the Chamber.[32] In the same year the statutes of the school were drawn up by the Chamber. In April 1634 an usher was added to the staff.[33] Some £400 had been expended on the school,[34] and its endowment of £500 put out at interest.[35]

While the Latin school prospered, the orphanage received a new lease of life from the benefaction of the widow of George Jurdaine, a grocer and member of an eminent city family. Her will provided £500 for charitable purposes. The feoffees consulted the Council before devoting these funds to a free English school and orphanage.[36]

---

[31] *Accounts and Papers*, 1–4.
[32] AB vii, 846.   [33] AB viii, 4.
[34] *Ibid.*
[35] AB vii, 850. This £500 was made up of £250 from the Walker heirs (AB vii, 853); £200 of Borough's money, £100 of the original gift and £100 by will (AB vii, 832); and £20 from Mrs. Modiford, widow of the rich merchant (AB vii, 853). The balance of £30 came out of the city funds (AB vii, 850). The money drew 6⅔ per cent.
[36] See PRO, PC 2/46, v. 12, fol. 56. There was a dispute between the Jurdaine feoffees and the Chamber since the latter wished to have unrestricted control over the fund, but the Council compelled them to accept the money for a free school. See Parry, *Exeter School*, 68–69.

The Chamber became the proprietor of the money, and the £500 of Mrs. Jurdaine's gift was let out at an interest rate of 6⅔ per cent.[37] In January 1638 a master was appointed[38] to the English school, which in the previous June had received incorporation from the Crown as St. Johns Hospital within the City of Exon.[39]

Endowments for the schools continued to come in. A rent income of £20 per annum originally given by Walter Borough in 1625 in case a hospital should be established, went to the school from 1638 on.[40] Mrs. Alice Heale left £300 for repairing the chapel in St. Johns, which was consecrated by the bishop on St. Bartholomew, 1639.[41] In 1637, Dr. Robert Vilvaine, alumnus of the old high school, gave the new Latin school tenements worth £2 13s. 4d. per annum.[42] Other city magnates of the period left money to the schools. Peter Tailor gave £100, and Alderman Nicholas Martin £200 (which came to the city on his widow's death in 1655 along with an additional £100 and various tenements). Contributions for building expenses were also generous. The gifts of land by the founding generation provided a yearly income of about £130 for the schools. By the time of the Revolution of 1688 this income had risen to £275. Besides this, by 1641 the schools had money out on loan to a total of £1,300 beyond the sums which had been expended on building costs. Between 1645 and 1661 another £1,590 in money was given. Within a generation of their founding the schools had a secure, indeed a handsome, endowment.[43]

[37] AB viii, 105.

[38] See AB viii, 135.

[39] *Accounts and Papers*, 4. See Parry, *Exeter School*, Appendix D, for full text of charter. It was to provide for the aged poor as well as for children, but this intention was never carried out.

[40] *Accounts and Papers*, 6.

[41] AB viii, 69. The sum of £20 left over from the chapel was credited to the general fund.

[42] *Accounts and Papers*, 6–7.

[43] *Ibid.*, 6–16. The gifts in land of the founding generation provided a yearly income of about £130 for the school. (This is the total income from the legacies of Vilvaine, Martin, the Tailors, Thomas Tucker, James White, Dorothy Mogridge, and Richard Crossing.) According to ECM, Book 148, fol. 112, the school enjoyed an income of £275 from land by the time of the Revolution of 1688.

The two schools were quite different in aim. The free school was a traditional grammar school for the ancient languages,[44] reading knowledge of English being a prerequisite. Greek and Latin were the staple subjects, but religion was not neglected with catechism once a week, and Communion at least once a year. The teachers were to instruct in the principles of the Church in obedience to the King, avoiding schism, error, heresy, or superstition. Power of government was vested in wardens appointed by the Chamber. Fees were to be charged only at entrance. The hospital,[45] on the other hand, was orphanage and school combined for children between seven and fourteen, where they were to be taught to read, write, and cipher before being apprenticed to some trade. Clothing, lodging, and food were of course provided.

The schools were the most permanent monuments of seventeenth-century philanthropy in the city. They satisfied the newer philanthropic impulse and its doctrine of self-help as well as the older religious drive of charity expressed through good works. But these foundations were also the expression of more secular drives. Once again the ruthless determination of the Chamber to assert its own will against any possible rivals was successfully manifested. Another province of city life was drawn within the orbit of the oligarchy's control, and the clerics driven from almost their last outpost in the city. Civic pride, which had been hurt by the knowledge that Exeter was more poorly served by schools than many smaller places, was gratified. In short, the new schools, although they served religious and philanthropic ends, were equally manifestations of the purposeful aggression we have seen in political and economic matters.

[44] See ECM, Statutes of Free Grammar School 1633, made by the Mayor and Twenty-Four of the Common Council. Entrants were charged 6d. if freemen's children, 1s. if those of other inhabitants, 2s. if those of strangers. The first wardens were appointed by the Chamber in November 1633 (AB vii, 858).

[45] See the statutes made 21 September 1638 in *Accounts and Papers*, 4.

Chapter Six

The Community in Action

The historian of sixteenth-century Exeter has few dramatic events or major changes to record. Much of his account must simply describe the immemorial rhythm of custom, the steady beat of an ancient and conservative community life. But there are some events, grand enough in scale and in consequence, to be worth observing in detail.

Two corporate undertakings, both of them aimed at augmenting the wealth of the mercantile class, were set afoot in the early 1560's. The building of the canal from the city to the estuary and the chartering of the Merchant Adventurers Company were the outstanding events during the latter half of the sixteenth century. They constitute in a sense the "history" of Exeter in this era, the major movements of change initiated and carried out within the community itself.

Part 1: The Building of the Haven of Exe

Chronologically, the story of the canal (the "Haven of Exe") begins earlier than the chartering of the Merchant Adventurers Company. The problem of the navigation of the Exe was an old and sore one, for, since the thirteenth century the Courtenay Earls of Devon had effectually blocked the river, cutting the city's ancient connection with the open sea.[1] Hooker relates this story with a

---

[1] Hooker, *History*, III, 626–664. This section, headed "The Haven and Ryver of Exe," is an account of the struggle over the stream from the days of Isabella de Fortibus down to the lawsuit with the Earl of Bedford. It includes inquisitions of the fourteenth century as well as the final judgment in the suit of the 1580's.

warmth of civic indignation which was felt even as late as his day. The conflict began in the thirteenth century when Isabella de Fortibus, heiress of the last male Redvers, Earl of Devon, lord of the manor of Topsham, constructed two weirs in the Exe to serve the manor mill. The countess left a thirty-foot gap through which boats could continue to pass to the city, but even this concession was lost when the earldom passed to the more unscrupulous Courtenays. The first of these earls, Hugh, closed the gap and stopped all traffic on the river above the estuary. The resulting disadvantages to the city are recited in documents copied by Hooker.[2] Not only was shipping up to the city stopped, but the taking of salmon and other fish above the weirs was prevented. Moreover, the merchants arriving by sea were stopped by the earl's officers and required to pay dues at Topsham. Edward I commanded that goods should be unpacked only at Exeter, but "because it was within no penaltie" he was disobeyed. In addition, the same Earl Hugh invaded the rights of the citizens in the suburb of the Westgate on Exe Island, taking over jurisdiction on the Island. The ancient rights of collecting stones, sand, and gravel from it were abridged.

These vexations continued unabated, for "noe Lawe coulde take place noe order be obayed nor Justice be executed by theym so Longe as anye of that Race & name lyved and continewed beinge Erles of Devon."[3] Not until 1537 with the fall of the house of Courtenay was this unhappy situation ended. The first fruit of freedom was the passage of the act of 1540 at the city's petition.[4] By this act Parliament authorized the city to clear the river of all weirs, rocks, sand, and other obstructions. Its passage opened the history of the Haven of Exe.

The intention of the petitioners was simply to remove the weirs that blocked Exe and thus to permit the unrestricted flow of the river and of the tides. Preparations were begun at once although

---

[2] *Ibid.*, 635f.
[3] *Ibid.*, 657. This sums up Hooker's (and probably his contemporaries') attitude towards the house of Courtenay.
[4] *Statutes of the Realm*, 31 Henry VIII, c. 4.

work probably did not begin until 1546.[5] The evidence of this early attempt to clear the navigation of the river is very fragmentary. About all we can say is that the city confiscated a large amount of parish church plate,[6] forestalling the government of Edward VI in this respect, and that work of some kind was done on the river, although it was unsuccessful.[7] Two causes probably account for this failure. The money from the plate was exhausted, and there is no evidence that other funds were raised. Of greater importance was the discovery that the task was far more difficult than anyone had foreseen. The money spent had to be charged to experience and a new start made.

Quite probably the overoptimistic undertakers had planned merely to remove the weirs and let the river take its natural course. With this in view they negotiated with the owner of the mills of Countess weir preliminary to destroying the weir.[8] Presumably the long continuance of the weirs had effected permanent changes in the river bed so that their mere removal left the stream as impossible of navigation as ever. In any case, the task of clearing it was beyond the scope of a body of amateurs; expert assistance had to be summoned.

In 1560 negotiations for engaging an engineer were opened. The first estimate they received put the cost at £1,500 and the time of construction at about ten years.[9] The actual contract made, with John Trew of Glamorganshire, was more hopeful but less realistic.[10] Trew promised to make the Exe navigable from Exmouth to the water gate of Exeter for ships of eight to ten tons burden, in return for £200, a ninety-nine year lease of the haven at an annual rent of £13 6s. 8d., and sufficient supplies of stone and timber. When he actually began work early in 1564 he made an important change in

[5] Hooker, *History*, III, 658. See also AB ii, 108, 180, for additional information on this early work.

[6] AB ii, 235, 15 December 1551. The total amount was 741¾ oz., which the Chamber sold to John Bodley for £191 (5s. 2d. per ounce). They also sold another 44 oz. from St. Petrock's for £37.

[7] See AB ii, 235, 223, and 231. See also Hooker, *History*, III, 658.

[8] AB ii, 231.

[9] AB iv, 89.

[10] ECM, Deed 1528d. See also AB iv, 278.

plans. Hitherto he had planned to go by the east side of the river.[11] As De la Garde, the nineteenth-century antiquarian of Exeter, conjectures,[12] Trew probably intended to utilize the course of the mill leat which ran from St. James weir to a point in the river just above Countess weir, eastward of the main stream. The justice of this conjecture is confirmed by an agreement of September 1563 with the lessees of the weir mills regarding the weirs in their mill leat.[13] They were to allow all stakes to be pulled up, in other words to allow the clearance of the leat so that it might be transformed into a canal. De la Garde assumes that Trew's plan was to build a sluice gate at the lower end of the leat, a kind of lock which would provide a sufficient level of water to float barges up to the main stream just below the city.

Now this plan was abandoned, and a new and bolder one adopted. Trew determined to utilize the west bank of the Exe where the lands of St. Thomas and Alphington parishes are considerably flatter. His scheme was to throw a weir across the river just below the city, in St. Leonard's parish, but above the St. James weir.[14] This would divert a flow of water which would be conducted through an artificial channel to the brook called Deep Pyll which empties into the estuary of Exe. Such a scheme would have the double advantage of saving the weirs and another mill lower down at Lampreyford as well as avoiding a stretch of the river above St. James weir which was notoriously swift, rocky, and liable to flood. On the other hand, it created an elaborate problem of construction. De la Garde thinks that locks were required, perhaps as many as seven. It is certain that pools had to be created which would be broad enough to allow the passage of two boats at once. Moreover, the new scheme required the purchase of various pieces of land

---

[11] AB iv, 278. Possibly the Chamber conceived this idea earlier when they bought the weir mills served by St. James weir about 1553 (see RR, 5–6 Edward VI, also 3–4/4–5 Philip & Mary).

[12] Philip Chilwell De la Garde, "On the Antiquity and Invention of the Lock Canal of Exeter," *Archaeologia*, vol. XXVIII (1840), 18–19.

[13] AB iv, 221.

[14] De la Garde, 19ff.; a canal 3000 yards long, 16 feet wide, 3 feet deep, was built (W. G. Hoskins, *Two Thousand Years in Exeter* (Exeter, 1960), 63).

in the two parishes through which the canal would pass.[15] In spite of these obstacles the Chamber consented to the proposal.[16]

The city's relationship with Trew was anything but happy. Their own limited resources and an overoptimistic estimate of the problems to be faced produced bad temper on both sides. The city was slow in its payments and impatient for completion of work. The canal may have been opened in 1566,[17] but by this time the city was involved in a lawsuit with the engineer. The precise issues are quite unclear, but Trew felt he had been treated badly. Both Cecil and the Privy Council were invoked by the outraged parties, and the lords ordered the justices of assize on the western circuit to look into the matter.[18] With the assistance of the Earl of Bedford they drew up a judgment which went against the city. A lump sum of about £230 plus a £30 annuity had to be paid Trew.[19] But once these payments were made it seemed as though the major anxieties of the undertaking might be past. As Hooker rather melodramatically says, "the whole controversies being nowe ended & concluded and the Citie in quiet possession of the watercourse: It was thought that nowe all occasions of further troubles were taken awaye and that nowe shoulde be at reste & quietnes, but they were no sooner Delyvered from the great perills & Daungers CHARYBDIS but THEREWITH also fell ynto the moste Daungerouse Gulff of Sylla."[20] What this Scylla was we shall soon see.

[15] AB iv, 15 December 1563. The reference to surveying land on the "further" bank of the river is the first direct indication of the intention to use the west bank.

[16] The new scheme threatened the city tucking mills just above the proposed new weir, leased out by the Chamber. Trew offered to save these for an additional £40 and fifty loads of timber (AB iv, 247).

[17] AB iv, 197.

[18] For the intervention of the Council see APC, ed. J. R. Dasent, 32 vols. (London, 1890–1907), VII, 222 (June 1565); VIII, 82 (February 1573); and VIII, 25 (9 July 1574). An agreement for an additional £200 to Trew is found in ECM, Deed 298, 1 June 1566, and a receipt for £100 in HMC Rep, 29, Letter 75. Trew's appeal to Cecil in the British Museum, Lansdowne MS., cvii, no. 73. The Act Books follow the struggle: see AB iv, 176, 300, 311, 317, 320, and AB iii, 317.

[19] Hooker, *History*, III, 658. Payments to Trew are in AB iv, 327, 336, and 337.

[20] Hooker, *History*, III, 658.

Actually, the difficulties now besetting the city were of two kinds. The first were engineering and maintenance problems; the second, to which Hooker referred, the attempt of the Earl of Bedford to extract a toll from the city's water-borne traffic at Topsham.

The engineering problem was not solved with any measure of success until the late 1590's. By 1566 the new water gate and the wharf of ashlar, 150 by 80 feet, had been completed,[21] but it was another ten years before goods arrived here with any regularity. In 1576 the canal was farmed to a consortium of nine at the yearly rent of £30.[22] This rent was paid until 1580. Then for seventeen years the canal was not farmed, and there are practically no records of receipts of toll. Heavy expenditures were necessary, and a permanent maintenance staff had to be enrolled. Banks broke with discouraging regularity; in 1578 floods from the river poured into the canal and swamped lands in Exminster parish; over and over again the clumsy efforts of these amateur engineers proved inadequate to hold the river in the course they set it. But by dint of unremitting effort and probably by constant trial and error, they won at least a partial victory over the waters. By 1597 the canal could be farmed again and from that time forward the steady return of £100 annual rent[23] suggests that the project operated with fair success. Large sums still had to be expended almost every year for maintenance of the Haven, and it would seem, as was suggested in Chapter II, that during our period the city expended about £2,000 more on the canal than it received in rents.

But while the Chamber struggled to hold the unruly Exe in check, they faced a new and hardly less vexatious set of obstacles on quite another front. Initially these arose from the shift in traffic that the new waterway produced. At the best larger ships could not approach

[21] See AB iii, 160; RR, 6–7 through 8–9 Elizabeth; and BM, Lansdowne MS., xxv, no. 2.

[22] AB iii, 458. See AB iii *passim* for the affairs of the Haven. The flood at Exminster is in AB iii, 415. For the staff see AB iii, 16. The years 1580 to 1582 were ones of very heavy expense (£562 according to RR, 22–24 Elizabeth). Possibly, as De la Garde speculates (see note 12 above), the sluices which were built in these years were really locks (see Isacke, *Antiquities*, 137).

[23] AB v, 396, 24 July 1597, to Thomas Pope, merchant, for eight years with fine of £100.

shore in the estuary of Exe; they anchored about three miles out,[24] transshipping their cargo to lighters which carried it to Topsham quay at the head of the estuary; thence it was borne on pack horse up to the city. Now transshipment could be made to lighters which would pass directly up to Exeter water gate.

The townsmen of Topsham, faced with ruin, determined to make a good fight.[25] The crane and quay as part of the manor of Topsham belonged to the Crown.[26] The farmer of the crane and quay now put forward his claim to receive the accustomed dues regardless of whether the goods were landed at Topsham or not. To enforce his claim he had his water bailiff stop lighters laden with the goods of Exeter merchants on their way up to the Haven. Hot words passed between the enraged merchants and the Topsham men; blows were struck; at least one man was seriously hurt. The upshot was a lawsuit at Westminster, initiated by the water bailiff of Topsham against the merchants involved in the initial fray. He demanded they be ordered to land their goods at Topsham. This in itself was a vexation; worse was to follow.

Before the suit was determined, the lease of the manor was offered for sale. The inhabitants of Topsham, eager to obtain a powerful patron in their struggle, urged the Earl of Bedford to take the lease. Whether he took the lease of the whole manor is unclear, but certainly he undertook to become the patron of the village by acquiring a sublease (and thence actual possession) of the quay and crane of Topsham.[27] And now "as the Erles of Devon in the olde tyme" he demanded that merchants load and unload all goods at Topsham. Upon the Chamber's refusal, he entered the suit already commenced at Westminster.

His motives were probably mixed. Hooker records an incident which had touched the Earl's pride. A culprit arrested by the city sergeants just outside the precincts of Bedford House sought relief

[24] See BM, Lansdowne MS., vol. xxv, no. 2.

[25] See Hooker, *History*, III, 65f for a full account of this affair and of the intervention of Lord Bedford.

[26] The manor of Topsham was part of the former Courtenay lands.

[27] See Bedford to Burghley, B M, Lansdowne MS., xxviii, no. 61, dated 1579.

from imprisonment by enlisting the Earl's favor. His pride pricked by the implied insult to the liberties of his house, the Earl required the prisoner's release from the city magistrates, without effect. But not only injured pride was at work. The Russells had in some measure taken the place of the Courtenays as the great lords of the West. Their relations with Exeter had long been intimate, but the Topsham incident gave the Earl the opportunity to acquire a kind of ascendancy in civic affairs he had hitherto lacked. The city had no intention of receiving a new lord after having escaped the Courtenays. So the struggle became a contest of strength.

The legal documents in the case are missing, but it is possible to piece together its main outlines from the appeals to Lord Burghley made by both sides.[28] The case turned on the legal question as to the appointed landing place in the port of Exeter. Officially the port included all the various creeks and bays of the estuary of Exe as far as Teignmouth on one side and Seaton on the other.[29] An act of 1 Elizabeth ordered that the appointed landing place in any port was to be where the customs officials had dwelt for ten years past. In the port of Exeter this was Topsham and the Chamber itself had acknowledged this in an Exchequer commission some years earlier. The city's legal position was weak, and they had to stand on the authority of the act of 1540 which permitted them to re-edify their port and on their equitable claim that after the expenditure of £3,000 they should not be denied the use of the Haven.

While the city was pressing these arguments on the Lord Treasurer, Bedford was making equally cogent claims to favor. The city backed up its suit for favor at court by positive action at home. An act was issued[30] setting up rates on all goods landed by Exeter inhabitants within the port at places other than Exeter quay. The rates ordered were heavy enough to discourage use of such landing places.

[28] See BM, Lansdowne MS., vols. xxv and xxviii, no. 12, no. 13, no. 61.

[29] See ECM, Transcript 58 (Com and Dep Exchequer QR 2880, probably 8 Elizabeth).

[30] AB iv, 110. It was couched in a very plaintive tone, complaining of merchants who continued to use Topsham quay, of the high cost to the city, and of lack of general support for the Haven.

The decision when it came in Easter term of 1580 was a compromise. Both sides had already agreed to refer the case to a special commission consisting of the Chancellor of the Exchequer, the Lord Chief Baron, the second baron, and one of the Queen's sergeants. This commission[31] ordered that all goods landed at the wharf of Topsham should pay the accustomed rates to the farmer, but that goods landed at the quay of Exeter or transferred from a ship in the estuary for delivery there were to be free of Topsham charges. The farmer of Topsham was recompensed for the loss of revenue by a yearly payment of £13 6s. 8d. from the city. The decree was given the same force as if it had been officially ordered by the court of Exchequer.

It was a partial but not unsatisfactory victory for the city. At least goods landed at Exeter quay would be free of Topsham charges. But the Chamber was not content. By a very shrewd maneuver they secured a full measure of victory. The city simply bought up the interest of William Stubbs,[32] who leased directly from the Crown, and sublet to Bedford. By this move they became lessors to Bedford and in 1584 received from him his first annual rent payment of £40.[33] It must have been a day of triumph for the city thus to turn the tables on their opponent by making him their tenant. It left them in the anomalous situation of paying Bedford £13 6s. 8d. per annum while receiving from him £40, but it was a strategic victory of the first order.[34] They had defeated one of the most powerful

---

[31] See Hooker, *History*, III, 661–663 for a copy of the judgment.

[32] AB iv, 397, and ECM, Deed 1623.

[33] AB iv, 452.

[34] This anomalous relationship is difficult to straighten out as there is no clear evidence as to what the Earl of Bedford's interest in Topsham was. Hooker says (III, 660) that the Earl bought the whole manor of Topsham, but the lease of the cranage certainly remained in the hands of Stubbs, from whom the city bought it. Bedford himself says (letter to Burghley, Lansdowne MS., xxviii, no. 61) that he was farmer to Stubbs for the cranage. It is clear enough from the receivers' rolls and the act books that the city received £40 a year from Bedford after buying the lease from Stubbs and that they paid him £13 6s. 8d. Therefore, we have assumed that he was sublessee to the city after 1584. Just how the payment to the city became the responsibility of the Warwicks by the 1590's is not clear.

nobles in the realm and strengthened their independence against any possible encroachment by him.

In 1587 the manor of Topsham passed by royal grant to the Earl and Countess of Warwick,[35] and although there is no direct evidence for it, Bedford's interest in the cranage also probably passed to them. When negotiations for the fishing of the river were in progress with the widowed Countess of Warwick an agreement was reached; both her sublease of the cranage and the payments due by the city were canceled.[36] The crane of Topsham now passed directly into the Chamber's hands. Goods quite apparently continued to pass through Topsham since the Chamber was able to farm the cranage for £20 per annum, but evidently the city no longer regarded this with a jealous eye. Possibly the Haven was unable to accommodate all the goods arriving by sea. At any rate, the Chamber allowed the lease of the crane to pass into other hands when their lease expired in 1614 without any visible concern.[37]

The city consolidated its control over the river by securing in 1588 from the Countess of Warwick the lease of the fishing of salmon in the river below the city.[38] The rent of £50 a year was a substantial increment to the city income; the mayor had the additional satisfaction of a free supply of salmon for his table, salmon reputed to be the best in England.

The construction of the canal was a major episode in the history of Exeter. It became possible through a radical change in the city's political position, but this change would have meant little had not the Chamber strained every nerve to exploit it. There was a new temper in these men; they were prepared to confiscate the plate of the churches, to spend the city's slender resources almost recklessly, and to fight the most powerful aristocrat in the West to gain their

[35] ECM, Law Papers, Martin vs. Worth.

[36] AB v, 187–188.

[37] An elaborate system of rates was set up in 1593 to control the transshipment of goods at the port. Dues for freemen's goods not landed at Exeter Quay continued; charges for use of the city's boats were set up as well as for other boats using the canal. Tolls were also levied on goods moving by horse from or to Topsham (AB v. 245, 293, 295, 298).

[38] AB v, 84.

ends. They showed tenacity, skill, and beyond that a boldness of purpose, a certain unscrupulousness, which their predecessors had not had. They were pushing forward to their aims with assurance and a newly found self-confidence. The sixteenth century was primarily a time when the citizens were laying the foundations of a new prosperity, but in this effort to push their fortunes, they already reveal the effects of a psychological revolution.

Part 2: Founding of the Merchant Adventurers Company

The ambitions of the merchants of Exeter were not limited to the canal project. They had already strengthened their position in the city's wholesale markets; they now determined to add a similar monopoly in the overseas trade flowing through the port. This was to be achieved by the chartering of a Merchant Adventurers Company modeled on that of London. This scheme, like that of the canal, formed another link in the whole pattern of economic expansionism which was a leading characteristic of the civic life during this epoch.

The first mention of the Merchant Adventurer incorporation is an entry in Hooker's *Annals* under the year 1558[1] which states that merchants trading to France were incorporated by Queen Mary. No such charter survives; perhaps the Queen's last illness interrupted a suit to obtain it. During this year the merchants did obtain incorporation under the common seal of the city as a company "in the mystery and trade of all wares and merchandise transported from beyond the seas within the city and county of Exeter."[2] But they wished to have their privileges guaranteed by higher and more unassailable authority. In December 1558, before the new reign was fairly begun, we find the mayor and aldermen writing to Sir William Cecil on behalf of a group of merchants in the city, who by the same bearer sent up their petition for incorporation.[3]

---

[1] ECM, Book 51, fol. 352. [2] AB ii, 329.
[3] ECM, Book 85 (Merchants Adventurers Papers), Document 4 and Document 22. PRO, SP 12/1/23.

This petition met with speedy response, for the charter preserved in the city archives is dated 28 January 1558–59.[4] The terms of this document included a grant of incorporation to sixteen merchants of the city under the style of the Warden and Society of the Merchant Adventurers of Exeter, with the right to hold property, sue and be sued, to rule and govern the merchants and apprentices of the city, and to make their own by-laws. But the core of the grant was a provision which forbade all inhabitants of the city who were not members of the society to sell *by wholesale or retail* any goods produced outside the realm or to export goods beyond the seas. It was a grant of monopoly modeled on the much older practices of the London Merchant Adventurers, reserving to the holders of the monopoly exclusive trading rights out of a certain port. In this case there was no specification of the ports of destination, but the trade of Exeter extended largely to those French ports lying along the Atlantic coast between Rouen and Bordeaux and to the Spanish and Portuguese wine-exporting centers. In one important way the Exeter charter was significantly different from the practice of London. This was the reservation to the monopoly holders of all retail trade in goods produced abroad. Such a provision went far towards concentrating a great part of the commercial activity of the city in the hands of the company members.

It was this latter provision that provoked the bitter civic feud of the next eighteen months. Fortunately profuse documentation on the subject was preserved by John Hooker, who himself played a prominent role in these events. These documents include copies of the petitions and replications sent to London as well as the depositions taken by the magistrates when matters reached a stage demanding their intervention.

The charter was sued out by the merchants with some secrecy.[5] But the tailors' company, aware of the grant, were able to procure copies of the charter out of Chancery,[6] which they then translated into English and distributed about the city. When the provisions of

[4] ECM, Book 85, Document 4.
[5] ECM, Book 85, Documents 4 and 22.
[6] *Ibid.*, Document 20.

this charter became known, they aroused the most violent reactions. There is a long petition addressed to the Lord Keeper Sir Nicholas Bacon, undated but belonging to some time between the issuance of the charter in January and early May 1559. Entitled "The Supplicacon of the Comoners agaynst the merchants,"[7] it is signed by the master and wardens of the tailors' company, the master of the weavers and tuckers, and the heads of the companies of bakers, brewers, cappers, dyers, and shoemakers "in the name and behalf of themselves and of their whole several companies as also for and in the name and behalf of all the residents and inhabitants within the county of the city of Exeter being free men of the same city." The petition recited that the petitioners were freemen of the city, sharing its common burdens. According to them, the recent charter was sought by a small body of merchants out "of a covetous and greedy desire of lucre" and was injurious to the interests of the rest of the citizenry. They were driven from "the exercise of their painful mystery by bargain sail and traffic of merchandise" and were faced with utter ruin and destruction. They, therefore, begged the Queen to act upon the provisions of a clause in the charter and to issue a commission *ad quod dampnum* for inquiring into the detriments occasioned by this grant.

The members of the new corporation countered with a replication defending themselves against the allegations of their opponents.[8] The substance of this answer can be summed up in three points: (1) that the new grant in no way infringed upon existing privileges; (2) that no actual organization under the new charter had taken place and consequently no regulation had been issued under it against which exception could be made; (3) that the complainants were not what they represented themselves to be. No such companies of brewers, cappers, or dyers existed; and the signers of the original complaint were claiming to represent many "honest diligent artificers . . . without their consents and agreement." The replication also pointed directly to the tailors as ringleaders in the agitation. According to the merchants it was chiefly this company of cutting tailors

[7] *Ibid.*, Document 6.   [8] *Ibid.*, Document 7.

who were behind the complaint—a group of "busy, seditious, and factious persons, neither minding their own occupations or the commodity of their neighbors, nor yet regarding their bounden duty towards their superiors."[9] But above all, the tailors, not content with their own trade, had taken to the occupation of drapers as well as of merchants, to the damage of the rightful exercisers of these trades.

It was now the turn of the tailors and their associates in this exchange of vituperations.[10] Their reply added little information, consisting mostly of emphatic denials of the merchants' allegations. However, it was plainly stated that the merchants, far from having done nothing under the charter, had actually inhibited various freemen in their lawful trades and even imprisoned one Hugh Simons. It was also said in this bill that the merchants had "procured unto their corporation" the mayor and aldermen, men of little substance themselves, but complacent towards the pretensions of the merchant oligarchy.

Against this we may weigh the replies of the merchants. Imposing both in volume and in style, they probably reflect the skillful hand of John Hooker. After restating their major arguments, the merchants went on to assail the tailors' company in particular.[11] To them, it was said, could be traced all the "promoting and maintaining" of the present agitation. They alleged concern for the common weal, but the truth was they had a factious grievance against the city fathers. Some two years back they had objected to the making of leather jerkins by certain shoemakers in the city, and when the mayor, basing his judgment on the custom of London, had allowed this practice as legal, the tailors became much incensed and continued to nurse their spite until the present occasion. This was not

[9] They went on to add: "which might have been better occupied in the exercise of their mystery and about the reformation of some uncunning and ignorant persons of their company as they permit to occupy rather than in the affairs of merchant venturers so far above their skill and ability, for no common wealth can flourish or be well governed where as every man will be a ruler and none contented with his condition."

[10] ECM, Book 85, Documents 8 and 9.

[11] *Ibid.*, Documents 22 and 2.

the tailors' only motive, however, for they had strayed from the proper exercise of their own trade to engage in others, such as those of drapers, merchants, and grocers. Now that their encroachments upon the trades of other men were to be suppressed, they cloaked their dismay in lofty appeals to principle and malicious assaults on their rivals.

Besides these fierce attacks upon the complainants as a mere jealous faction, representing no one but themselves, the merchants offered more positive arguments to support their own project. They based their assertions primarily on the claim that good order would be obtained and preserved by the new corporation. Men would be kept to their own proper tasks, for which their individual skills fitted them. Moreover, apprentices would receive "godly education" and be kept in good order; artificers would be set at work; while those who suffered loss at sea would be relieved by the benefactions of the new company; and there would be "many other like godly orders which must tend to the increase of a commonwealth and prosperity of the members of the same."[12]

The arguments sometimes ascended to even higher levels of consideration. In one such argument it was asserted that trade was peculiarly advantageous to a commonweal.[13] The proposition was developed under the three general heads of knowledge, wealth, and commodity. Under the first it was pointed out that princes receive from merchants full knowledge of neighboring countries and are thus able to estimate justly whether they are to be feared. As for wealth, beside the obvious income from customs duties, there was the increase of riches through an exchange by which commodities not otherwise obtainable were procured. And, of course, this flow of commerce set on work the cloth workers and other artisans and thus aided in preserving the good order and prosperity of the community.

In the meantime, while the opponents engaged in this war of words, the magistrates of Exeter made examinations to determine how the petitions against the new company had originated and how

[12] *Ibid.*, Documents 22 and 1.   [13] *Ibid.*, Documents 22 and 2.

they had been circulated. The depositions[14] taken at these examinations give us a glimpse of the complainants' methods and the character of the opposition. In the extramural area of the West Gate the work of organization was done by Ambrose Howell of the tuckers' company.[15] Going to the house of John Borne, a brewer on Exe Island, he gave him a petition already signed by all the tuckers and asked him to procure the signatures of his neighbors. To Borne's question, "Wherefore shall I do it?" Howell's response was, "Because there is many good householders without the West Gate that have great families and that shall not henceforth be able to buy at Topsham any grain or malt or salt neither the dyers may buy any alum, woad, or madders with divers other things without they must first have license of the merchants corporation." It was a persuasive argument.[16]

In the Bishop's Fee there was a general summons of all the tenants.[17] The head bailiff spoke to them, saying that the bishop had received a request to know the will of his tenants regarding the new charters.[18] He then read the charter, pointing out that it prohibited anyone's selling any merchandise within the city or at Topsham unless he were a member of the merchants' corporation. Some six or seven score apparently signed this petition. In the parish of St. Sidwell,[19] the bishop's holding to the east of the city, a jerkin maker appeared at the steward's court and circulated a copy of the charter among the suitors.

Various maneuvers had evidently been used to secure the consent

[14] *Ibid.*, Document 10.

[15] *Ibid.*, Deposition of John Borne, brewer, of Exe Island.

[16] The argument takes a more direct form in the speech of the bailiff of the Bishop's Fee, reported by one of his tenants (Deposition of Richard Pettie): "the corporation of the merchants of the city have gotten a corporation and charter that no man shall buy or sell any Rouen wares at Topsham but only the merchants of the city and by such encroachment all they should be annoyed and not suffered to occupy as they were wont to do."

[17] ECM, Book 85, Document 10, Deposition of John Langford, tucker, and Richard Pettie, glazier.

[18] Bishop Turberville, the Marian incumbent of the see, was still in office.

[19] ECM, Book 85, Document 10, Deposition of Hugh Symonds, jerkin maker.

of members of the tailors' and weavers' companies. One tailor,[20] who had absented himself from the meeting called to discuss the charter, was accosted in the street by Richard Prowse, warden of the company, reproached for his absence, and solicited to sign. The absentee, fearful of some fine for his nonattendance, subscribed without reading. The master of the weavers and tuckers, Symon Jane,[21] complained bitterly that Richard Maunsell, alleging a power of deputation, had usurped his place, and had even gone so far as to sign his—Jane's—name to the petition.

Mere rumor, too, had played its part in stimulating excitement. A goldsmith, Penfolde, had declared[22] in casual conversation that the rich merchants would repent themselves, for the handicrafts would band together to have "the statute upon them." Another, complaining that prices of all commodities would now rise, added that there were 5,000 in the town who would stand against the merchants.

Several things appear plainly from these depositions. The ringleaders in the agitation against the charter were members of the two artisan companies of the tailors and the weavers and tuckers, men of some substance, forming the second stratum of the city's economic structure. They had not hesitated to use political trickery of a sort to obtain signatures. And there was an interesting demonstration of the power of calculated rumor in a society lacking any regular sources of information.

The Council in London, bombarded by the petitions and counterpetitions of the Exeter factions, decided in May that further consideration should be given to the matter. A letter under the signet was issued 12 May 1559,[23] suspending the grant of incorporation since "it should seem that the said incorporation is not like to lead to so good a purpose as it was first by the said merchants pre-

---

[20] *Ibid.*, Deposition of John May, tailor.
[21] *Ibid.*, Confession of Symon Jane, sheerman.
[22] *Ibid.*, The saying of one John Collyer, capper. This Penfolde seems to have been something of a trouble maker. See above Chapter II, p. 39.
[23] PRO, SP 12/4/19.

tended."[24] This stay was obtained largely by the action of the tailors and was a clear victory for their side. They signaled their victory with more exuberance than discretion. The letter announcing it was sent by their representatives in London in the hands of one John Webbe,[25] a member of the tailors' company who "used both unseemly and uncomely order in delivery thereof." Accompanied by a crowd of about thirty, he waited for the mayor to come out of church, whereupon he presented the letter in the open street, demanding an immediate answer. Being denied it, for the letter required none, he came again later to the mayor's house and demanded an answer within two hours. One can imagine the angry vexation of the humiliated magistrate. In an age so respectful of ceremony and among a class particularly sensitive to any slight to its dignity, such humiliation must have wounded deeply.

The Privy Council now sought to find a compromise. It is contained in a document headed "The offers made unto the tailors and other artificers of the city by the merchants of the same city."[26] According to the terms of this proposal the tailors and other artificers desirous of trading were to be admitted to the merchants company, but if any of them could not pay the entrance fine, he was to be allowed to continue trading providing he made an annual contribution to the company for a "knoledge." Second, each artificer was to be free to buy any kind of merchandise for use in his craft. Lastly, it was agreed that all the freemen should be reduced into companies which would be invested with all the freedoms and liberties held by the London companies. For reasons which we do not know this offer was not accepted.

In the meanwhile, sometime before December 1559, the Council took another step, by summoning representatives of the disputants

[24] There is an interlined sentence "and that ye deliver out of prison any merchant or person who is imprisoned by force of your said corporation."

[25] Book 85, Documents 22 and 3.

[26] *Ibid.*, Document 19. From a letter written in the following year (Document 16) it seems that a commission of London merchants were appointed by royal charter to come down to Exeter, to hear the disputants and attempt to arrange a settlement on the basis of the custom of the London merchant adventurers.

to appear personally before a committee of its own members.[27] The committee included Sir William Petre, Sir John Mason, and Sir Ambrose Cave. The first of these was closely connected with Exeter affairs through his brother John Peter, the customer, and his brother-in-law, John Peter, the mayor in 1557. It was before them that Richard Heliard, Thomas Hawes, and Thomas Byrde appeared as representatives of the complainants. Why or how these three men were chosen we do not know. The purpose of the councillors, apparently, was to act as arbitrators rather than as judges. In any case they advanced a compromise proposal. In substance they suggested that, while the merchants' company should be given a monopoly of overseas trade, freedom of retail trade in all kinds of goods should be allowed to every freeman as heretofore.[28] Asked how he liked this arrangement, Heliard answered that he thought the commons would not like it, whereupon Sir John Mason called him "a busy and prating fellow and a vauntparler."[29] Heliard remained silent under the rebuke.

The representatives of the complainants returned to Exeter, and the city awaited the final judgment of the royal councillors. When the letters from the Council came down, heralded by rumor, an order was issued that all freemen should assemble at the Guildhall to hear them read by John Hooker. He was also to deliver an oration urging upon the citizenry obedience and reconciliation. The terms of the letters[30] were those of the compromise stated above. A new company with a monopoly of wholesale, but not of retail, trade in foreign products was established. It was also provided that not only the original petitioners but also any other freemen desirous of being an adventurer might sue for admittance gratis. A committee, consisting of the mayor and chamber with ten principal commoners of the city, was to pass upon their eligibility for admission.

After the reading of the letters and Hooker's oration, the heads

[27] *Ibid.*, Documents 11 and 12. Here we are inferring from later and indirect evidence.

[28] *Ibid.*, Document 12, Deposition of John Hooker.

[29] *Ibid.*

[30] William Cotton, *An Elizabethan Guild of the City of Exeter* (Exeter, 1873), 104f.

of guilds and the complainants' three representatives before the Council were ordered to remain behind for further instructions.[31] They were told that since not all the freemen were present, it was their duty to communicate the tenor of the Council's letters to the absent and to enjoin obedience upon the members of their respective companies. As for the three delegates, since they had been present before the Council committee and had there given consent to the arrangement, they were now to exhort their fellow citizens to like agreement. The irritated deputies, particularly Heliard, declared they had given no such consent and further maintained that the Council letters were to be understood not as a command but as a suggestion. Heliard, under questioning, admitted that the lords had made the compromise proposal contained in the letters, but declared that he, cowed by Mason's harsh words, had merely remained silent without intending by this silence to give tacit consent.

This continued resistance on the part of the ringleaders of the complainants roused the magistrates to action. Depositions were taken from the principal participants in the scene at the Guildhall, including Alderman Hurst, the sheriff, Richard Prestwood, and the chamberlain, Hooker, as well as numerous other witnesses, and the whole was dispatched to London with a lengthy letter.[32] The gist of this letter was that the continued opposition was of a purely factious nature, designed rather to embarrass the civic authorities than to resist a settlement which harmed no one. Such restraints to trading as were imposed by the Council's decision possessed the same general character as those limiting trade with Flanders or Russia to a certain body and did no harm to the privileges of the Exeter freemen. Resistance raised on the pretense of such harm was but opposition to the Council's orders, veiling itself under a claim of threatened privilege. There was also a letter from the wardens of the new company to the Council, written in much the same vein.[33] From it and from some of the depositions it is evident that the opposition

---

[31] ECM, Book 85, Document 12, particularly the deposition of John Hooker and that of Alderman William Hurst for these details.

[32] *Ibid.*, Document 16.

[33] *Ibid.*, Document 17.

now disclaimed that any powers of representation had ever been given the three men who went up to London. Another delegation was already on its way to the capital to make this claim before the lords and urge revocation of their order. The letters of the Exeter magnates had their intended effect in London. Early in February the three, Helliard, Hawse, and Byrde, were bound over in £20 each to appear on demand before the Council.[34] This was the usual penalty imposed in such cases, and, no doubt, was as effective in this one as in others. The way was now open to the merchants, and on 17 June 1560 the Queen signed the new charter.[35]

Some of the provisions of the charter are worth noting in detail. The stated motives of the Queen in granting the charter fell under two heads. The first was the loyalty of the city as demonstrated in the times of King Henry VII and again under Edward VI. The second was to take away "sundrie obsurdities and inconveniences which of late within the saide Citie hath cropen and growen by reason of the excessive nomber of artificers and other inexpert ignorante and unworthie men which doo take upon them to use the arte scyence and mysterie of merchandise."[36] In order to correct this a monopoly of wholesale trade in overseas commodities was granted the new company. No citizen not a member could participate in this trade. The general provisions that followed duplicated those of the earlier charter of 1559 except that the name of the society was now "Governor Consuls and Societie of Merchant Adventurers of the Citie of Exon traffiquinge the realme of Ffraunce and dominions of the Ffrenche Kinges" and the number of grantees was enlarged from sixteen to forty-nine.[37] Nor was this number a maximum, for it was also provided that during the next three years any artificer who gave up his craft was to be admitted gratis.[38] The final clause of the charter provided that the company was to provide yearly twelve garments for a like number of poor people, as well as to provide for any of their own members who might be ruined by

[34] *Ibid.*, Document 18.
[35] Cotton, *Elizabethan Guild*, 1–10. The charter is printed in full here.
[36] Cotton, *Elizabethan Guild*, 1.
[37] *Ibid.*, 2. [38] *Ibid.*, 7.

accident at sea.[39] The charter reflected an interesting effort to dress
the new company in the garb of a true guild fellowship. Not only
was the fiction of "an arte scyence and mysterie of merchandise"
carefully maintained, but also the customary act of charity, here
reduced to a mere formal gesture, was preserved. In the same way
the company was listed by Hooker along with the city guilds of
artisans, bakers, and brewers. It would be presuming too much to
accuse him of deliberate hypocrisy in assimilating this trade monopoly of the merchant oligarchy to the humble artisan guilds familiar
to the city. Doubtless, it was still possible to think of the merchant's
calling as a craft, but there was also here an attempt to accommodate
public opinion by presenting the new monopoly in the familiar
features of a city guild.

Looking back over the history of this bitter struggle one sees
several important facts. The fundamental issues lay between two
competing economic groups rather than between various social
classes. It is fairly clear from the evidence that the protest against
the new charter did not arise from the spontaneous indignation of
the whole artisan class, but rather that it was systematically and
skillfully stirred up by the interested party of the tailors. Their best
efforts could not make the contention that they represented the civic
guilds and the whole body of freemen a convincing one. The core
of the opposition was among three groups, the tailors, the weavers,
and the tuckers. They represented the particular economic stratum
that would suffer by the new restrictions, especially by those on
retail trade in foreign goods. It is clear from the testimony in the
various documents of the controversy that these groups were in the
habit of dealing as traders, but probably not on a large enough scale
to support themselves. In other words, they still had to divide their
efforts between their craft and their trading activities. The new
company, with its original limited membership, would have excluded them from trade altogether. Hence arose their particular
bitterness about the restrictions on retail trade. The royal government, called in to solve the problem, moved cautiously. Although
desiring to do justice, it was probably sympathetic to the aspirations

[39] *Ibid.*, 10.

of the merchants. To the Council the latter represented the most
solid and reliable element in Exeter, who, in their magisterial
capacities, were the guarantors of order and the executors of royal
policy. It required skill to satisfy both sides, but the councillors hit
upon the central issue, the jealous discontent of the tailors and lesser
traders, and by removal of the restrictions on retail trade and en-
largement of the company's membership, they were able to satisfy
most of the discontented. It is significant that the last stage of resistance to the charter was conducted by a new group of leaders, men
of less prominence than those who earlier supplied leadership to the
agitation. By this time most of the influential men of the city were
in one way or another drawn to support the amended charter, and
after the spring of 1560 the agitation melted away and seemed
forgotten.

Already, before the signing of the second charter, organization of
the new company had taken place; but it was not until 6 August
1560 that the first regular elections under the new charter were held
in the chapel chamber of the Guildhall, and William Hurst was
sworn in as first governor in the presence of forty-three of the sixty
members.[40] The charter provided for the annual election of the
governor and four "consulls." To them was entrusted the general
governance of the company, but by the statutes and ordinances of
the society, they were to make no regulations unless twenty or more
of the company joined with them.[41]

In the oaths[42] required of the officers as well as of the members,
obedience was promised, significantly enough, to the Queen and

[40] *Ibid.*, 25.
[41] *Ibid.*, 15, in "Statutes and Ordinances of said Societie devised by the
Governor, Consulls, and Companie." Additional ordinances provided for the
maintenance of order at meetings; no one was "to be talkatyve or yangeling
upon payne to paye for everye such offence two pence." No one was to be a
member unless he was a freeman of Exeter dwelling in the city, or became
one within a month. The eldest son of every freeman (or woman) was allowed
to succeed upon the death of his father, provided he remained a merchant,
while apprentices or members were admitted after seven years' service.
Another remnant of guild organization was the provision that at the burial
of any member all the other brethren should attend at the church.
[42] *Ibid.*, 19.

her successors, and to the Mayor of Exeter, her lieutenant in the city. An additional promise was made, not only to obey the ordinances of the company, but also to report any unlawful gatherings. The company was evidently considered a public body, a part of the legal structure of government.

Other provisions for the ordinary functioning of the company were made. Income was derived in part from entrance fines and penalty fines, but more largely from the "average money," a levy of 1d. per tun of wine and per fardel of cloth passing inward or outward.[43] Later this was farmed, first at £10 or £12 per annum. By 1587 with the levy doubled to 2d., it was farmed at £17 10s. per annum. A meeting hall was also leased; its location cannot be ascertained, but it was close enough to the Guildhall so that the chapel bell there could be used to summon meetings. Although entrance into the company remained restricted, the membership grew considerably, and admissions were relatively numerous at the end of the century. In 1596 seventy-one members were listed in a subscription list for the purchase of corn.[44] The entrance fines were apparently not fixed, but were voted by the members on the occasion of each admission. In 1599 a draper, William Newcombe, who applied for entrance, was fined twenty marks but the fine was later reduced to £10.[45] A random list of admissions from 1562 to 1597 reveals fines varying from £8 to a few shillings, but they were seldom less than £2. The main hurdle to be leaped in entering the society was not a financial one but rather the approval of the members.

The charter settled the main questions at issue in 1560 but it left unclear some very important problems. The charter of the company was issued to the merchants of Exeter trading with France. But what about those trading with Spain, or later on, with the Low Countries? And what was the relation of this company to the Merchant Adventurers of England? To these questions we can give only confused answers.

[43] *Ibid.*, 28–29. [44] *Ibid.*, 152.
[45] *Ibid.*, 169.

There could be no doubt as to the company's jurisdiction over
the French trade, although even here it had some preliminary difficulties since the great Exeter merchant, John Periam, remained outside the company until 1574.[46] But from that time forward its
control over the trade with France was secure. Once, indeed, in
1633 it was necessary to invoke the Privy Council against a recalcitrant, and in this instance the Council firmly backed the company's
claims.

When the company was founded, the other main trading area of
the Exeter merchants besides France was Spain. The company was
certainly concerned with the Spanish trade. On at least one occasion
its officers organized a joint-stock venture to Spain,[47] and in 1572
and again in 1587 it acted as representative for those merchants
who had suffered loss by confiscation in Spanish ports. There is
some slight indication that there may even have been a separate
Spanish company, but this is very uncertain.[48] But after 1603 there

[46] He became free of the company in 1574. See fol. 50 in Act Book of the
Company of Merchant Adventurers trading to France, deposited in the
Tuckers' Hall, Exeter. There were other interlopers who tried to ignore the
company's jurisdiction from time to time. See fol. 15d and 20d for the case of
John Pyll who was imprisoned by the magistrates for his failure to pay the
£10 fine levied by the company. Usually the company's authority was sufficient to bring the offender to heel, but in 1633 the company had to petition
the Privy Council for redress against Malachi Dudney. Although a sidesman
of St. Olave parish, he claimed not to be under the company's jurisdiction.
The company was upheld by the Council (PRO, SP 16/251/65 and SP
16/259/7). The Chamber fined him £200 but remitted all but £3 6s. 8d.
(A.B. viii, 4).

[47] See Merchant Adventurer Act Book, fol. 21, 22, and 23. On fol. 21 there
is an order that no member is to lade a ship to Spain or Portugal in partnership with a nonmember. He could trade only by himself or in partnership
with another member.

[48] There are inconclusive letters relating to this matter in the Merchant
Adventurer Act Book. In 1577 a letter was received from the new company of
merchants trading Spain from London (fol. 69). An answer was returned
(fol. 70d) which seems to imply that merchants who wished to enter the company might do so individually. Later there is a note (fol. 83, March 1579) in
which rent for the company's hall is shared between the "Merchant Adventures of Exeter" and the "Spanish company." And another entry on fol. 88
(1580) refers to the treasurer of the Spanish company. There is one additional
reference to a payment by the Spanish company in 1587 (fol. 143). In 1587
also there was a letter from the President and Fellowship of Merchant

is little evidence that it took any interest in Spain. It was not the company but an informal group of shipowners and merchants who were consulted when the charter of the Spanish company of London was before the Council in 1637.[49] Indeed, in the seventeenth century the company is most usually referred to as the merchants trading with France.

The ambiguity of the situation became an urgent question only when the Exeter merchants began to participate in the Low Countries' trade in the late 1630's. The issues were put in a case originally brought before the Privy Council in 1633.[50] At this point the complaint was simply against artificers who traded with France and also exercised their regular craft. The Council peremptorily forbade such combinations of occupation; the offenders were to exercise one calling or the other, but not both. But the case was not ended, for one defendant continued to exercise both trades, claiming that since he did not deal in French commodities, he was not violating the charter. The prohibition against simultaneous retail and wholesale dealings in foreign goods applied only to French commodities, he argued. On this larger question the Council accepted the judges' opinion that the company charter gave jurisdiction over all merchant adventurers in any parts.

Thence the company's concerns were largely with the French trade. But what were its specific functions? On occasion it could be a joint-stock venture.[51] But much more commonly it served the usual purposes of a regulated company. In the main this meant that it was what we should call a trade association. Sometimes lobbyist,

---

Adventurers trading Spain and Portugal in London, asking for certificates on losses by Western merchants in Spain and wrongs done by the Inquisition, but this was addressed to the Merchant Adventurers of Exeter. It seems possible that the Exeter merchants were allowed to participate individually in the parent company and possibly there was some local branch organization, but the subject really remains mysterious.

[49] APC, PC 2/47, v. 13, fol. 46, and fol. 289.

[50] For the protracted course of this case see APC, PC 2/43, v. 9, fol. 473; PC 2/44, v. 10, fol. 472; PC 2/45, v. 11, fol. 127, 171, 198, 211; PC 2/47, vol. 13, fol. 32, 217, 275. The Council eventually took the opinion of the justices on the western circuit who were ordered to investigate the case.

[51] See p. 169.

sometimes attorney for the merchants, it was always the guardian of their collective interests. Through its agency they carried their grievances to the Council, sought redress against French exactions or pirate depredations, or urged alterations in English trade policy. It coöperated frequently with the London merchants trading to France, and acted as the leader of the smaller southern and western ports engaged in the same trade.

Foreign trade always gave rise to frictions, but the Exeter merchants might feel they had more than their share during this century. Civil disorder in France from 1560 to 1598 made their important trade there precarious at the very period when war canceled out the Spanish trade altogether.[52] With the coming of peace with Spain and the end of civil war in France conditions improved, but sources of friction remained abundant in France. Moreover, throughout the century, piracy in the Channel was at its worst. These problems demanded the constant attention of the company.

Exeter merchants abroad were helpless in the face of the arbitrary actions of the French government, or more frequently, of local authorities. Even in peacetime, ships and goods were seized and held by the French officials and in the decade of the 1630's the state papers are full of complaints about the unsettled condition of the French trade.[53] In the absence of consular authority, merchants had to fend for themselves, and here the company proved its value. Working in close coöperation with the London merchants dealing in France and with those of the smaller ports, it provided an organization through which the tedious and intricate negotiations at London, Paris, or the various French ports could be carried on.

[52] The records of the company are extant only to 1603. Much of their content over the long period of the French civil war deals with the vexations of trade in Brittany and Normandy. Agents were appointed to follow specific suits in the French courts, proposals were bruited for removing the trade to the Channel Islands, and constant communication was maintained among all West Country merchants concerned. Many of these documents are published in Cotton, *Elizabethan Guild*.

[53] The most famous case was the De Launay seizure which involved £150,000 of English goods, of which Exeter merchants may have owned £30,000. The settlement of the suit which followed cost £1,500, shared between London and the West Country. See SPD, Charles I, 364/31, ccxix.

Expenses were high, and in order to meet them authority was obtained from the Council to levy a rate on goods passing through the ports. The Council had general knowledge of these matters, and part of the negotiations was carried on through the English ambassador, but much of the work had to be done by the companies' own representatives.

Control of the trade from the English side also preoccupied the company. Facing competition of Londoners and of the other Western outports, it aligned itself with the former. After the 1606 act granted free trade with France and Spain, Exeter secured statutory confirmation of its charter privileges.[54] Thus assured, it did not join the Western outcry when London got a charter for French trade in 1611. After 1630 Exeter repeatedly tried to control the other Western ports, and persuaded the Privy Council to allow levy of duties in them to pay for Exeter's lawsuits in France. In 1633 they boldly proposed a shared monopoly of French trade—northern and eastern traders under London, southern and western under Exeter, each company authorized to tax the ports in its area. The scheme failed but did result in provision for joint action and membership exchange between Exeter and London.[55]

In the 1630's Exeter's invasion of the Dutch trade, begun in the French wars of the 1620's, disrupted friendly relations. London, alarmed at the new competition, urged the Council to exclude Exeter from this trade. That in turn put in doubt the relationship of the two companies. Clearly Exeter was not a branch of the Merchant Adventurers of England, with automatic membership in it, but certainly some Exonians had been members of both. The 1638 Council decision giving them full rights in the national company (they were to buy Spanish cloth only in Devon) inaugurated a major extension of Exeter's trade.[56] But not all the company's energies went to defense of its rights. It had many workaday functions; the seas were filled with pirates. The complaints of the merchants were frequent and heartfelt, but

[54] *Statutes of the Realm*, 4 J. I, c.6, c.9

[55] For this and the following paragraph I have relied on W. B. Stephens, "Merchant Companies," TDA 86 (1954), 141–48.

[56] See SPD, Charles I, 298/98, ccxli; PRO, SP 16/380: 85, 86, 87.

relief was painfully slow in coming. In 1578 the merchants' company petitioned for a Queen's ship to be stationed off the Devon and Cornwall coasts as a guard against pirates, and they levied £100 among themselves to cover expenses.[57] Elizabeth, with a touch of cautious economy, sent down a commission allowing them to fit out a vessel with all the privileges of a royal ship at their own expense. To this proposal the citizens answered with a host of objections, which boiled down to the fact that no one was prepared to put up money to protect himself from a catastrophe much more likely to strike someone else. Later, Queen's ships were stationed along the coast, but without much effect, and in one season, that of 1602, the Western merchants fitted out a ship of their own.[58] The situation did not improve. In 1619 the government initiated a general effort to suppress the Barbary pirates, and Exeter, with some reluctance, put up £500 (out of £1,000 assessed) for an expedition that did not take place.[59] In 1630 the Chamber pleaded for protection against the Dunkirkers,[60] and in the following year the merchants petitioned for a general rate on the south coast merchants to finance private ships.[61] The petition was granted, but nothing seems to have come of it. In 1635 the company armed a ship of its own to carry goods to Morlaix and St. Malo, no merchant being allowed to ship otherwise, and a rate being levied for expenses.[62] The following year all the western ports joined in a petition for protection against the Sallee pirates. At the very end of our period in 1639 we find the Admiralty assigning four ships to the Western coasts but complaining that on the last ship money levy Exeter had paid but £100 out of £350.[63] The problem was obviously much too large for local

---

[57] Cotton, *Elizabethan Guild*, 138f and fol. 82d in the Merchant Adventurers Act Book, where apparently the money was given over to the use of the poor.

[58] Cotton, *Elizabeth Guild*, 167.

[59] APC, III, 218; IV, 360, 414, 421; V, 62. See also SPD, James I, 26/45, cvii.

[60] SPD, Charles I, 232/39, clxiv, and 241/15, clxv.

[61] *Ibid.*, 28/84, clxxxiv.

[62] PRO, SP 16/535/155, and APC, 2/47, v. 13, fol. 31.

[63] PRO, Acts of the Privy Council, PC 2/51, Pt. 2, vol. 17, fol. 590.

authorities, and the government of Charles I was not prepared to put its full efforts into solving it.

The company's importance to Exeter's trade was considerable. The national government did not provide necessary services; it could not adequately protect its subjects' commercial services abroad nor their shipping on the high seas. The company had often to act as a makeshift substitute, doing what it could to protect mercantile interests. In this capacity it was not always adequate, but it did much to establish the leadership of Exeter among the Western merchants and to secure the place of the Exeter merchants in the national mercantile community.

The merchants' company did not confine its representations to foreign matters or to piracy, however. It also concerned itself with domestic policies of the royal government. Their objections to the new customs rates of 1600 were of this type. In September of that year[64] the Lord Treasurer ordered new customs on certain kinds of wool cloths, to last for four years. The company wrote off to the other Western towns for support in urging that these duties be lowered and their duration shortened. We do not know the result of their representations. In 1595, when for two years the ports of the West had been paying a duty of 10s. per tun of Gascon wine, for the Queen's household expenses, they were able to make an arrangement to buy up the tax from the farmer, for a lump sum of £75.[65] In order to do this they made a special levy of their own for one year on wine entering the port.

The Council was not the only body to be influenced. When Parliament met, the company delivered its instructions to the Exeter burgesses. In 1580 along with Totnes the company proposed an act requiring that all traders be residents in an incorporated town, and another regulating the making of Devon kerseys.[66] For the Parliament of 1584 there is extant a copy of the company's instructions to the burgesses, Brewerton and Prowse.[67] Again they were to demand town residence of all traders beyond seas and, in addition,

---

[64] Cotton, *Elizabethan Guild*, 145.   [65] *Ibid.*, 147.
[66] *Ibid.*, 129.   [67] *Ibid.*, 159.

clauses that none should be merchants who had not been traders overseas for eighteen years past or apprentices to an older merchant for at least seven years.

The merchant company, besides the dual aspect of its activity as a commercial association, retained some remnants of guild organization. Control over its apprentices and over the conditions of their service was a right firmly exercised. And disputes between members were settled by umpires appointed by the company. The company, although not in any sense a religious association, still took seriously its duties of providing charity. Each year a certain amount of wood was provided for the poor of the city.[68] Specific donations for needy cases were fairly numerous. Even the Portuguese sailors in Exeter gaol in 1585 were beneficiaries of such a donation.[69] The unfortunate of their own company were objects of concern, too. A fund known as the house money had been set up, and from time to time loans from this were made to those who had suffered loss.[70] In 1585 it went to Morrice Downe who had suffered loss at the hands of pirates; in 1592 to a widow; and in 1593 to John Sampford "in consequence of his great losses by sea."[1]

More important, however, were the major public functions that were undertaken by the company. Dignified by its royal charter, endowed with coveted privilege, which included limited but effectual punitive powers, the company doubtless appeared to contemporary eyes almost as much a public body as the Chamber itself. This impression must have been heightened by the fact that the personnel of both was nearly identical. The magnates sitting in the Guildhall or holding company court embodied power and responsibility in the Exeter community. And they themselves doubtless drew no clear-cut line of separation between their functions in the two bodies. In instructing the burgesses or in prosecuting a suit for the mitigation of a French customs duty, they felt they were acting for the public good as well as pursuing a private advantage.

We may note some instances of their action as a purely public

[68] *Ibid.*, 120.
[69] *Ibid.*, 154.
[70] *Ibid.*, 175.

body. There were such items as the purchase of gunpowder for the use of the Queen. When this was done in January 1590 some £50 was expended,[71] a sum collected by a rate on the members. In October, the danger for the season being past, the members were reimbursed by the sale of the gunpowder. But as occasion arose again, they purchased more with the understanding that if it were used the loss would be shared. When the new Guildhall was under construction in 1593 they subscribed £40 for the work.[72] And, more important, they were forward in the movement for a lecturer in the parish churches. As early as 1580 they discussed how much each would contribute[73] towards the stipend of a preacher "to enstruct the youth of this Citie as well their Catechesme as also their dutie and obedience towardes God and their parentes." Such an appointment was not made until 1599 when the company agreed to contribute £10 yearly for a preacher nominated by the Chamber. The money was to be raised by an additional levy of 1d. on each ton, pack, or fardel.

Their action in providing grain in times of scarcity was of great importance to the community. In 1586, for instance, a shortage of grain occurred, and the company made a purchase of rye and wheat.[74] Each man who contributed to the expense of purchase was promised one bushel of wheat and one of rye for each pound subscribed by him. More serious, however, was the shortage of 1596.[75] In August it became apparent that a shortage would occur as a result of the bad weather that summer, and the company decided to purchase rye from Danzig or elsewhere in the amount of 100 tons. This time the contributors were to receive back one-third of their money in grain; the other two-thirds were to be sold to the poor at cost. A contract was made for 3,600 bushels of rye at 4s. 6d. a bushel, a total of £810. In this year rye was selling locally at 9s. Delivery of this cargo was to be made before 15 May following. In the meantime, additional grain was needed and had to be bought with a subscription raised in the company. In February 1596–97,

[71] Cotton, *Elizabethan Guild*, 140.   [72] *Ibid.*, 90.
[73] *Ibid.*, 156.   [74] *Ibid.*, 150.
[75] *Ibid.*

£550 was raised in this fashion. Presumably the additional money necessary was raised by the sale of the grain. It was agreed that if the poor people refused to take the corn coming in May at 5s. 4d., each member of the company was to have one-half of the grain at that price. Actually 800 bushels were reserved to the company, and the balance made available to the city.

The new company, like the canal, marked an era in Exeter's history. Exeter's economic development during the late Middle Ages had probably been somewhat retarded as a result of the blockage of the river and perhaps also of its isolation from the great trade routes across the North Sea. The foundation of the company was a token of the Exeter merchants' determination to make good lost opportunity. It is significant that the Exeter merchants should have chosen the already somewhat archaic form of the regulated company to advance their commercial interests. It points both to a certain backwardness in their economic outlook and to the weakness of their financial position. They still needed the strength afforded by the adventurers' organization; very few of them could venture alone into the commercial struggle for overseas markets. Nevertheless, the company proved to be a very useful and effective form of economic organization during troubled years. It filled not only the role of a commercial combination for overseas trade, but also that of a trade protection association, and on occasion it acted as a kind of auxiliary to the civic corporation in performing public services.

The bitter struggle which surrounded its establishment aroused much passion in the city, but it did not leave permanent scars. The eventual compromise provided satisfaction to all those who were important enough economically to share in the overseas trade and left unharmed the position of the small retailers and the artisans. There may have been underlying social discontents in the community, but they did not find articulate expression in the dispute over the charter.

The initiation of the merchants' company was a long step forward in the foundation of Exeter's later prosperity. It strengthened the trading position of the merchants at a time when they were still individually weak, and through it they became a more self-conscious economic class; they learned how to protect their group interests and how to pursue group objectives. In short, the company provided them with the opportunity to serve their apprenticeship in the expanding economic world of the Elizabethan era.

Chapter Seven

The Trade of Exeter

It is much more easy to describe the formal framework of economic controls than it is to give an account of the actual business activity of the community. What commodities were traded in the markets of Exeter? What was the volume of trade? Where did exports go and from whence did imports come? And what about the individual merchant? How did he organize his business? How much trade did he handle in a year? How did he make his profit? To all these and many other related questions we can give only very partial answers. Our sources of information are disappointingly few. The royal customs books and those of the city petty customs give us some information. Unfortunately, only a half-dozen years are still extant in the royal customs books, and a mere scattering, largely concentrated in Elizabeth's reign, in the city books. These can be supplemented by occasional information in the act books or other official documents, but the sum total of our knowledge is very sketchy.

The basic characteristics of Exeter's economic life were naturally determined by the province of which it was both capital and entrepot. Devon's prosperity was built largely upon one commodity, wool. It was, as Hooker said, "the best commodity that this country doth yield and which keepeth most part of the people in work."[1] In this region enclosure had long been common, but not to the utter ruin of agriculture. The sheep, rather than being concentrated in great flocks, were scattered among the small individual holdings of many small farmers who combined sheep raising and agriculture.

[1] BM, Harleian MS. 5827 (*Synopsis Chorographical of Devonshire* by John Hooker), fol. 8d.

Similarly, the production of woollen goods was on a family basis. "Wheresoever any man doth travel ye shall find it at the hall door as they do name the hall door of the house, ye shall find, I say, the wife, their children, and their servants at the turn spinning or at their cards carding and by which commodities the common people do live."[2] The work of manufacture went on in the households, but the purchase of raw materials and the sale of finished products took place in the various market towns, and above all, in Exeter on market days. Hooker describes the process: "For first the merchant or weaver buyeth the weaver his cloth and payeth present money, the weaver buyeth the yarn of the spinster and payeth present money; the clothier he sendeth his clothes to the tucker or fuller and he when his work is finished hath likewise his money; and then the merchant or clothier doth dye them in colors . . . or send them to London or elsewhere to his best advantage."[3] The merchant clothier was as yet only a trader, dealing in the finished product. In the seventeenth century the patterns of organization began to change: the entrepreneur emerged as purchaser of the raw material, owner of it throughout the entire manufacturing process, and employer of the erstwhile small producers who had formed the basis of Devon's regional export trade to the rest of England and overseas.[4]

Further changes in the industry came about as new types of cloth were developed between 1500 and 1700. After 1530 the Exe and Culme valleys became centers for manufacturing the specialized Devon kersey, and a century later the Ottery St. Mary area was producing a colored version of the cloth. North Devon produced coarse bays; in the Taunton-Chard area the specialty was "cottons," used for lining; and Collumpton turned out stockings as well as kerseys. In Devon serges, thicker than most of the new draperies, took on a local form, the perpetuano. All these cloths required both more variety and greater quantities of wool than the sheep of Devon could provide, and dependence on weekly supplies from nearby counties, as well as from Wales, Ireland, and Spain

[2] *Ibid.*, fol. 7d.
[3] *Ibid.*
[4] Stephens, *Exeter*, 50.

increased.[5] This trend, coupled with the greater specialization of labor, could only hasten the decline of the small producer.

The expansion of cloth production in Devonshire was working changes in the economy of the region which were felt during our period. Hooker boasts of his native county as a great producer not only of sheep but of cattle and corn. Westcote, writing a generation later,[6] regretfully notes the change that had come about. No longer, he sighs, can Devon export corn, beeves, and mutton; now it can barely feed itself, and the frequent shortages of grain on the Exeter markets confirm his assertion. Still the regional economy was a mixed one in which neither tillage nor pasture absolutely overshadowed the other. There were other activities of some importance. Tin was being mined on Dartmoor, and at least one Exeter merchant, George Smith, had interests in this industry.[7] But the export of tin through the port declined sharply between 1550 and 1600, and in general London merchants rather that West countrymen seem to have exploited tin mining. Beyond this the sea itself was of great importance in the Devon economy, providing "sea-faring men as well for merchandise as for fishing." It supplied the principal livelihood for every village and hamlet along the deeply indented coasts of the county.

Exeter was the distribution center for a prosperous regional economy, and its inhabitants were busily engaged in providing goods and services for the two western counties. The city was the funnel through which moved both the exports and the imports of the whole area, and regional commerce was the economic lifeblood of the city. Table V reveals how this fact dominated the civic economy. The figures presented there are drawn from the freemen admission lists for the decades 1620–40, contained in Book 55.

The primary fact which emerges is the overwhelming predominance of the merchant. Almost a third of these new businessmen were to become wholesalers either of general commodities, such as

---

[5] See Stephens, *Exeter*, 47–50, and Thomas Westcote, *A View of Devonshire in 1630...*, ed. George Oliver and Pitman Jones (Exeter, 1845), 59–61.

[6] *Ibid.*, 55.

[7] Historical Manuscripts Commission, *Cecil Papers*, V, 162.

TABLE V.—*Admission of Freemen to Exeter Trades,*
1620–40

Trade	Admissions	
	Number	Percentage
Wholesalers	173	31
Textile processing	88	16
Building	64	12
Provisioners	62	11
Retail Clothing	59	11
Leather-workers	43	8
Miscellaneous	62	11
Total	551	100

"merchants" proper (68 admissions); grocers (33); or as more specialized dealers: chandlers, ironmongers, or stationers. The chief commodity in which most of them dealt was cloth, a fact reflected in the city's second major group of occupations, textile processing. Of the 88 included in this total only 14 are actually weavers; the majority (40 admissions) were engaged in fulling or tucking along the river banks or on its islands. The only other manufacturers in this group are the felt makers (11 admissions) and the silk weavers (18). It is clear that industry took second place to commerce in Exeter.

Wholesale distribution and textile processing thus account for about a half of the new freemen. It is not surprising to find that most of the rest were to be engaged in providing the everyday necessities of life—food, drink, clothing, household or farm needs, and houses themselves. Besides butchers (23 admissions), bakers (26), glovers (16), or haberdashers (14), all of whom served a general clientele, there were members of the luxury trades like the goldsmiths (6), clockmakers (2), a limner, or an embroiderer, catering to a more exclusive market. For the rest there was a miscellaneous assortment, ranging from apothecaries (12 admissions) and barbers (7) to a solitary fletcher, still pursuing his dying trade, a musician (perhaps one of the city waits), and a parchment maker. The lingering rural character of the city is recalled by two admissions of husbandmen, and five of yeomen.

The intimate relations between the urban economy and the hinterland which it served are clear enough. The Exeter merchants depended upon the populations of the western counties both as suppliers and as customers; the fullers and tuckers looked to them for the materials of their trade. But even many of the provisioning and service trades in the city must have been equally dependent on country custom. Dr. Hoskins points this out in his study of sixteenth-century Leicester,[8] a town which subsisted largely by providing goods and services to the consumers of the neighboring countryside. It is interesting to compare Leicester figures with those for Exeter. The former town, perhaps no more than a third the size of Exeter, contained only a small merchant class; the major groups were those in the clothing, provisioning, and leather trades. The contrast with Exeter is evident. Not only had the latter a substantial industrial interest, but its citizens were primarily engaged in the wholesale movement of commodities. Leicester existed to serve directly the consumers of a small local area; Exeter to provide wholesale distributive services for a major region.

Exeter did not lack some of the features of Leicester's economic life, however. For instance, the building trades at Exeter admitted 12 per cent of the new freemen in the decades 1620–40, and we can hardly suppose they labored solely within the city precincts. As has been said above, Exeter also provided consumer goods and services for the surrounding area, fulfilling at one and the same time the roles of a local market town and a regional trade center.

One striking comparison may be made between Exeter and Leicester. The latter town numbered about a third the population of Exeter, yet annual admissions to the civic freedom during Elizabeth's reign averaged about 20. In Exeter, in spite of its larger size, the annual average is only about 28 for the decades 1620–40. This discrepancy may be partially accounted for by the depressed state of Exeter trade during much of the twenties, thanks to plague, war,

[8] See *Studies in Social History*, ed. by J. H. Plumb (London, 1955), "An Elizabethan Provincial Town: Leicester" by W. G. Hoskins, 33–67.

and the resulting business decline. But a more significant reason probably lies in the economic structure of the two towns. In commercial Exeter with its busy seaport and its numerous merchant warehouses there must have been a very large class of "common servants," members of no guild and not, of course, freemen. They performed the wearing, monotonous tasks of wharf, warehouse, and shop as well as providing servants for the households of Exeter. The existence of a rich merchant class in the Devon capital (quite lacking at Leicester) created a demand for extensive household staffs. This submerged class of the bigger cities emerges into the light of history only in the poor accounts or the court records; we should not forget that it contained a substantial portion of the city's inhabitants.

In the bustling commerce of Exeter one commodity clearly reigned—cloth. With the establishment by the Chamber of separate wool, yarn, and cloth markets in the city a considerable proportion of the county's output of these articles changed hands there. Hooker asserts that the weekly turnover of cloth in his time was about twenty-five or thirty packs, each worth from £20 to £30.[9] In other words, from £500 to £625 worth of business was done in this commodity each week prior to 1600. There can be little doubt that the figures would be larger at a later date.

Where the cloth went from Exeter is something of a mystery. Of course, much of it went overseas, but whether the city merchants had an inland trade in cloth is not clear. The very scanty evidence at hand suggests they did not. By the 1630's they were enjoying a larger and larger share in the export of colored cloth to the Low Countries, much to the irritation of the Londoners. The evidence taken in hearings on the London petition to the Council[10] is significant. The Exeter merchants objected most strongly to being compelled to deal at Blackwell Hall, which suggests that they did not usually trade there. Clearly their main interest was in export, and they bitterly disliked the prospect of having to shift to the position of suppliers to the London market. Whether the Londoners

[9] BM, Harleian MS. 5827, fol. 7d.
[10] PRO, SP 16/380/85, 6, 7.

bought their cloth on the Exeter market or preferred the smaller market towns (or dealt only through Blackwell Hall) is also unclear. Their main interest in the Exeter fairs seems to have been in the sale of goods, and they could not have dealt in the market as buyers at any other time.[11] It is significant, too, that cloth does not appear in the intercoastal trade with London,[12] which again suggests it was not purchased in the city by Londoners, but rather bought in the country markets. All this must remain a very obscure question but one can make a tentative guess that the cloths purchased in the Exeter market were mostly destined for overseas sale.

But finished cloth was the end product of a long manufacturing process. The other stages of manufacture were also important to Exeter. Besides the sale of raw wool and yarn, which we have no means of measuring, the city's mills on the Exe were centers for fulling and dyeing, and engaged some of the merchant capital in the city. The merchants were also importers on a large scale of woad for dyeing, which they sold not only locally but even in London.[13] A smaller but quite essential item of import was wool cards from Normandy. Wool itself, the soft fleece of Spain, was brought in from San Sebastian and other Biscayan ports.

But if wool served to set flowing Exeter's commerce, many other commodities poured in to add to the flow. For Exeter's real economic importance was as a distributing center, and cloth was only one of the many commodities handled there. In the first place Exeter served as an intrepot for foreign goods. The merchants who imported canvas and linen, paper and glass from Normandy, wine from Bordeaux or the Canaries, sold to a clientele scattered all over the western peninsula. Retailers, and possibly consumers, in Plymouth, Bodmin, Lympston, Ilfracombe, Barnstaple, Taunton, Tiverton, Crediton, and many smaller places bought from them.[14]

[11] See above, p. 86. See also PRO, Acts of the Privy Council PC 2/47, v. 13, fol. 366.

[12] See the Port Books of the royal customers and the Exeter petty customs rolls.

[13] See ECM, Inventory 143, Thomas Amy. Amy had 12 tons of woad on hand in London at his death.

[14] See the accounts receivable of various Exeter merchants listed in their inventories. See particularly Inventories 101, 127, 132, and 152.

Not only foreign imports, however, but English goods as well were distributed by them. Manufactured articles, books, and spices from London, hops from Kent, coal from Wales, Newcastle, or Scotland, were brought in by coastal shipping. Much of this trade was handled by Exeter merchants, but it was shared with those of the other Western ports and with Londoners. Retailers in Exeter could buy directly from the Londoners at fair time, and apparently had standing accounts in London.[15]

The port books do give information as to the kinds of goods shipped (although not as to their value) and also indicate where they went (or came from) and who shipped them. The commodities do not vary widely across the period from 1565 to 1640. Devon dozens, the woollen cloths for which the county was famous, formed the largest item in export in each recorded year. But they were rivaled by other West Country cloths, bays, Dunster cloth, perpetuanoes, and serge; and another woollen product, stockings, appears steadily in the returns. Tin, an item of some consequence at the beginning of our period, fades out of the picture altogether by 1640. Fish from Newfoundland, for re-export, appears as a new item towards the end of the sixteenth century. The destinations of these cargoes varied considerably as to individual ports, but at the beginning of our period they fell into three groups. Most important were the Norman-Breton towns from Rouen to Nantes (including the Channel Islands). Morlaix and St. Malo were the most frequently visited. The second group was that of the mid-Atlantic coast, Bordeaux, Rochelle, and Oleron, the sources of Gascon wines, woad, and salt. The third group was the Iberian ports, which, temporarily cut off by war, reappeared in the books after 1603. They included harbors all around the peninsula from Bilbao to Alicante, as well as the Atlantic islands. Beginning in the 1590's the Low Country ports, particularly Rotterdam, formed a fourth group, and by the 1630's these were of major importance. Besides these major areas there was a small trade with Ireland and with the Baltic, both appearing about 1600. The New World figured slightly in Exeter's

[15] See Inventory 150, that of an apothecary who had a running account in London, on which he made monthly payments.

commerce, with fish from Newfoundland and an occasional vessel from Virginia.

The cargoes brought home on return voyages varied according to the points of origin. From Brittany and Normandy came the heavy linen and hempen cloths made in those regions, probably the largest single item in Exeter imports,[16] and one which was sold on a large scale outside the Exeter market area. More probably intended for local consumption were the miscellaneous processed items brought in from Normandy: paper, brushes, combs, wool cards, thread, soap, alum, vinegar, glass, licorice, wax, aniseed, and much else besides. Wine came from Gascony but also from Spain and the Atlantic islands, while raisins, figs, oranges, and lemons came from the Iberian peninsula which also provided Spanish wool and iron from Bilbao. Woad, all-important for the dyers, was purchased in Bordeaux, and from the same area came large quantities of salt. The Low Countries provided madder, hops, and (as re-exports) masts, spars, beams, pitch, and tar. Baltic cargoes were usually grain from Danzig or Elbing.

Besides the foreign commerce there was a considerable and varied coastal trade. In part it was reshipment of imports to smaller Devon and Cornwall ports, but there was a large movement of goods from southeastern England, hops and malt from Kent, and manufactured articles or imports from London.[17] Coal came around from Wales or from Newcastle (or occasionally from Scotland).

Of the foreign trade about a third moved in ships owned in the ports and creeks of Exeter, particularly Topsham. Probably most of the Topsham ships were small. A survey of the 1580's, listing ships of 100 tons or more in the various ports of England, gave a tonnage of 440 for Exmouth as well as sixteen topmen (ships with

---

[16] See PRO, SP 12/281/107, an account of customs on all linen cloth of all types brought into England during the seven years ending Michaelmas 43 Elizabeth. Exeter and Poole were rivals for second place after London as centers of linen import. For later 17th-century trade, see App. III.

[17] See Exeter city petty customs rolls 31–32 Elizabeth for a typical cargo from London. It included: 13 tons iron, 13 tons grocery wares, 8 bbls. soap, 4 lasts pitch and tar, 7 ballots fat madder, 3 bbls. candles, 1 ton vinegar, frying pans, pots, brimstone, candies.

tops on masts) under 100 tons. This contrasted with the 1,520 tons of Bristol, which boasted only twelve topmen, or with Hull's 1,270 tons and forty topmen.[18] The number of ships registered out of the creeks of Exeter remained steady at about 40 for each extant year in the port books of the early seventeenth century, and this may very probably represent the bulk of Exe shipping.[19]

Naturally we should like to know something about the individual businessmen engaged in this commerce, but here again the evidence is fragmentary. No one of the Exeter merchants was probably dealing on a very large scale as compared with the great London exporters. Aside from a few major figures, they were unable to command any large amount of capital. Relatively few were shipowners, and even fewer could finance singlehanded the venture of a whole shipload of cargo. Hence the Merchant Adventurers Company, at least on some occasions, became a joint-stock company.[20] Once agreement had been reached as to destination and cargo, the officers of the company were left to organize the voyage, hire the ships, and settle freight rates. Each participating merchant then arranged for the portion of the cargo he was to provide. There is an example of this kind of venture in the year 1566.

In that summer the Governor and Consuls contracted for five ships, four of sixty and one of forty tons burden. All were scheduled to sail to various Iberian ports for cargoes of wine, raisins, and figs. There are extant the accounts drawn up for these ships, listing the merchants venturing in each one. In these five ships twenty-six

[18] PRO, SP 12/91/217. The other ports listed were as follows: Southampton & Portsmouth, 340 T., 10 topmen; Plymouth, 700 T.; Dartmouth, 730 T., 22 topmen; Ipswich, 1,230 T., 5 topmen; Yarmouth, 540 T., 10 topmen.

[19] The shipping was as follows:

Tonnage	Number of Ships		Tonnage	Number of Ships	
	1611	1637–38		1611	1637–38
12 tons	—	1	50 tons	3	7
18	2	—	60	7	5
20	3	6	70	3	1
26	4	—	80	1	—
30	8	10	100	2	1
40	5	7	120	—	2
45	1	—			

[20] See Merchant Adventurers Act Book, fol. 22–24.

merchants ventured, five of them with goods in all five ships, four in four ships, ten in three ships, six in two, and one in one ship only. The individual tonnages shipped varied from the 43 tons of William Hurst to Richard Swete's three tons.[21] This particular enterprise involved a distant destination and a single return cargo: wine. For such a venture joint arrangements were both necessary and convenient, and trade with southern Spain may have had a particular type of organization. This is hinted by a regulation of 1566 prohibiting any member of the company from trading with Spain in partnership with a nonmember—which suggests that the trade was usually on a joint basis. In the more diversified trade with France, involving a shorter distance, individual enterprise may have been more common, but even here from the entries of the customs books, joint ventures of several merchants seem to have been frequent enough.

The customs books give us some notion of the distribution of trade among individual citizens. In Table VI are figures for the

TABLE VI.—*Individual Payments to Customs*[a]

Period (Christmas to Christmas)	Over £100		£100–£50		£50–£1	
	Number	Amount	Number	Amount	Number	Amount
1611–12	8	£1,748	21	£1,305	48	£687
1614–15	8	1,251	21	1,554	52	812
1616–17	14	2,138	20	1,410	63	771
1627–28	1	109	4	370	27	258
1635–36	19	4,202	8	537	78	1,238
1637–38	15	2,824	15	1,098	61	812

[a] This table is based on Port Books (PRO, E 190/941/4; 942/11; 943/10; 947/3; 949/9; 950/7). Note that 1628 was a year when there was war with France and Spain.

years extant, showing the division of shipments in terms of customs duties paid. The large role played by the bigger merchants is immediately apparent; those paying more than £100 per annum in

[21] Eight shipped 10 tons or more; eleven 5 tons or more; and the remaining seven less than 5 tons.

customs duties were doing nearly half the business of the port. Nevertheless, there was still room for a sizable number of smaller dealers. Within the circle of the company free competition for trade existed. What is more striking is the large role in the Exeter overseas trade played by merchants from other places, particularly the small market towns of the West and the suburbs of Exeter. Taunton, Tiverton, Chard, Barnstaple, Totnes, South Moulton (of which only Totnes and Taunton were free of Exeter city custom) were among the former; St. Sidwell parish, Heavitree parish, Exminster, and—at the top of the list—Topsham, among the latter. As much as a third of the trade was in their hands. A few London and a few Bristol merchants traded through the port, but their share was insignificant compared with that of the West Country dealers.

One can make only a few surmises as to how the overseas trade was conducted at the other end. Exonians were frequently passing overseas, as the reports on foreign affairs transmitted through the mayor to London indicate, but whether or not a particular individual was designated to act as agent for the rest of the venturers in a particular cargo, cannot be determined. Some of the larger merchants maintained an apprentice abroad who acted as factor for their affairs. Simon Knight (mayor in 1570) served William Hurst in this fashion before starting out on his own account.[22]

The area of trade of the Exeter merchants expanded very slowly beyond the traditional limits within which they had dealt for centuries past. They showed themselves more conservative than their colleagues of Bristol or Plymouth in exploiting the possibilities of the newly opened trans-Atlantic commerce. The first opportunity for entering the American trade came with the expedition of the Gilberts in 1584.[23] Although the Exeter merchants who engaged in this enterprise did so as individual members of the Gilberts' company, the negotiations were handled through the Exeter Merchant Adventurers society. When Sir Walter Raleigh proposed their entry into his Virginia venture in 1585 the Merchant Adventurers replied

---

[22] ECM, Book 51, fol. 360 (sub anno 1569).
[23] See Merchant Adventurers Act Book, fol. 116. Seven merchants participated in this voyage, contributing £12 10s. each.

that they were already participants in Adrian Gilbert's voyage to China and would await the outcome of that before venturing in others. They did, indeed, join in the second Gilbert expedition of 1586. Out of £1,175 subscribed for this venture, £475 came from Exeter merchants.[24] The ships used were those of the five Exeter investors, of whom the most prominent was John Periam. In December 1587,[25] a third voyage was discussed in the company but there is no evidence as to the action taken. Later, in 1588, the matter again came up with the receipt of a letter from William Sanderson, the uncle of Davis, the explorer.[26] The letter proposed that all members of the Company of North-West Discovery were to hand over decision-making power to eight persons, including Walsingham, Raleigh, Thomas Smith, and, among others, John Periam. The Exeter company emphatically refused to adopt the proposal, and this was the end of the matter.

Outside of these ventures, where the influence of the Gilberts, locally well-known and respected, prevailed, the Exeter merchants showed little interest in such speculative activity. Towards Sir Walter Raleigh, in spite of his local connections, they showed positive dislike.[27] Probably it was largely occasioned by the privileges which the Queen had granted him in the port. He had permission to export cloth from Exeter, controlled the vintners' licenses, and had certain customs perquisites. In 1586, money was collected to support a suit against him for collecting fees upon the cockets and customs certificates.[28] A proposal of his to the company in 1588, offering them the benefits of his American discoveries, met with an almost contemptuous refusal.[29] Two proposals from Sir Francis Drake, one in 1588 and one in 1589,[30] touching expeditions into Spain, were read in the company but apparently found no response.[31]

[24] *Ibid.*, fol. 133b. Of the balance, £370 came from Totnes; £160 from London; £24 from Collumpton; £37 from Chard; £24 from Tiverton; and £75 from miscellaneous participants, including Mr. Duck of Heavitree parish just outside Exeter.

[25] Cotton, *Elizabethan Guild*, 84.   [26] *Ibid.*, 149.

[27] *Ibid.*, 80.   [28] *Ibid.*, 145.

[29] *Ibid.*, 80.   [30] *Ibid.*, 87.

[31] Exeter merchants showed a mild interest in Virginia. They subscribed £97 for the Virginia company's lottery in 1614. See ECM, Letter 167.

Exeter's economic development during our century was steady and substantial. There were no dramatic changes, but a healthy growth fostered by the expansion and specialization of the Devon cloth industry. The merchants themselves continued to trade in their old markets but from the turn of the century onwards were cautiously pushing out into the rich market of the Low Countries. But although the increasing prosperity of the city was based on the cloth trade of Devon, the city was not properly a wool or cloth town. These commodities created the prosperity of Devonshire and gave it a surplus to export, either abroad or in London. The surplus made possible the demand for commodities imported from outside the shire. It was here that Exeter played its role as the middleman who marketed the cloth and brought home the imports. The city's economy rested on this distributive function and was commercial in the strictest sense. The Chamber recognized this fact in its unremitting efforts to encourage more trading in the city. In other words, the city presents an interesting although not uncommon type of economy, resting not on the production of a particular commodity, nor on the exploitation of a new market, nor indeed on any special advantages. Such advantages as the city possessed arose simply from its importance as an established marketplace, a center of exchange and distribution. The prosaic secret of its success was the careful exploitation of these modest opportunities in the fullest possible measure.

Chapter Eight

The Reformation in Exeter

The religious life of Exeter offers a body of historical data easy enough to observe but difficult to interpret. The piety of the Middle Ages had here, as everywhere, reared an impressive institutional structure, which during the mid-sixteenth century underwent profound alteration. It is easy to catalogue these alterations: the disappearance of the monasteries and the dispersal of their property, the impoverishment of the bishopric, the confiscation of the parish church plate, the drastic revision of the liturgy, and the other changes in the daily life of worship. But along with these outward changes in the institutional structure of religion one senses an inward alteration of the religious attitudes and of the unenunciated beliefs of the population which is much more difficult to assay. In Exeter these latter changes left no literary monuments, indeed no history, by which to measure their development, and we can make only the most cautious guesses about their nature.

In the early sixteenth century the Christian life of Exeter centered, as it had for centuries, around the magnificent cathedral of St. Peter. Governed by a bishop whose revenue was among the largest episcopal incomes in England, and served by a well-endowed chapter of canons, the cathedral overshadowed all other religious establishments in the city and its vicinity. Under the bishop and dean were a chapter, nominally numbering twenty-four prebendaries, a college of vicars choral, also nominally listed as twenty-four, besides a subsidiary body of scholars and choristers. In actual fact this establishment centered in the dean and his officers, the chaunter (precentor), the chancellor, the treasurer, the four archdeacons of Exeter, Cornwall, Totnes, and Barnstaple, and the subdean. In addition an indeterminate number of vicars choral, stipendiary priests, and a body of attendants were resident in the close.

The incumbent of the bishopric from 1519 until 1549 was John Veysey. In more ways than one, he was the last of the Exeter bishops of the medieval tradition. Like his predecessors he played a great role in the state and was a prominent figure at court. By training a doctor of law, he was fitted for administrative posts and held the great office of Lord President of Wales at the time when Mary was Princess of Wales. He lived in great state and dignity, but his residence, after the early years of his tenure, was seldom at Exeter. He became more and more devoted to his native town, Sutton Coldfield in Warwickshire, on which he lavished his benefactions. The cares of his diocese were left to subordinates. When the years of spoliation began, he was ill-equipped to resist the importunities of the King or his courtiers. His very familiarity with them, as Hooker suggests, made it harder for him to deny them. Before his deposition by Edward VI's government, in 1549, the see's properties, once numbering thirty-two lordships and manors, were reduced to about three or four, and of the twelve episcopal residences only one was left.[1] The income, listed at about £1,500 in the *Valor Ecclesiasticus*, was no more than £500 by Elizabeth's time. But before describing the great changes of the Reformation decades, we need to survey the state of affairs as they were in 1530.

The cathedral establishment of Exeter had no monastic rivals either in the city or in the county of Devon. Western houses, with few exceptions, did not rank among the great foundations of England. Within the city there stood one modest Benedictine foundation, St. Nicholas, a cell of the Abbey of Battle. In the *Valor Ecclesiasticus* its income appeared as £147 12s.[2] The Prior of St. Nicholas controlled a small walled area within the city and held separate jurisdiction over his tenants there and in St. David's Down.

---

[1] This sketch of Veysey is derived in part from Hooker, Book 51, fol. 351, in part from Boggis, *Diocese of Exeter*, 330–335.

[2] *Valor Ecclesiasticus*, II, 313.

He also owned the fair of Lammas.[3] His relations with the Chamber, like those of the cathedral liberty, were not always friendly for his separate jurisdiction was resented.[4] The only other strictly monastic foundation in the close vicinity of Exeter was the little nunnery of Polslo, about a mile from the East Gate, noted in the *Valor Ecclesiasticus* at £164 8s. 11¼ d.[5] The nuns' steward was the eminent Devonian courtier and Recorder of Exeter, Sir Thomas Dennys. At the Dissolution the nuns numbered fourteen, including the prioress and subprioress.[6] Besides these two houses there was the Hospital of St. John just inside the East Gate. Inhabited by a prior and three brethren at the Dissolution, it possessed an income of £102 12s. 9d. of which £29 13s. 8d. went towards the maintenance of thirteen paupers and nine students of grammar.[7] The friars, both Dominican and Franciscan, had establishments in the city,[8] the former near the East Gate, the latter just outside the city walls on the southwest. These were modest foundations; in 1538 the Dominicans numbered fifteen, the Franciscans only ten. Two of the wardens of the Grey Friars were religious figures of some importance in the city's life; one, who welcomed Latimer in 1534,[9] suffered under Mary for his Protestantism; the other, also suspected of heretical leanings, abjured, and lived to be sought by warrant in 1561 as a "common mass-sayer."[10]

Both the episcopal and the monastic establishments stood apart from and above the daily lives of the citizens. Staffed in large part by strangers whose ties of interest and of affection were elsewhere, they belonged to the great complex of the English ecclesiastical world

---

[3] Hooker, *History*, III, 652–653.

[4] See AB i, 46 and 102. See also ECM, Miscellaneous Deeds, 220 and 221, for a settlement of disputes between the city and the priory in 1528.

[5] *Valor Ecclesiasticus*, II, 315.

[6] George Oliver. *Monasticon Diocesis Exoniensis* (Exeter, 1846), 164.

[7] *Valor Ecclesiasticus*, II, 314.

[8] See A. G. Little and R. C. Easterling, *The Franciscans and Dominicans of Exeter*, History of Exeter Research Group, Monograph No. 3 (Exeter, 1927).

[9] John Cardmaker alias Taylor. See Hooker, Book 51, fol. 342 (sub anno 1534).

[10] Little and Easterling, *Franciscans and Dominicans*, 28.

rather than to the Exeter community. Hence the parish churches, even though overshadowed by the wealth and dignity of their great neighbors, probably touched much more directly and frequently upon the religious lives of the citizens. There were, in the sixteenth century, no fewer than nineteen parishes, counting St. Sidwells and St. Davids,[11] which lay without the walls but formed part of the County of the City of Exeter. This rather large number is to be accounted for by the haphazard foundations of the earlier Middle Ages, for all of them had come into existence by the beginning of the thirteenth century. Naturally both the extent and the population of each parish was small, and this, along with the proximity of the cathedral, seems to have had the effect of discouraging the generous benefactions for fabric which characterize even much smaller towns than Exeter. In any event none of the churches was distinguished in either size or style; most of them were built out of the local red stone, startling in color but not a particularly satisfactory building material. Some, at least, were in serious disrepair in the sixteenth century, and civic pride in them was not strong enough to bring forth an effort at restoration. Most of them were buildings of fourteenth- and fifteenth-century construction although the original dedications went back in several cases to the Dark Ages.[12]

Control of patronage in these parishes was vested largely in the cathedral authorities.[13] The dean and chapter of Exeter were patrons of eight of the intramural parishes, and at the end of the century were presenting to Heavitree, the Devon parish in which the chapels of St. David and St. Sidwell lay. These eight included the three richest livings, St. Mary Major, St. Petrock, and Holy Trinity. The

[11] St. David and St. Sidwell were technically chapels dependent on the vicarage of Heavitree in the county of Devon, but they were commonly spoken of as parishes and treated as such in matters of parochial administration. St. Edmund's parish was also extramural, covering Exe Island, while Holy Trinity and St. Mary Steps were in large part extramural.

[12] For a general account of the parish church buildings, see Beatrix Cresswell, *Exeter Churches* (Exeter, 1908), published as vol. V, part 2, of the *Devon Notes and Queries*.

[13] For patrons, see *Devon and Cornwall Notes and Queries*, XV–XVII, 1928–1933, *passim* under series "Rectors of Exeter Churches." See also BM, Harleian MS. 5827, fol. 79.

bishop presented to two, his ancient charge of St. Stephens and St. Mary Arches. The Mayor, Bailiffs, and Commonalty were the patrons of St. Edmund on Exe bridge. The living of St. Mary Steps was controlled by a Devon family, the Southcotes of Shillingford. Two churches were in the patronage of monastic foundations: St. Olave,[14] in that of the Prior of St. Nicholas, and St. Lawrence, in that of the Prior of St. John's Hospital.[15] All Hallows in Goldsmith Street was in the presentation of the Courtenay family early in the century, but it is not clear who made the last presentation recorded there in 1547–48. For one parish, St. John Bow, there are no records of institution during this whole period, so it is impossible to say who the patron was.

The value of these livings varied considerably.[16] The largest was that of St. Mary Major which brought in £15 13s. 9d. per annum. Close behind it was St. Petrock with £14 10s. 2d. Holy Trinity was worth £11 6s. 5d., and St. Edmund on Exe bridge, £10 6s. 8d., but none of the others reached the sum of £10 per annum. St. Pancras was worth but £4 13s. 4d. Compared with the average level of livings in the archdeaconry of Exeter these were rather low. For the 137 livings in the archdeaconry outside the walls the average income was £18 18s.[17] For fifteen intramural parishes[18] the average reached only £8 8s.

To point up the comparison it is necessary also to observe the differences between the sources of urban and rural clerical income. In the country parishes it arose from the glebe lands, the freehold of the incumbent, and from the tithes, both protected by law. This left the clergyman in a position of relatively great independence vis-à-vis his parishioners. The position of the urban incumbents was quite different. In Exeter their incomes derived from three sources.

---

[14] *Devon and Cornwall Notes and Queries*, XVII, 174.

[15] *Valor Ecclesiasticus*, II, 314.

[16] See *Valor Ecclesiasticus*, II, 316–317, for a list of their incomes in 1535.

[17] In calculating these averages I have relied on Hooker, *History*, II, 244–249, for the Archdeaconry of Exeter.

[18] This excludes St. John Bow and St. Lawrence, neither of which appears in *Valor Ecclesiasticus,* as well as the two chapelries of St. David and St. Sidwell.

In most of the parishes there was some income from tithes, but only in four did it approach one half of the total. The other sources were the so-called dominical oblations and the offerings on the four principal feasts. The nature of the oblations is made clear in an order of the Chamber of 1582.[19] By its terms the incumbent in each parish was to have from each separate house a penny or a halfpenny weekly, depending on the size of the establishment. The penny houses were those with a kitchen, chimney, and hall. Beyond this all persons of lawful years admitted to the Communion Table were to pay 2d. yearly for offering days. Such a system must have been open to abuses; one cannot but suspect the incumbent's income was often uncertain in amount and difficult of collection.

The parishes themselves had their own income. Besides endowments for charitable purposes, several Exeter parishes possessed some property devoted to church maintenance.[20] Of equal importance was the stock of plate which each parish possessed. Gifts of plate were at once pious works and tokens of civic distinction; the giver not only performed a good deed but displayed its effects before the admiring (or envious) eyes of his fellow parishioners. A certain amount of social competition among individuals and among parishes probably existed in this regard. The plate had other functions as well, for it was a kind of common store or bank which the parish could draw upon in an emergency.

For the Exeter parishes the published inventories of the Edwardian commissioners for church plate of 1552 preserve an account of this congregational wealth just before its confiscation.[21] Among the

[19] See Church Wardens' Account Rolls, Parish of St. Mary Major, fol. 40, bound out of date order. A controversy between the parson of St. Mary Major and a parishioner had been referred by the Bishop and Lord Bedford to Mayor Thomas Martin and Alderman Nicholas Martin. The judgment is given with consent of the Twenty-Four and is to hold for all the city parishes.

[20] St. Mary Steps had about £5 income from property in 1552–53; see Church Wardens' Accounts for that parish in Exeter City Library. Annual ale wakes brought in another £2. St. Mary Major had between £6 and £7 per annum in rents (Church Wardens' Accounts, 1530, fol. 187d). St. Kerian possessed income of about £2 10s. These are the only parishes whose accounts survive.

[21] See Cresswell, *Edwardian Inventories*, for details.

parishes St. Mary Major was the wealthiest with 355 oz., St. Paul's
the poorest with only 12 oz.; but the average wealth was high, for
thirteen had more than 100 oz., and seven had more than 200 oz.
Calculated at 5s. per ounce (the price of plate sold by the city in
1551) the total value was £744.

When the commissioners arrived this plate was no longer intact.
The city itself had confiscated for the new Haven somewhere between 800 and 1,100 oz., while the parishes themselves had spent
heavily for other purposes. At All Hallows in Goldsmith Street a
cross and chalice had gone for the building of a new tower; another
chalice had gone for soldiers' wages during the Rebellion of 1549;
and a censer, ship, and spoon had been disposed of to pay for pews.
In several other parishes plate had been sold for the relief of the
poor during and after the Rebellion. The religious changes themselves had occasioned expense at St. Olave where 48 oz. were sold
to pay for painting the Scriptures on the walls, and 6 oz. more for
a reading desk, font, and pulpit.

These common funds for emergency use were swept away by the
wholesale confiscation of the Edwardian government. At almost the
same time, the seven parish chantries vanished. The result was not
only the impoverishment of the parishes, but the destruction of a
major object of congregational pride and interest. Some of the decay
of parish life in Exeter during the next generation may be the result
of this factor.

Little can be said about the clerical personnel of the Exeter
churches before the Reformation. As far as the records go,[22] there
is no evidence of the pluralists in the early part of the century. The
succession of incumbents was regular enough in the various parishes,
but one cannot be certain about possible vacancies between the death
or resignation of one and the installation of the next. Nor is there
evidence as to absenteeism during this period. Most of the parish
clergy were humble men with little chance of preferment beyond
their present livings. Few are shown as having university degrees.
The most notable exception was Dr. John Moreman, so much

---

[22] See notes on rectors of parish churches of Exeter in *Devon and Cornwall
Notes and Queries*, (as above, n. 13) and BM, Harleian MS. 5827, fol. 79.

admired by his pupil, John Hooker.[23] Moreman was rector of Holy Trinity in 1528 and 1529, later a canon of Exeter and a sufferer for the Catholic cause under Edward VI.

Besides the beneficed clergy there was another group of clerics in the city. These stipendiary priests were of two types, those who served the chantries and those who held curacies. We possess a list of the chantry priests made when they were pensioned in 1548.[24] They numbered twenty-one, all but one serving various chantries. The exception, William Morrice, is listed as a priest stipendiary in *Domus Elimosinar' in Exon*. The pensions varied from 53s. to £5 per annum. The institution of the chantry was well represented in Exeter.[25] The cathedral alone numbered nineteen chantries with a total income of £95. Seven of the parishes possessed chantries in their churches. Elyott's, in St. Petrock, with an income of £4 15s., had passed to the Crown under Henry VII, who took it in payment of £171 owed by the founder to him. At St. Mary Arches there were three, one worth £19 4s. 8d., which supported a priest and provided alms for twelve poor men; another with an income of 27s. 6d. for the priest; and that of the Weavers and Tuckers Company, which provided its priest with £6 9s. 4d. a year. The largest priest's stipend was that of the chapel on Exe bridge, which was worth £11 19s. 7d.

The number of curates was much smaller, as a list for 1540 indicates.[26] At St. Mary Major, St. Petrock, and St. Edmund the rector maintained an assistant. At St. Lawrence, impropriate until that year to St. John's Hospital, the parish employed a curate, and the same was the case at St. John Bow. (This is the only evidence for the whole century of a priest in the latter parish.) At St. Sidwell and St. David, chapels of the parish of Heavitree, the vicar of the parish maintained two priests, and at St. Sidwell the wardens employed a second one. There were three priests privately employed by individuals, probably in the execution of wills which provided

[23] BM, Harleian MS. 5827, fol. 37.

[24] Exch. accounts, King's Remembrancer, Bdl. 75, No. 9, 22 June 1548, quoted in *Devon and Cornwall Notes and Queries*, XVII, 334.

[25] The chantries are listed in Oliver, *Monasticon, Supplement*, 472–474.

[26] See *Devon and Cornwall Notes and Queries*, XVII, 82.

for the saying of masses for the dead. In the cathedral, Canon Horsey employed three priests. In all, then, there were thirty-two unbeneficed clergy in the city.

In this complex of ecclesiastical institutions the first element to be affected by the sweeping changes of the Reformation was the monastic foundations. Under the act for the dissolution of monasteries under £200, both St. Nicholas Priory and the nunnery of St. Catherine, Polslo, were swept away. The former surrendered to the King's Commissioners in 1536; the latter, with the aid of court friends,[27] lasted until 1538. The Prior of St. Nicholas received a pension of £20, while pensions were similarly granted to the Prioress of Polslo and to her thirteen sisters.[28] The suppression of St. Nicholas was not accomplished without a disturbance which occurred when the commissioners came down to view the monastic property.[29] Having viewed the priory, they retired to dinner, after giving order that in the meanwhile the rood loft in the church should be pulled down. Hardly had the workman started on his task when he was assaulted by a group of five or six women, who pursued him with such fury that he had to jump from a window for his life and broke a rib doing so. Alderman John Blackaller was similarly driven from the church. At this point the mayor himself arrived, anxious to suppress the trouble before the commissioners became aware of it, but he had to use force to break into the church and seize the offenders, whom he hurried off to ward. The commissioners, apprized of his action, thanked him and begged that the women be let off. It was a minor incident, but probably indicative of the general attitude toward the fate of the priory. If among the faithful there were those who grieved for the fate of the old religion, their opposition was completely unorganized, while the whole weight of the magistracy was at the disposal of the King's commissioners.

One matter did concern the Chamber vitally: the disposition of

[27] See ECM, Book 51, fol. 343 (sub anno 1535).

[28] For pensions see Oliver, *Monasticon*, 164 (for St. Nicholas), and 115 for Polslo. The prioress received a £30 pension.

[29] ECM, Book 51, fol. 343 (sub anno 1535). The actual year of the occurrence is probably 1537.

the priory lands. They were anxious to acquire these properties, both the site of the priory itself and also its tenements in St. David's Down, north of the city. With this end in view they dispatched the town clerk to London in 1538 to make suit to Lord Russell and the Council for the purchase of these lands.[30] They were not successful in this effort. Some of the buildings were demolished rapidly, for in 1539 the warden of Exe bridge bought stone from the priory for the repair of an arch of the bridge, swept away in a November storm.[31] In 1540 the Crown sold the site to Sir Thomas Dennys.[32]

The other houses in the city were not long in succumbing to the same fate as the priory. Both the friars' houses surrendered on the same day, 15 September 1538.[33] The Dominicans' house, near the East Gate, passed almost immediately to John, Lord Russell,[34] while that of the Franciscans was bought in 1543 by John Hull of Larkbeare from the previous grantee.[35] St. John's Hospital was the last to surrender, for it survived until 1540. As we have seen, that part of the endowment which went toward the support of thirteen paupers escaped confiscation. The hospital buildings were granted to Thomas Carewe of Bickleigh in 1540.[36]

These grants, however, left unaffected the major part of the monastic lands in the city. More important than the monastic buildings and their sites were the various tenements in the city belonging not only to the Exeter foundations but also to other Western houses. The Abbots of Ford, Dunkeswell, and Newenham had town houses as well as other holdings in Exeter while Plympton Priory, Pilton Priory, Launceston Priory, and St. John's Hospital

---

[30] AB, i, fol. 152, printed in HMC, 304.

[31] ECM, Book 51, fol. 343 (sub anno 1539). At the same time the receiver bought some more of this stone for repairs on the walls.

[32] See TDA, LXXXIV (1952), 131. The thorough and illuminating article by Dr. Joyce Youings, "The City of Exeter and the Property of the Dissolved Monasteries" appeared after I first wrote this chapter. It has been most useful on all matters connected with the fate of monastic properties in the city.

[33] *Calendar of Letters and Papers, Henry VIII*, XIII, ii, 354, for the Franciscans; *ibid.*, XIII, ii, 489, for the Dominicans.

[34] *Ibid.*, XIV, i, 586.

[35] *Ibid.*, XVIII, i, 198.

[36] *Ibid.*, XV, 299.

at Bridgwater all possessed tenements within the walls.[37] For a time the Crown retained these properties within its direct control, entrusted to various stewards. The principal steward of these lands in Devon was John Greynfeld,[38] burgess for Exeter in the Parliaments of 1545, 1555, and 1558. In 1545 all the monastic properties in the city of Exeter were sold by the Crown as one parcel to John Haydon and Thomas Gibbes of Clyst St. George, for the sum of £899 1s. 11d.[39] In the following year these men transferred their interest to another pair, Sir John Williams, Treasurer of the Court of Augmentations, and Henry Norryce.[40] The Chamber were still interested in acquiring the properties, not only for the latter's value, but also because they feared the possibility that they might pass to some great local magnate, who would then be too prominent in the city for their comfort.[41]

In 1549 their chance to buy came. On 13 May of that year the town clerk was sent up to London to negotiate with Williams about the purchase of all the monastic lands in the city and suburbs.[42] He was to offer at the most sixteen years' purchase for one half the total value, and seventeen for the other. At the same time thirteen members of the Chamber bound themselves to stand good for the payment of the purchase price. The sale was quickly negotiated on the buyers' terms. On 20 May 1549 a contract was completed by which the lands passed to five feoffees for the sum of £1,460 2s. 3d., which was to be paid in installments over three years.[43] The rents of these lands amounted to something between £90 and £95 a year, so that the Chamber had paid a little more than sixteen years' purchase.[44]

The problem of financing this transaction was not an easy one for

[37] For a complete list of these holdings see ECM, Book 184b.
[38] *Calendar of Letters and Papers, Henry VIII*, XVIII, i, 546.
[39] *Ibid.*, XX, i, 298.
[40] ECM, Deed 1452.
[41] At one time it seemed as if Sir George Carew of Mohun's Ottery would become the proprietor of all the monastic lands in the city as well as of the manor of Polslo. For details see Dr. Youing's article cited above, p. 133f.
[42] AB ii, 204.
[43] ECM, Deeds 1464, 1465.
[44] ECM, Book 184b.

the city, but it was solved by a combination of civic and private interests. In order to meet the purchase price and attendant legal expenses, the bulk of the monastic lands were sold to various private citizens of Exeter, but the remainder, which were secured to the Chamber, cost it nothing.

About £76 worth of the rental was sold to thirty-two citizens, in parcels which varied in size from the £16 10s. of Maurice Levermore to several of 6s. each.[45] The five largest purchasers divided about £36 in rentals between them; the rest went in relatively small lots. These sales more than covered the purchase price and left unsold about £17 in annual rentals. The properties had been bought at sixteen years' purchase, but the purchasers paid for their parcels at the rate of twenty years' purchase, to the city's profit. These unsold lands were now transferred by the feoffees to the Chamber,[46] which thus secured an increment of some £17 in yearly income without having laid out a penny. The benefits of this transaction to the Chamber are obvious. But the interests of the individual citizens were also served; in the hands of the city the single block of monastic lands could be broken up and made available to small investors. Even the most modest citizen now had a chance for his share in monastic spoils. Economically, the Dissolution meant in Exeter, as elsewhere, the appearance of a large amount of rental property on the market, which the action of the Chamber secured to itself and to the inhabitants. Thus the civic corporation and a body of its wealthier citizens were added to the already large and certainly influential group which had an economic stake in the maintenance of the Reformed religion. Politically, the purchase extinguished a rival jurisdiction, both within the walls and in St. David's Down.

The monks were not the only sufferers at this time. The cathedral establishment also received severe blows. Under the aging and pliant Bishop Veysey, the see lost one manor after another and from being one of the wealthiest in England sank to be the poorest of

---

[45] There is a list of these sales in ECM, Book 184c.
[46] ECM, Deed 1498, 7 October 1555.

those of pre-Reformation foundation.[47] The status of the episcopate generally declined much during these years, but the poverty of the see emphasized the change at Exeter. The dean and chapter also suffered spoliation. In 1560 the new bishop made a statute by which the number of canons residentiary was reduced to nine, the four officers being given precedence of choice.[48] For the time being the endowment of the college of vicars choral was in the hands of the Crown as was that of the annivellars. The chantries, of course, vanished, and with them the body of stipendiary priests who served them. The wealth and numbers of the episcopal establishment were greatly reduced, but its jurisdiction remained intact, and it continued to stand as a distinct and rival community beside its secular neighbor. Nevertheless, the bishop, dean, and chapter—members of a shorn and fettered body—were no longer such formidable neighbors as in the past, and from this time forward a subtle but certain diminution of their prestige was to take place.

It is, however, in the parish churches that one can trace the main lines of the religious changes in Exeter. The disappearance of the church ornaments and treasure and the dissolution of the chantries have already been recounted, but quite some time before those events took place preliminary stirrings of the Reform had agitated the community. In 1531 had taken place the burning of Thomas Benet, a Master of Arts of Cambridge.[49] A friend of Bilney and a member of the Reforming circle at the university, he was not a local figure but had taken refuge in Exeter in the obscurity of a small school. He was apprehended by the diocesan authorities after posting anonymous attacks on various Catholic doctrines on the cathedral doors. He was condemned to the usual penalty, but the Chamber would not—for what reason is not clear—permit the stake to be set up in the city, and so the sheriff shifted it out to Liverydole in Heavitree parish, where Benet suffered.

There were also local heretics in the community. The most emi-

---

[47] The revenues of the see decreased by about two-thirds, from £1,500 to £500. See Boggis, *Diocese of Exeter*, 347.

[48] Freeman, *Exeter*, 203.

[49] ECM, Book 51, fol. 341 (sub anno 1531).

nent was John Cardmaker (alias Taylor), Warden of the Grey Friars. Hooker relates a little incident which occurred when Latimer came to preach at Exeter in June 1535.[50] He spoke in the churchyard of the Grey Friars to the indignation of several of the brethren who "cursed and banned the man," and rejoiced in the nose bleed which cut short his sermon, as a sign of Divine disapproval. The bishop, however, had the support of the warden, who apparently was converted to the Reformed doctrines at this time. Shortly afterwards Cardmaker left his native Exeter for London, where he died a martyr's death under Queen Mary.[51] His successor, Gregory Bassett, was also suspect as a reader of Luther, but he recanted after imprisonment and was a leader of the Catholic reaction in the city.[52] Another Reformer appeared upon the scene soon, Dr. Simon Haynes, appointed Dean of Exeter upon the dismissal of Reginald Pole by the King in 1537.[53] Haynes was a man of marked Protestant inclinations and a vigorous temper. His entry into office was signalized by a quarrel with the chapter, in which, among other things, he refused to maintain any longer the sanctuary light (hitherto the obligation of the Dean), which he regarded as a superstitious practise.[54] His disputes with the chapter continued throughout the rest of Henry's reign and on into Edward's. In 1540 they accused him of having, among other things, destroyed images of the saints, removed iron and brass memorials (including that of the revered Bishop Lacy, a popular shrine), as well as having taken down the sanctuary light.[55] He also presented to the King a "Proposal for the Government of the Church of Exeter,"[56] which would have substituted for the dean and chapter a pastor and twelve preachers of the Gospel, along with a free grammar school for sixty boys and twelve exhibitions at Oxford and twelve at Cambridge.

---

[50] ECM, Book 51, fol. 343 (sub anno 1535).

[51] Little and Easterling, *Franciscans and Dominicans*, 27.

[52] ECM, Book 51, fol. 350 (sub anno 1553).

[53] *Ibid.*, fol. 349 (sub anno 1551).

[54] Herbert Reynolds, *A Short History of the Ancient Diocese of Exeter*, 368–369 (Exeter, 1895).

[55] Boggis, *Diocese of Exeter*, 313.

[56] *Ibid.*, 369.

He lived on until 1551, and his influence during the hectic days of the rebellion was strong in support of the magistrates. The continued opposition of the chapter officers brought several of them to prison under Edward VI.

It is hard to form an estimate of religious opinion in the city. What little we know of the professors of the Reformed opinions in Exeter has been indicated, but we know even less as to how these opinions were received by the mass of citizens. In 1534, when Latimer came to preach in Exeter, he aroused much curiosity. Besides the sermon at the Franciscan house, mentioned above, he preached at St. Mary Major on the feast day of the dedication of the church. Hooker tells us[57] that the clergy much resented this intrusion into the customary ceremonies of the day and alleged that there was no time for a sermon along with the processions and masses. Nevertheless, Latimer preached to an "audience so greate and the Churche so full that the Churche glass wyndowes were broken open for the people to hear the sermon; who the more he was heard the more he was lyked." The only interference came from a certain Thomas Carewe, who protested against the contents of the sermon and threatened to drag the preacher from the pulpit. The bishop, nevertheless, finished his sermon. As Hooker was but an infant at this time, one can trust him only for the general outline of the event; one cannot be sure how far his own Protestant preferences carried him away in describing the reactions of the congregation.

The minor riot at the time of the dissolution of St. Nicholas has already been noted. The most serious religious movement in the West Country was, of course, the rebellion of 1549.[58] This broke out at Sampford Courtenay, only sixteen miles away, and the rebels soon encompassed the city. At that time, Hooker tells us, they had great hopes that the Catholic party within the city would open its gates to them. Indeed, some of the magistrates were friendly to the old religion, and even Hooker admits that the city was divided into

[57] ECM, Book 51, fol. 343 (sub anno 1533).
[58] The contemporary account of this is Hooker's. For a modern account see Frances Rose-Troup, *The Western Rebellion of 1549* (London, 1913).

two parties, the larger being that of the Catholics. Several plots were laid during the siege by this group, and they apparently included in their number the prominent merchant, John Wolcot, and one of the clothiers, Richard Taylor. The balance between the two parties was evidently close, and it was a sense of responsibility for good order and fear of a general sack of the merchants' houses and shops, rather than enthusiasm for the Reformed doctrines, that kept the magistrates steady in their loyalty.

The Reform party in the city was much strengthened when, in 1550, Miles Coverdale, the translator of the Bible and a thorough-going exponent of change, replaced Veysey. John Hooker was one of a party in the city which had intimate relations with this prelate, who undoubtedly left behind him a core of convinced Protestants.[59] His stay was brief, however. On a July day in 1553, while he was preaching in the cathedral, the news of Mary's accession arrived. The congregation, save for a few "godly men," trooped out of the church.[60] Shortly afterwards Bishop Coverdale fled the kingdom.

The Marian reaction brought little active persecution in Exeter, but there was a definite Catholic party in the city, led by William Smythe, a goldsmith, mayor in 1553–54. Hooker portrays him as plotting the entrapment of the professors of the Gospel—particularly the great merchants, John Bodley and John Periam—at a game of bowls with his cronies, Canons Southron and Blaxton, and the ex-friar, Gregory Bassett.[61] But these plots came to little. In the following year a "Gospeller," John Midwinter, was mayor,[62] and the following year the office was held by a man who perhaps typified the general attitudes of the wealthier classes. Walter Staplehill (mayor, 1556–57), though a hearty Catholic, was tolerant of his reforming friends and "did friendly and lovingly bear with them and wink at them."[63] Thus, pronounced Protestants held office under Mary, while at least once, in 1565–66, a notorious Catholic

---

[59] ECM, Book 51, fol. 350 (sub anno 1552).
[60] *Ibid.*, fol. 349 (sub anno 1552).
[61] *Ibid.*, fol. 350 (sub anno 1553).
[62] *Ibid.*, fol. 350 (sub anno 1554).
[63] *Ibid.*, fol. 351 (sub anno 1557).

was mayor under her sister.[64] The merchants of Exeter, however united in most of their sentiments, assumed widely divergent positions on the religious issue. But, what is perhaps more important, these divergences of opinion did not impair the working unity of the community in other matters. However important the religious problems of the century were for individuals, they were not an occasion for major social disagreement among the ruling classes of the city.[65]

We know very little of parish life during this period. In one parish only can we trace, at least in dim outline, the alterations in routine parochial affairs which the Reform brought.[66] Fortunately, this parish is St. Petrock, the home of many of the leading citizens. Hence events here probably reflect in some degree the sentiments of the dominant group in the city. At the very least, the parish records (principally churchwardens' accounts) provide some account of the religious changes of the century as they affected a particular Exeter parish.

The religious revolution can fairly be said to have begun here in 1538–39 when the parish purchased its first Bible. Significantly, it is in the same account that the King is first referred to as Supreme Head. The next alterations in parish life followed in the first year of Edward VI's reign. The last year in which obits were celebrated also witnessed the removal of the rood. In 1548–49 the paintings on the walls were washed away and covered with white lime, while the

[64] John Wolcott. See Book 51, fol. 355 (sub anno 1565).

[65] In 1564 the Bishops were required to report to the Privy Council a list both of those favorable and those unfavorable to the new religious order. The Bishop of Exeter's list includes very few from the city. No one was listed as being positively favorable to the Reformed faith, but two were listed as unfavorable, Robert Midwinter, a Justice of the Peace (mayor in 1559), and Richard Hert, the Town Clerk. We have no other information to indicate that these two men were opposed to the religious settlement. Hert continued to hold his office for many years; Midwinter died before 1571. See Camden Miscellany, vol. 9, *Collection of Original Letters from Bishops to Privy Council, 1564*, 1–83.

[66] See the transcriptions of Church Wardens' Accounts and other documents in Robert Dymond, *The History of the Parish of St. Petrock* (Plymouth, 1882). This is a reprint from the *Transactions of the Devonshire Association*, XIV (1882), 402–492.

parish purchased the new Prayer Book and Erasmus' *Paraphrases*. The year following that the images in the church were sold, and the altars pulled down. Like the other parishes, it disposed of its plate, in part to the city for the canal, in part by direct sale. With the plate went also the vestments and some of the bells.

This process of change was abruptly reversed by the accession of Mary. The Catholic reaction was signalized by the purchase of incense, candlesticks, and a Paschal candle for the first Easter of Mary's reign. In the following years a pyx, a rood loft, an alb, and altar cloths were added along with missals and other books necessary to the restored Latin rite. Contributions from the parishioners were not lacking.

But hardly had the restoration of ornaments been completed when the pendulum swung once again, and the story of Edward's reign was repeated. The Book of Common Prayer was brought back; the rood loft came down again (but not until 1561–62); a book on the Ten Commandments was purchased; and the Scriptures were painted about the church. These entries bear dumb witness to the progress of religious revolution in the turbulent years between 1535 and 1560. The alterations of ornaments and of liturgy followed royal commands with creditable alacrity, but one can only wonder whether or not the parishioners' religious sentiments varied with the same promptness.

The priest of the parish, who had been instituted in 1528, served faithfully through every change in religious polity until his death in 1566. A glimpse of his attitude and that of some of his parishioners is given by an anecdote of Hooker in which he records an incident of 1554.[67] The mayor then, John Midwinter, was a "proffessor of the ghosple" under King Edward and a close friend of the parson of St. Petrock, William Herne. The latter had declared to Midwinter that he would be torn with wild horses rather than say mass again. Nevertheless, Herne conformed readily enough under Queen Mary. Midwinter, coming upon the parson robed for mass, "poynted unto him with his fynger remembringe as it were his olde protestations that he wold never singe masse agayne; but parson herne

[67] ECM, Book 51, fol. 350 (sub anno 1553).

openly yn the churche spak alowde unto hym. It is no remedye man, it is no remedy." St. Petrock's was probably more prompt in its response to royal policy than the humbler parishes of the city, but there is no reason to think that attitudes varied significantly elsewhere.

Our knowledge of the rest of the parishes is slight. One clue to the advance of the Reform is afforded by the church inventories of 1552, which also listed the books owned by each parish church.[68] If they are complete for each parish, they indicate a very slight compliance with the royal injunctions of preceding years. Only four churches, including St. Petrock, possessed an English Bible, and the same four were the only ones which owned copies of the Book of Common Prayer and Erasmus' *Paraphrases*. In the majority of the city's parishes the prime documents of the English Reformation had not yet made their appearance.

We can say but little about the parish clergy of this epoch. None of them figured in the Rebellion of 1549. The parson of St. Thomas the Apostle, the parish west of the river, was hanged from his own church steeple in full canonicals for his share in the revolt,[69] but of the intramural clergy we hear not a word. As far as the scanty evidence of the Bishop's Register goes, it provides little definite evidence of deprivations in the city, under either Edward or his sisters. At St. Martin's, Gregory Bassett, the former warden of the Franciscans, had been appointed rector in 1544 by the dean and chapter,[70] and he may have resigned under the Edwardian regime, for in 1554 the parish was vacant by resignation and had to be filled again. His successor, Thomas Smythe, resigned sometime before February 1559–60,[71] but there is no indication that he did so because he objected to the new religious order. A more certain case is that at St. Mary Steps, where on 26 May 1554 the new incumbent Hugo Collyns was instituted *per privatione* William Austyn.[72] Otherwise, although there were numerous institutions in the city churches, all

[68] See Cresswell, *Edwardian Inventories.*
[69] Hooker, *History*, II, 94.
[70] *Devon and Cornwall Notes and Queries*, XV (October 1929), 380.
[71] Bishop of Exeter's Register, Book 16, fol. 28b.
[72] *Ibid.*, Book 16, fol. 19b.

took place in the normal course of replacement of deceased or resigned incumbents. Other evidence of the religious changes of Edward and Mary is scant indeed.

In 1559 the Elizabethan settlement ended the hectic alternations of the previous decade. In September of that year the Bishop-elect of Salisbury, Jewel, came down with other visitors of the Queen's commission to supervise the removal of images and their burning in the cathedral churchyard.[73] The prevailing temper of compliance was again illustrated. "They which yn Quene Mary's Dayes were accompted to be more forewarde yn erectinge theyme up and yn meanteanynge of theym were now made the Instrumentes to make the fyre and to burne theym." The new liturgy was accepted only after some difficulty. Hooker reports that various devices were used by its enemies to hinder it. They prevented the ringing of the bell at morning prayer, refused to let the new liturgy be used in the chancel, or objected to the singing of psalms. The ringleader was the chancellor of the cathedral, and the Council's authority had to be invoked to establish the new order. Early in 1560 a certain doctor Gammon, one of the canons, "maynteend certyn artycles of popery which upon soneday the X of marche by Order he was commanded to recant it, and dyd." Turberville, Veysey's successor, along with the other Marian bishops, had been deprived in 1559. His successor, William Alley, arrived in 1560, accompanied by the Earl of Bedford.[74]

Our knowledge of the religious life of Exeter grows even slimmer during the first years of the Reformed establishment.[75] Only one informative document is left to us, the visitation of the clergy of 1561.[76] Here we have the only full account available of the condition

[73] These details are taken from ECM, Book 51, fol. 352 (sub anno 1558).

[74] ECM, Book 51, fol. 353 (sub anno 1559).

[75] The St. Petrock accounts are not very interesting for the years between 1560 and 1590 (when they break off). The principal item of interest is the addition of the new south aisle to the church in 1587–88 (Dymond, *St. Petrock*, 69) at a cost of £33 9s. 6d. This is one of the few evidences of church construction during our period. The only other major one was the reconstruction of the tower of St. Mary Major at the cost of £186.

[76] Photostat of Visitation of Devon Clergy, 1561, in Exeter City Library. The original is in the possession of Corpus Christi College, Cambridge. It

of the Exeter clergy in the later sixteenth century. Six parishes were vacant. The remaining eleven incumbents were all priests and all but one were in residence.[77] Three of the incumbents were pluralists; two of them held parishes in the Exeter diocese; the third, the rector of St. Mary Major, was a vicar choral of the cathedral. They were not a learned clergy. None of them held a degree, and of the eight whose learning was evaluated, six were noted as *mediocriter doctus*, one as *satis doctus*, and one as *studiosus, non Latine doctus*. None of them preached. The length of incumbency of these priests is of interest.[78] One of them, instituted in 1528, had served through the whole succession of religious revolutions; two were instituted under the Henrician regime; two under the Edwardian; and of the rest all but two had come in under Mary's Catholic dispensation.

For the balance of the sixteenth century the thin entries of the Bishop's Register preserve to us little but the succession of incumbents in each parish. For three parishes, St. Lawrence (formerly impropriate to the Hospital of St. John), St. John Bow, and All Hallows, Goldsmith Street, there are no entries whatsoever. At St. Olave, where the Prior of St. Nicholas had been patron, the Crown made no appointments during the sixteenth century. At St. George the situation is confusing. The incumbent listed in the visitation of 1561 does not appear in the Bishop's Register, but three years later there was an entry of the appointment of Thomas Cole to the living, vacant by the death of the incumbent.[79] After that there is no more information on this parish. Similarly the situation is unclear at All

---

provides information on the seventeen parish churches, but not on the two chapels dependent on Heavitree.

[77] The exception was the rector of All Saints in Goldsmith Street, who was thought to be somewhere in London.

[78] The rector of St. Petrock had held his parish since 1528; the rector of Holy Trinity since 1542–43; the rector of St. Mary Arches since 1537. At St. Edmund the incumbent had been instituted in 1554; at St. Stephens in 1556; the absentee of All Hallows, Goldsmith Street, in 1547–48; the rector of St. Paul in 1557, and the rector of St. Mary Steps in the same year. In two parishes the appointments had been made under Elizabeth: St. Martin and St. Mary Major. For these data see the Bishop's Register, Books 16 and 17, *passim*.

[79] Bishop of Exeter's Register, Book 18, fol. 82.

Hallows on the Wall. The only two entries relating to it are for the year 1563; one noted that the living was *certo modo vacans*[80] (a phrase which usually refers to a deprivation); the other, a second appointment following upon the resignation of the incumbent.[81] At St. Stephen the last known incumbent until 1635 was the Thomas Petre mentioned in the 1561 visitation. St. Kerian presents a similar case. The incumbent appointed in 1567 (also rector of St. Leonard) was the last until 1845.[82] At St. Mary Arches the incumbent William Vaughan died in 1569–70,[83] and after that there is no notice of a new appointment, although in 1601 a certain Hugh Geare signed the marriage register as incumbent.[84] Again at St. Martin no institution was recorded between 1572 and 1634. There is a sixty-year gap without institutions at St. Pancras, from 1575–76 to 1637, and no curates appear before 1617. St. Petrock had a more regular line of succession, but even here there were long vacancies. In 1602 a new appointment was made by the Queen *per lapsum temporum vacan'*,[85] the last incumbent having died in 1597. A similar story is to be told of St. Paul's, where a vacancy lasted from 1585 to 1593,[86] when the Queen made the new appointment.

The parish in which the most regular succession of incumbents appears is St. Edmund, which was in the Chamber's patronage. This living was apparently held along with the curacy of St. David's chapel, a dependency of the parish of Heavitree in the county of Devon. The dates and names of the incumbents correspond exactly in these two churches. Besides this there are few instances of the holding of more than one city parish by the same incumbent. The most spectacular example is that of John Williams, incumbent of St. Edmund's and curate of St. David's from 1554,[87] rector of St.

[80] *Ibid.*, Book 18, fol. 80b.
[81] *Ibid.*, Book 18, fol. 82.
[82] *Ibid.*, Book 19, fol. 21b, but in 1598–99 Jasper Robinson, chaplain to the Bishop, was licensed to serve the cure. See *Devon and Cornwall Notes and Queries*, X, 323.
[83] *Devon and Cornwall Notes and Queries*, XVI, 140.
[84] *Ibid.*
[85] Bishop of Exeter's Register, Book 20, fol. 75b.
[86] *Ibid.*, Book 20, fol. 54b.
[87] *Ibid.*, Book 16, fol. 6a.

Mary Arches 1562–66,[88] who resigned the latter to take St. Petrock's[89] which he held until his death in the following year.[90] Both the livings of St. Petrock and of Holy Trinity, with two of the largest incomes in the city, may have been held by John Hunt[91] between 1587 and 1597.

The only other information about the Elizabethan clergy provided by the Bishop's Register concerns their education. Out of the fifty-eight institutions to Exeter parishes between 1552 and 1602 all but eleven were of priests simply listed as *clericus*. The others included eight M.A.'s and three B.A.'s. Notable, however, is the fact that all but two of these degree-holding clergy appear after 1585; in other words, out of the fourteen appointments of these final years of the century, eleven were of university graduates.[92]

The general state of the parishes is best summed up in a draft act of Parliament of 1601.[93] Here the Chamber, estimating the population of Exeter at 16,000, complains that none of the churches held above 200 to 300 apiece, that in any case they were without incumbents and so had to be served by reading curates, each curate having from two to three parishes in his charge. For want of time these curates omitted part of the service in each church in order to hasten on to the next, and the cathedral (which held but a thousand people) was the only place where sermons were regularly appointed. This state of affairs seems to have evoked little active complaint from the laity until late in the sixteenth century. The first attempt to improve the situation came about 1580. A bill was put forward in the Parliament of 1581[94] by the Chamber, which proposed the consolidation of the city parishes into five or six, each with an enlarged church, under the corporation's patronage. The bishop was

[88] *Ibid.*, Book 18, fol. 79b.

[89] *Ibid.*, Book 19, fol. 16.

[90] *Ibid.*, Book 19, fol. 16.

[91] Instituted at Holy Trinity, 1589 (Bishop's Register, Book 20, fol. 32); no record of institution at St. Petrock, but appears as rector in the burial register; successor at Holy Trinity recorded in Bishop's Register, Book 20, fol. 62.

[92] These figures include not only the city parishes but also the suburban parish of St. Leonard.

[93] PRO, SP 12/282/49.

[94] Act Book of the Bishop of Exeter, Book 41, pp. 155–163.

immediately aroused to opposition largely because of jealousy of the corporation[95] and the bill came to nothing. The proposal made in 1601 got so far as a second reading in Commons before being committed. This bill would have suppressed six parishes and replaced them by a single parish under borough patronage with a new and larger church, capable of holding 2,000 people. Property in the new parish would be assessed tithes in addition to the customary payments. Quite probably the failure of this bill can also be traced to episcopal hostility.

As early as 1580 agitation for a city lectureship had begun, indicating for the first time a new and intense religious feeling in the community. The Chamber agreed in 1599 that it was "very acceptable to ... the commonwealth of this city and to the praise of God and the reforming and abolishing of divers disorders" that "a learned person shall be procured with the consent of the Bishop to preach every Sabbath day ... and to do other godly exercises in St. Peters Church and other parish churches."[96] The Chamber sought the counsel of the Lady Paulet and the Countess of Warwick, a daughter of the house of Russell and closely identified with left-wing Puritan piety.[97] On their advice Edmund Snape, D.D., was appointed in 1600, at a stipend of £50 a year.[98] The choice was significant. Snape had a long history of radical dissent from the Elizabethan establishment, having been deprived in 1590 for his activity in the Northampton classis and suspended from the clerical order for a period of ten years, during which he had served the presbyterians of Jersey in collaboration with Cartwright, his former colleague. Thus Snape's appointment was an open challenge to the ecclesiastical establishment and to William Cotton, Bishop of Exeter, who, with some hesitation, soon inhibited him from preaching.[99]

---

[95] *Ibid.*, 164, Instruction to Bishop's procurators to be used against said bill.
[96] AB v, 435.
[97] AB v, 502, 506, and Cotton, *Elizabethan Guild*, 91.
[98] The city provided £20, as did Periam; the Merchant Adventurers, £10.
[99] *DNB*: "Edmund Snape."

It was 1610 before another appointment was made;[100] this lecturer stayed three years and, when he departed, was replaced by a morning preacher and an afternoon preacher.[101] In 1616 the legacy of Canon Lawrence Bodley made possible the appointment of a third lecturer;[102] his maintenance would be provided by the income from £400 to be invested in land.[103] But the first Bodley lecturer, John Hazard, encountered opposition from Bishop Cotton, who had ordained him. On appeal from the Mayor and Twenty-Four, the Archbishop of Canterbury granted license for the appointment over the head of Cotton, who could counter only by weakly accusing Hazard of false doctrine. Hazard elected to go to Awliscombe, and the Chamber agreed to seek a University divine for the post, which seems to have had a regular incumbent from the 1620's forward.[104]

While these provisions were being made for preaching and teaching the Gospel, another even more positive evidence of a new and Puritanical religious zeal appeared. In 1615 rigorous orders were passed by the Chamber to protect the sanctity of the Sabbath Day.[105] "Forasmuch as the Holy Sabbath Day sanctified by God Himself is much violated and broken by sundry people" the city magistrates forbade the sale of any foods, prohibited barbers from polling, trimming, or barbering; merchants from buying and selling; artificers from working with their hands, all on stiff penalties. Informers were encouraged by promise of half the fine.

The condition of the parish churches improved somewhat at the same time. In 1622 all the parishes were at least provided with

---

[100] AB vi, 367.

[101] AB vii, 72, 73. See AB vii, 117 for extra ten marks given morning preacher over and above usual £20; apparently the afternoon preacher was receiving £50.

[102] The merchant Thomas Moggridge left £200 for the endowment.

[103] The funds were for some years let out among the members of the Twenty-Four at 6⅔% interest. In 1631 the £600 was invested in the impropriated rectory of Hennock, Devon, which produced £40 p.a. for the lecturer (AB vii, 289, 799).

[104] Paul S. Seaver, *The Puritan Lectureships* (Stanford: Stanford University Press: 1970), 47–48; AB, vii, 104, printed in HMC rep., 93–96.

[105] AB vii, 161 and 171.

curates although only three had rectors.[106] By 1638 only four were served by curates.[107] A deliberate effort to remedy the situation from above seems to have been made in the mid-1630's when no fewer than seven presentations were made by the King although he was patron in only one case. Parishes such as St. George, St. Martin, St. Stephen, All Hallows in Goldsmith Street, All Hallows on the Walls, and St. Olave, which had been without an incumbent for two generations, were filled up.[108] It is impossible to say who was the moving spirit behind these appointments; possibly it was Bishop Hall, after the visitation of 1631.

The Reformation in Exeter emerged in forms characteristic of the intensified religious feeling of the age. Taking root in the mid-sixteenth century, it remained a sickly plant until the 1580's. From then on it began to thrive. After failing to reorganize the local parishes so as to provide a strong base for a preaching ministry, the local leaders turned to lectureships. It is impossible to gauge motives in the Snape appointment. It may have been a deliberately partisan move, but it is also quite possible that the Chamber, relying on Lady Warwick, blundered into a situation which they really did not understand. But as the Snape episode and the Hazard affair developed, the old hostility towards the Bishop and the irritabilities connected with it reappeared. Puritan piety and anti-clericalism were then so mingled that one cannot judge which predominated. There was certainly abroad in the leading circles of the city an earnest, sober and purposeful religious spirit, as the philanthropy of the period bears witness. But there is very little evidence of overt discontent with the religion established by law. The one recorded instance is an obscure episode of 1639.[109] At the reading of the royal proclamation on the Scottish revolt, the mayor, James Tucker, and two senior aldermen, Ignatius Jurdain and Thomas Crossing, remained covered. The Privy

---

[106] Visitation Book, 218, p. 12.

[107] Visitation Book, 1638 (no pagination), under Deanery of Christianity. The curate at St. Petrock's was the Bodley lecturer.

[108] The evidence is in the Bishop's Register, Book XXII, *passim*.

[109] See PRO, SP 16/420/153 and APC 2/50, v. 16, fol. 244, 294, 348.

Council, informed of this, demanded their attendance and their explanations. All hastened to apologize, declaring that they had remained covered only because of the cold day and not with any intent of irreverence. We may or may not accept this somewhat disingenuous explanation, but it is quite clear that if they did have any convictions in the matter, they held them rather timidly. It certainly does not provide evidence that there was any organized Puritan party in the city.

Throughout this period, relations between the city and its ecclesiastical neighbors, the bishop and the chapter, continued in their old course of irritating but not dangerous friction. The city since its creation as a county had a permanent advantage in the struggle, for both the episcopal fees were within the bounds of the county. Nevertheless, the ecclesiastics stood firmly on their ancient rights, resisting as well as they could every encroachment of the civic authorities. The resulting quarrels fill a good deal of space in the city archives, but they are of small interest. The same issues, petty at best, monotonously recur at each reopening of this chronic sore. Both sides showed a tendency to resort to extremes and to make the quarrel as unpleasant as possible. A mere chronicling of dates indicates how this squabble dragged on. There was a major dispute in 1560 with the new Elizabethan bishop, then relative peace until the late 1580's when various disputes broke out, coming to a head at the end of the century. In the seventeenth century relations were, if anything, worse; in 1605, in 1614 and 1615, in 1618 and 1619; again in 1622 (a major struggle); after a ten-year lapse, in 1632, 1633, and 1634; and finally in 1637 quarrels with the bishop engaged a major share of civic attention.

The issues varied from one year to the next. The chief was always that of jurisdiction, the city claiming that criminals took refuge in the close while the action of the city officers was obstructed by the episcopal officials. The bishop answered by accusing the city of encroaching on his liberties. In truth, the legal picture was anything but clear. The city cited its position as a county while the bishop referred to agreements of the fifteenth century freeing him from direct interference.[110] Two bishops, Alley in 1560 and Cary in 1622, tried to secure appointment to the civic commission of the peace, a proposal furiously resisted by the city in both cases.[111] Bishop Cotton tried to obtain a separate corporation for the episcopal fee.[112] As far as we know, these attempts came to nothing, and on the whole the city maintained a permanent advantage in the struggle.

There were subsidiary disputes further to exacerbate feeling. In 1586 there was a rancorous quarrel over a piece of ground contested between the vicars choral and the city, which ended with the incarceration of several of the vicars in the city gaol.[113] The bishop and chapter accused the citizens of irreverent behavior and of arresting clerics when robed and on their way to divine service. When Bishop Cary sought the favor of a postern door through the city wall for his private use, it took royal authority to coerce the city to agreement.[114]

On the more important topics of parish boundaries and patronage, of the lecturerships, and of the free school, we have seen how fiercely city and bishop wrangled, and how the city showed an increasing tendency to go its own way in these matters with little regard for the bishops. One issue at stake between the chapter and the citizens was settled after no more than the usual amount of bickering and by mutual concessions. A new cemetery was badly needed; the city agreed to relinquish its rack-yards in Friernhay at a loss in yearly rental of £13 for this purpose, while the chapter paid £150 towards the costs of establishing the new burying ground.[115]

[110] See M. E. Curtis, *Some Disputes between the City and Cathedral Authorities of Exeter*, History of Exeter Research Group Monograph No. 5 (Manchester, 1932), *passim*. Documentary evidence will be found in ECM, Law Papers, particularly Exeter v. Bishop of Exeter, 1615, and Miscellaneous Roll 103, and in the act books.

[111] See ECM, Book 51, fol. 353, sub anno 1560, for Alley's attempt; the quarrel with Bishop Cotton is recorded in HMC Rep., the letters of William Prouze.

[112] See ECM, Miscellaneous Roll 103, Salisbury to Ellesmere, 10 Dec. 1610.

[113] See AB iv, 289 and Miscellaneous Roll 103, 20 and 21, for very divergent accounts.

[114] HMC Rep., L. 240 and Privy Signet, 6 March 1623, James I, in AB vii, 486.

[115] AB viii, 85, 86, 89, and 168.

Our survey of the Reformation in Exeter is disappointingly incomplete, for the data are scanty and unsatisfactory. The great religious storm swept over the city, leaving behind very few traces, least of all those which might etch in the subtle but striking change in religious sentiment which is the most important fact of the English Reformation. Nevertheless, some conclusions may be drawn.

Religious parties appeared in the city as early as Edward VI's reign, but their divergences on religious issues were never allowed to split the unity of the ruling group. Two sentiments took precedence over religious convictions. One was loyalty to the state power, regardless of the religious outlook of those who exercised it. The other and deeper sentiment was a carefully calculated regard for the interests of the local oligarchy. The protection of their privileges, their influence, and their property was the very core of their attitude, in this as in all other matters. Consequently these provincial merchants were quite as convinced *politiques* as the most accomplished courtier. For them the Reformation in its first stages was a matter of careful calculation in order to be on the right side at the right time. Their other great concern was to benefit from the great property redistribution which followed the Dissolution, and particularly to secure themselves against the intervention of any magnate who might seek to succeed the vanished ecclesiastical proprietors in the city.

Later, when real religious feeling touched the ruling group towards the end of Elizabeth's reign, there was the same resolute assertion of civic interest. The oligarchy was determined to have its own way in the refashioning of the city's religious life. They would have brought the parishes directly under the Chamber's control if they could have done so; failing that, they turned to the sponsorship of the lecturers. In education it was the same story; the new schools were to be municipal institutions, entirely free from clerical interference. Throughout there was a determination to supplant ecclesiastical authority wherever possible, and to substitute for it that of the Chamber. Religion was to become another province in the all-embracing realm of civic control.

Chapter Nine

The Civic Community and the Royal Government

At the end of the sixteenth century Exeter was still a tightly knit and self-contained society. For most of its inhabitants this little world embraced the whole range of their hopes and cares. Almost all the important events of their lives transpired within it. The city was the political and economic unit within which their daily existence was carried on. Nevertheless, it was also part of a greater world—the kingdom of England. From the Crown came the decrees altering the religious establishment; the foreign policy of the royal government affected the whole course of Exeter's foreign trade; and the magistrates of the city were not likely to forget, under the vigorous prodding of the Tudor government, that they were its agents as well as the elected heads of the corporation of Exeter.

But it is precisely in defining the relations between the royal government and the city that difficulties arise. In a legal sense there could be no doubt of the subordination of the municipal corporation, either as borough or as county. In both capacities it was but a chartered liberty, enjoying certain privileges and exercising certain powers by the grace of the monarch. But in fact Exeter was, as we know, a semiautonomous community, with its own corporate life and its own special interests. The natural corollary of this fact was that the average inhabitant of the city found his prime social identification in the community of Exeter, while his identity as an Englishman was only secondary. This did not mean that the two loyalties were in any way mutually exclusive; it simply indicated that the second was a less familiar one. A citizen's loyalty to England was less frequently called upon, was far less prominent in his daily life, and likely to be regarded as irksome when its demands disarranged the pattern of his existence. Moreover, these dual loyalties point up the fundamental problem in understanding the relationship between the local and the national social units. Neither was quite what it appeared to be in legal or constitutional terms. In fact, one is not dealing solely with the relations between a central government and a subordinate administrative unit, or between a highly integrated society and one of its constituent parts. England was a hybrid political society in which a centralized monarchy existed side by side with a kind of confederation of local political interests, municipal, regional, professional, and class, all held together in a certain rough unity by the powerful hand of the monarchy, yet stubbornly retaining in wide areas independence of aims and of action. The political life of England was thus conducted in an arena where the various interests on the one hand struggled among themselves for the favor of the Crown, and on the other carried on a struggle with the Crown in which they yielded to its demands only in return for the favors which it could grant. As a member of this turbulent society of competing interests, Exeter had to find means to make its own way.

Insofar as Exeter was merely a local government unit, exercising delegated powers or carrying out direct commands of the Crown, the magistrates were civil servants obeying orders, and a discussion of their relations with the Privy Council demands no more than an account of their efficiency in executing royal policy. But since the city was at the same time a semiautonomous community with its own communal interests, its relations with the royal ministers involved not only obedience to the Council's orders, but also a constant effort to extract favors of various kinds from the court. While such interchange can hardly be called bargaining, the royal government could not resist the importunities of those political groups that were ultimately the guarantors of its own power. Hence, the relationship between Exeter and the royal government needs to be discussed under two heads. The first is the mobilization by the city of all the influential interests which it could command at court; the second, the execution by the city magistrates of Crown policy.

A discussion of the first aspect involves, of course, the formal constitutional channels through which the city sought to further its interests: Parliament and the courts. But to act effectively here something more than mere official procedures were necessary, for the governance of England was conducted within the great complex of personal relationships which bound together the dominant social groupings all over England. This political maelstrom centering in the court drew into itself all the lesser political forces of the country.

Exeter was too far removed both by geography and by its modest status in the official hierarchy to have a direct entrée at court. Its official status as a borough and as a county served, of course, for normal relationships, but when some extra privilege was sought, a new grant or a release from some burden, it was necessary to find an intermediary able to exert the additional pressure required.

Hitherto, the city's two great neighbors had been the Courtenays and the bishop, both of great influence at court, but enemies to the city. With the disappearance of one and the marked decline of the other, the city's prestige as a political power in the West increased, while at the same time the new families who rose on the ruins of the Courtenays and of the ecclesiastical power were its potential allies. The advantages of this new situation were revealed by the grants of 1535 and 1537, but the revolt of 1549 really displayed the development of the new alignments.

The most powerful single figure in the West after the fall of the Marquis of Exeter and the suppression of the monastic houses was John, Lord Russell, afterwards first Earl of Bedford. He had already acquired huge landed interests in the county, as the new proprietor of the Tavistock Abbey lands; nearer at hand he was the lord of the manor of Cowick, just west of the city, and within the walls he had built a town house on the site of the old Dominican priory. Moreover, as Lord President of the short-lived Council of the West, he became the representative of royal power in Devon and Cornwall. Although this body seems to have lapsed before the death of Henry VIII, it was to Russell that the Council of the young King turned in the crisis of the 1549 rebellion. The Lord Privy Seal, armed with special commission from the Council,[1] advanced with a small force as far as Honiton, where lack of equipment and money halted him in a most dangerous situation. At this juncture, he received much-needed financial aid from a group of Exeter merchants who were attending on him. These three— Thomas Prestwood, John Bodley, and John Periam—levied on their credit at Bristol, Lyme, Taunton, and elsewhere to provide him with funds.[2] With this money he was able to put his force in motion and to undertake the successful campaign which followed. But no less valuable to the Lord Privy Seal and to the government than the timely loan of the three merchants, was Exeter's stout and effective resistance to the rebels. They were thus held before the city walls through the dangerous weeks when they might have moved eastward unopposed and spread revolt far and wide in their path. Moreover, the city apparently afforded Bedford additional financial support, for in the Acts of the Privy Council there is an order[3] for the payment of £1,000 to the Mayor of Exeter, lent by him to the Lord Privy Seal.[4]

There can be no doubt that the rebellion marked the establishment of a firm connection between the city and the house of Russell. The confidence he reposed in them is suggested by a letter of the same year as the rebellion, in which he praised their "valiaunt maintaigning of this citie to the Kinges Majestis honour and your owne comon welthe" and blamed the gentry for their failure in the crisis.[5] In the following fall he borrowed some of the city's ordnance, with a promise to return it the following Easter.[6] A clear picture of the relationship is contained in a letter of 20 January 1549–50, to the mayor and his brethren, informing them that he has to leave

---

[1] Hooker, *History*, III, 60.
[2] *Ibid.*, 83.
[3] APC, II, 318, 26 August 1549.
[4] This might represent the repayment of the three merchants, but it may also represent a collection in the city. See AB ii, 210, note of £20 owed John Rowe lent the King during the late "Commotion."
[5] HMC Rep., 20, Letter 20.
[6] *Ibid.*, 22, Letter 23. See also AB ii, 211.

London for the negotiation of the French peace.[7] Hence he has requested his loving friends, the two burgesses of Exeter "who have behaved themselves vearie thankfullie in the service of you all" not to wait at Westminster but to return when he comes back for the advance of the city's suits "which all my Lordes of the Councell favor the more for that your faithfull constancie and defending of the late rebelles in those parties from your Citie." In this year the grant of the manor of Exe Island was received by the city.

The next decade was one of constant intercourse between the Russells and the city. There exists a series of letters from the earls,[8] dealing mostly with petty matters, but typical of the relationship. In 1550 the Earl asked them not to charge more than 20s. to 40s. a year rent for a tilt yard to be built in the Southernhay.[9] In 1553 he recommended to their care a servant of the Prince of Piedmont who was shortly to pass through on his way to Plymouth.[10] In the following year he took the trouble to write from Spain warning them that Prince Philip might land there and bidding them be ready to receive him.[11] This was the last letter the city received from the first Earl, for he died in March 1554–55. But his death changed little in the relationship. His son Francis, the second Earl, was a strong Protestant, and in 1560 he recommended to the mayor one of his chaplains, a certain Mr. Huntingdon,[12] trusting that the latter would be accepted as a "good workman in God's harvests" and assisted "in all things within your libertie and charge for the better setting forthe of God's truethe and the Queen's Majesties godly proceedings." (Huntingdon had just been appointed a canon of Exeter.) A request of a much different sort concerned Edward Bridgeman, one of the Chamber, who was about to be chosen receiver.[13] Bedford asked for his release from this duty, since Bridgeman was a servant of his and likely to be absent from the city.

[7] *Ibid.*, 22, Letter 27.
[8] Russell became Earl of Bedford in 1550.
[9] Printed in *Notes and Gleanings*, I, Part 2 (1891), 75.
[10] HMC Rep, 34, Letter 33. [11] *Ibid.*, 35, Letter 34.
[12] *Ibid.*, 41, Letter 41. [13] *Ibid.*, 43, Letter 52.

Again, two years later, he interceded for the same man, and asked that Bridgeman be relieved from the burden of any office as he could not sustain it.[14] The Chamber consented, but imposed a fine upon Bridgeman, who invoked the Earl's assistance again.[15] Again the Chamber yielded and lowered the fine from £40 to £16 13s. 8d.[16]

This Earl, like his father, was Lord Lieutenant of Devon and Exeter, and this official connection occasioned many exchanges, alike of business and of ceremony. Gifts of wine or sugar loaves were courteous expressions of the city's regard for the Earl, but an actual visit from him was the occasion of such ceremonial display as the age delighted in. In April 1558, when the second Earl came to Exeter, he was received with great dignity[17] at the East Gate and accompanied by the mayor and his brethren to Bedford House, where the next day he received and entertained them. A more substantial token of mutual trust was the Earl's action in entrusting to the city half his ordnance and in presenting them as an outright gift with one piece of ordnance. On another such occasion in 1577 the guns were fired in salute, sixty pounds of sugar and two gallons of hippocras were presented to the Countess, and a tun of Gascon wine to the Earl, while the corporation and the guilds went in their scarlet gowns to meet the visitors.[18] The greatest of all these occasions was doubtless the marriage of William Earl of Bath to the Lady Elizabeth Russell, daughter of the Earl of Bedford, in 1583,[19] when the city presented to the bride a silver bowl of 90 oz. gilt silver.

But aside from these exchanges of favors and of courtesies, not to be too slightly regarded in that age of high ceremony, there were other items of business transacted between the two parties. The Earl was the patron to whom the city looked in time of special need. In the long dispute over the Merchant Adventurers charter, for instance, they turned to the Earl for support. The merchants proposed to their opponents that the whole matter be left to the determination

---

[14] *Ibid.*, 43, Letter 71.
[15] *Ibid.*, 43, Letter 72.
[16] AB ii, 155 and 163.
[17] AB ii, 324.
[18] AB iii, 380.
[19] AB iv, 420.

of Bedford upon his coming into Devon,[20] and it is significant of their relationship that the merchants' opponents firmly opposed the offer. Bedford was also entrusted with the final judgment of the case between the city and Trew concerning the Haven, for it was he, sitting with the justices of assize, who made the final settlement.[21]

Relations with the Bedfords, however, were not always amicable. The Earl in 1562 attempted to obtain the nomination of one of the burgesses in the next Parliament, but he was refused by the city. He complained in a letter, "I thought my goodwill towards you somewhat better deserved than in so triffeling a matter to have suche a repulse."[22] The story of the Topsham cranage has been told elsewhere. In this case, there is some evidence of a deliberate attempt by the Earl to obtain a measure of control over city affairs.[23] In the quarrel over the liberties of Bedford House, which preceded the cranage dispute, there is an indication that the Earl claimed a separate jurisdiction within the city.[24] At the same time that the Topsham suit was going forward, another incident disturbed the normally good relations between the two parties. Some time in 1567 the Earl had granted one Rowe the right to erect a grist mill in St. David's Down just outside the city.[25] Such a mill would have ruined the city's own grist mill at Duryard, and the lessees complained to the Chamber, which enacted an ordinance prohibiting the citizens from grinding grain anywhere except at Duryard. This hit directly at the Earl's mill at Exwick, up the river, which had hitherto been the only place outside the city mills where citizens could grind. Bedford capitulated rather rapidly and revoked the lease to Rowe "out of his accustomed goodness to the said city," whereupon the

[20] Book 85, Document 22.
[21] AB iii, 337.
[22] HMC Rep., 143, Letter 64.
[23] Hooker, *History*, III, 660.
[24] There was a similar dispute in 1577 when one of the Earl's servants at Bedford House fell into a quarrel with several citizens, which soon involved others. In the skirmish that followed, Alderman Brewerton was hurt. The Earl was absent at the time, but upon his return he severely punished the servants responsible for the outbreak. See Book 55, sub anno 1577.
[25] The whole affair is rehearsed in AB iii, 238.

Chamber repealed their act and expressly included the Exwick mills among those to which citizens might take their grain.

In 1575 this act was renewed[26] with the additional statement that the city "hath always found the said earl and his noble father deceased their very good lords touching their liberties and lands, and divers others their business or suit." The Bedfords were the most important of the city's intermediaries in high places, and during the decades of the 1550's and 1560's might be said to have been its patrons. But the relationship was not a one-sided one, and the city retained a safe degree of independence in its dealings with the Earls. In such matters as Parliamentary patronage they resisted his interference whenever it did not suit their own convenience, and they kept open other channels of influence at court. When, at the time of the Topsham dispute, the second Earl showed some tendency to seek a dominant role in the relationship, they firmly resisted and successfully defeated him. The second Earl died in 1585, and the long minority of the third Earl ended for some years the Bedford influence at Exeter.

The Russells had been useful and powerful friends, but in the long run their ambition, coupled with their power, made them uncomfortable neighbors. The more intimate and more enduring relationships of the city were those between the city and the neighboring county families of Devon. Of modest fortunes but gentle birth, and often related to Exeter families, these men belonged to that rising class of gentry whose new power at court is one of the most striking features of the Tudor monarchy. One of the most prominent of them was the Carewes, and with that house the city cultivated a long friendship. The family had enjoyed a prominent position in Western affairs for several generations, but it was only in the middle of the sixteenth century that they became major figures not only in the county but also at court. The two who made the family fortunes were Sir Gawen Carewe (d. 1583) and his nephew, Sir Peter (1514–75).

---

[26] AB iii, 342.

Of the latter we know a good deal, for his biographer was the indefatigable Hooker, his confidant and agent.[27] Peter Carewe's connection with the city of Exeter began early, for he went to the Exeter school, lodging while a pupil with the draper, Thomas Hunt, alderman and mayor in 1515.[28] His subsequent career was among the most spectacular even in a generation rich in flamboyant careers. After a series of adventures fit for the most extravagant of novels, he returned to England in the 1540's.[29] By 1548 he was back in his Devonshire house, Mohuns Ottery, and served as sheriff in the first year of Edward VI.[30] Both he and his uncle played a prominent but ineffectual role in the Prayer Book Rebellion, after having been sent down specially by the Council. Their failure cost them a reprimand and loss of favor at court. Upon the death of Edward, Sir Peter was among the first to proclaim Mary in Devon,[31] but within a short time he, his uncle, and his cousin Champernoun were all involved in the plots against her throne, and Sir Peter had to flee to France. Before his departure he was engaged in an obscure scheme to seize Exeter, which was thwarted by the civic authorities, but he was able to borrow money there before leaving.[32] After a sojourn in Venice and Strassburg, where he stayed with Ponet,[33] he made his

---

[27] This biography has been published twice, once in *Archaeologia*, XXVIII (1840), 96–151, and also as a separate volume, *Life and Times of Sir Peter Carew Kt.*, ed. Sir John MacLean (London, 1857).

[28] See edition in *Archaeologia*, 97.

[29] After a term of service as page in the French court, he came back to serve Henry as gentleman of the Chamber and then went off to Turkey with his cousin John Champernoun, scion of another prominent South Devon family. They visited Constantinople before returning to Venice and thence went to serve under the Imperialist captains at the siege of Buda. Upon his return to England, Carewe was knighted in 1545 while serving as captain of one of the King's ships in the war against France, and in 1547 he married an heiress, Alice, Lady Tailboys, a widow of a baron, whose lands lay in Lancashire. See *Archaeologia*, 98–115.

[30] Isacke, *Antiquities*, "A Catalogue of all the sheriffs of Devon," sub Edward VI.

[31] *Archaeologia*, 120.

[32] *Ibid.*, 120–121.

[33] *Ibid.*, 123.

peace with Paget. He had yet to endure an imprisonment in the Tower and a heavy fine before returning to his restored lands at Mohuns Ottery.[34] After some employment in Elizabeth's Scottish wars, he engaged in a venture in Ireland, where he died in 1575.[35] Both Carewes seem to have been zealous Protestants and were strong supporters of Dean Haynes in Edward's time as well as of the preacher, William Alley (later Bishop of Exeter).[36] When the latter preached there and was ill received, they went up to the pulpit to protect him.

The first evidence we have of the city's relations with the Carewes is in 1549 when Sir Peter borrowed £40 from them.[37] He made some sort of arrangement with Alderman Griffin Ameredith, who was to undertake the repayment. In the same year the city granted him a pension of £2 a year for life with a hogshead of wine at the sealing of the grant,[38] "for his great travail and good will to the city and for his counsell hereafter." This pension ceased in the first year of Philip and Mary, when the Carewes were involved in the conspiracy mentioned above.[39] The nature of the plot remains obscure, but from a surviving report sent by the Exeter magistrates to the Privy Council[40] we gather that a report went abroad that in the week after Christmas sessions (mid-January 1554) certain gentlemen of Devonshire would try to seize the city. Attempts were made by the Carewes to smuggle arms into the city while Gawen Carewe, who was then within the walls, attempted to bribe the porter to let him out during the night, alleging that a ship waited to carry him overseas. Eventually he did escape to Mohuns Ottery, only to be arrested there. In the meantime the city authorities made a thorough search during the night of 19 January, and on 20 January instituted regular watch and ward. As in the past the city remained faithful to constituted authority.

As we have seen, the Carewes were pardoned before the end of Mary's reign and were received back into favor by her sister. Imme-

[34] *Ibid.*, 124–125.
[36] *Ibid.*, 147.
[38] AB ii, 219.
[40] PRO, SP 11/2/14.

[35] *Ibid.*, 144.
[37] AB ii, 212.
[39] RR, 1 Mary—1 & 2 P & M.

diately the city resumed the old connection, and in the first year of the new reign Sir Peter Carewe and his uncle, George Carewe, already a canon of Exeter and later to be dean, received £3 3s. 11d. for their favor and good will.[41] Peter Carewe's pension reappears on the rolls henceforward until his death, and in 1566 he was elected burgess in Parliament.[42] Sir Gawen was honored in 1574 by being elected a freeman of the city and granted a pension of 40s. per annum.[43] The Carewes, like the Bedords, played a role both in the dispute over the Merchant Adventurers' charter and in the litigation with Trew. In the former case, Sir Peter was put forward as an arbitrator by the merchants,[44] and in the latter he interceded for Trew in 1567, persuading the city to give the engineer additional time to complete his work.[45] Moreover, he was to judge whether or not the work was finished according to the contract, when the additional time expired. It was also Sir Peter who recommended Sture (later recorder) to serve as legal counsel to the city.[46]

The Carewes were not the only county family that played the role of counsellors to the city of Exeter. In such matters as that of the canal, Carewe's cousin, Sir Arthur Champernoun, shared with him the task of judging Trew's work, and was likewise proposed by the city for the arbitration of the merchants' charter. Sir John Chichester was another Devon gentleman who shared in these tasks. More closely connected with the city were the Dennys family, the first of whom, Sir Thomas, began his long and successful career as Recorder of Exeter (1514-44),[47] while his son followed in the same office from 1574 to 1592.[48] Lewis Pollard,[49] a member of another distinguished Devon family was the successor of the elder Dennys in the recordership before he resigned to become a Justice of Common Pleas. Another member of the same family was burgess for Exeter in 1555 and 1559.[50]

[41] RR, 5-6 P & M—1 Elizabeth. [42] AB iii, 151.
[43] AB iii, 335. [44] Book 85, Document 22.
[45] AB iii, 197. [46] HMC Rep., 24, Letter 25.
[47] Oliver, *History*, 236. [48] AB iii, 328.
[49] Oliver, *History*, 236.
[50] J. J. Alexander, "Exeter Members of Parliament, Part III, 1537 to 1688," in TDA, LXI (1929), 199–200.

The role of these gentlemen in Exeter affairs was much more modest than that of the Bedfords. But their influence at court, especially that of the Carewes, was not negligible, and they provided an important link with the center of power. They filled a place which few of the Exeter citizens had sufficient dignity or experience to occupy, and thus provided an entrée into court and official circles where the city had to do business.

There were a few exceptions to this generalization. At least two of the merchant families had connections in high places. William,[51] son of the John Periam who was mayor in 1563 and 1572 and brother of the John who held that office in 1598, made his place in the legal world, rising to be Lord Chief Baron in the last years of the century, and thus constituted a valuable connection for the city in the high official world. John Peter, the merchant (mayor in 1557), married Wilmot Peter, the sister of the other John Peter of Exeter, the Queen's customer and of Sir William Peter (Petre) the secretary.[52]

The city also sought to maintain personal connections in the highest quarters. In an age which did not look askance at the acceptance of pensions by ministers, even from foreign rulers, it was natural that the lesser political interests should use the same methods to obtain favors from those in power. Exeter was not behindhand in such practices. In 1533, a pension of £4 per annum for life was granted to Thomas Cromwell.[53] In 1561, a more auspicious choice was made. In that year the Chamber decided that since Sir William Cecil "hath been our especial friend in our affairs and suits as well for suit for Exiland, confirmation of charters and new grants in same and hath received no reward so in consideration thereof we grant him an annuity of £5 for life."[54] In 1565–66, this pension was doubled, and it continued to be paid until the end of his life.[55]

---

[51] *DNB*: "Sir William Peryam."

[52] See Oliver, *Monasticon*, Additional Supplement, 29, for table of Peter genealogy.

[53] AB i, fol. 15.

[54] AB iii, 61.

[55] RR, 7–8 Elizabeth.

Nor did that sever the Cecil connection, for on 23 January 1598–99 the Chamber agreed that the same pension should be paid Sir Robert Cecil for life.[56]

A little later he became the city's first lord high steward.[57] He was followed by a series of great courtiers, the Howard Earls of Northampton and Suffolk, the Earl of Pembroke, Lord Treasurer Weston, and the Earl of Pembroke and Montgomery.[58] Of these Suffolk proved but a slender reed. In 1622 a great suit with the bishop came on. The city's agent in London saw there was little to hope for from Suffolk and wrote down in despair, "your adversarie is potent and hathe manie eminent friendes to backe his enterprises; wherein he hathe the advantage of you your Chamber standing upon bare feete and is without a pillar to leane unto in this daie of neede."[59] Worry had muddled the poor man's metaphors, but the point was clear enough. The Chamber demanded Suffolk's resignation of his patent and opened negotiations with Cranfield as a replacement. But Suffolk's dignity was not to be so ruffled, and only after several years of controversy and the payment of £70 was he induced to give way.[60]

But the city kept open more than one door to the court circle. A natural intermediary was the Lord Lieutenant of Devon and Exeter. The Bedfords held this office until 1585 and again after 1622; in the interval it was filled by the Earl of Bath. Relations with these noblemen were generally amiable, and there are many instances of reciprocal favors. The Earl of Bedford, for instance, received £10 and the city's thanks, for securing the removal of troops billeted in Exeter in 1627.[61] Beyond these official connections regular relations were maintained with Lord Keeper Coventry, who received £20 in

[56] AB v, 438.
[57] Letter 116.
[58] For Northampton's appointment see AB vii, 49 (1613); for Suffolk, AB vii, 176 (1616); for Pembroke, AB vii, 624 and 650 (1625); Weston, AB vii, 754 (1631); and Pembroke and Montgomery, AB viii, 38 (1635).
[59] Letter 220.
[60] Letter 205 and 238, AB vii, 677.
[61] AB vii, 683.

plate for favors to the city in 1628 and occasional New Year's gifts of equal value.[62]

No other local family ever played such a dominant role as the Carewes had done in the sixteenth century, but the city remained on friendly terms with many. Sir John Acland was an active benefactor to the citizens, and on one occasion a recommendation on his part was accepted in appointing a new sword bearer.[63] The same man was also recommended by Sir Amyas Bampfeld who occasionally acted as mediator in civic affairs. Sir Roger Fulford and William Cary were elected freemen in 1613.[64] But beyond such courtesies as these there is little evidence of any close connection with a particular family; it is significant that all the Parliamentary burgesses from 1603 onwards were citizens or recorder.[65]

During the century of our study the city advanced steadily in prestige and influence at court. The disappearance of local patrons like the Carewes is one token of this; the city could afford to dispense with their patronage now that it could be easily secured in more influential quarters. (Moreover local patrons might demand such favors as one of the borough seats in Parliament, a price dearer than the city wished to pay.) The relative ease with which Prouze, the city's London agent in 1622, was able to obtain admission in many important quarters indicates that the city now enjoyed enhanced status in court circles.[66] One reason for this was the greater number of Exeter families with high connections. A Periam was Lord Chief Baron of England, a Martin Recorder of London, and a Hakewill tutor to the Prince of Wales. Moreover, the merchants of Exeter themselves had unquestionably gained in experience and self-confidence.

---

[62] AB vii, 687, 859, and viii, 193. In 1634 the recorder recommended holding up the gift until the end of the next term since the city had a suit pending.

[63] Letter 151 and AB vii, 106.

[64] AB vii, 106.

[65] A quite different kind of attempt to win favor at court may be mentioned. At the accession of Charles I £300 was given as a free gift to the new sovereign. This may have been related to the plans for securing a new charter. See AB vii, 623.

[66] See sequence of Prouze letters, HMC Rep., Letters 217–233, *passim*.

We can conclude this discussion of the informal connections between the city and the court by two concrete examples which illustrate happily the way in which business was done in London. The first dates from Mary's reign. By means of the inventories of 1552, the Privy Council had discovered the Chamber's requisitioning of church plate and had the latter bound in a recognizance to settle with the parishes for this plate.[67] Anxious to escape from this obligation, the Chamber used every channel of influence possible to win a release. How this was accomplished is revealed by the accounts.[68] The largest payment went to John Pollard, later the city's burgess, who received a sum of £20 "for obtaining the request of Lord Pembroke." Certain of Pembroke's servants were paid £8 "to buy them each a gelding." The Clerk of the Council had £6 "for keeping the suit in remembrance." The secretaries to the Treasurer, the Chancellor, and the Lord Admiral also took their tribute, another £6 in all. Even the porter of the Treasurer had his 2s., and the servants of the keeper of the Council chamber, 5s. But besides these direct payments gratitude had to be expressed to the more lofty intermediaries in more delicate terms. Both the Earl of Bedford and Sir William Petre, the Secretary, received suitable gifts of sugar loaves. Nothing could more precisely exhibit the structure of political machinery than this little incident. Court officials of varying dignity—and varying price—had to be conciliated. A courtier of sufficient influence had to be employed to press the suit; and one or more of the great officers of state had to be approached. It was no accident that the courtier whose services were engaged in this case was a member of a local family already connected with the city. And among the lords of the council whose aid was sought, one was the Lord-Lieutenant of Devon and Exeter and the second the head of a prominent Western family, one of whose members was a city officer.

The first case was of a common and relatively simple type. The

[67] See copies of this recognizance and the Council's decision to release the Chamber in Book 55 under date 18 May 1555.

[68] For this account see Book 55 under date 1 & 2 P & M.

renewals of the charters, the grant of a new charter in 1627, the alleviation of tax or military obligations were among the many such favors sought at the hands of the Crown. Such cases required the conciliation of various court magnates and their satellites and often cost dearly, but they did not involve a contest for favor. Let us look at the more complicated situation where the city carried a dispute with a rival or a neighbor to the Crown for settlement.

Our second illustration comes from a later period. In 1622, Bishop Valentine Cary sought to be appointed a justice of the peace in the city. This was a shrewd move by the Bishop in his unending squabble with the city over jurisdiction. The whole advantage of the civic magistrates lay in their commission of peace in the county of the city which gave them superior rights over any immunities of the Bishop's Fee. The Chamber soon had wind of the episcopal maneuver and promptly dispatched to London as their agent, William Prouze, member of a very prominent civic family. A sequence of his letters enables us to follow some of the intricate details of negotiation.[69]

Prouze stayed in Aldersgate Street with his cousin George Hakewill, who was brother to John, one of the Exeter Twenty-Four. Together with Hakewill and the recorder, Nicholas Duck, he planned the city's strategy.[70] Siege was laid to all the major figures in the Council. The Lord Keeper, Bishop Williams, was approached both through members of his staff and directly, but unhappily was not to be won, and indeed had soon to be counted of the enemy's camp.[71] The Lord Treasurer was to be conciliated by the prompt dispatch of the lately collected benevolence accompanied by a letter urging the city's case.[72] Another letter was to go from the Chamber to the Lord President. Secretary Calvert was approached directly by

---

[69] This sequence of letters (217, 218, 219, 220, 222, 223, 226, 227, 229, 230, 231, 232, 233) runs from 4 May through 13 July 1622. They are printed in HMC Rep., 115–123.

[70] Prouze was given a credit of £100 by the Chamber for this business, AB vii, 475.

[71] Letters 218 and 226.

[72] Letters 219 and 220.

Prouze and won to a promise to "take upon him the patronizing of your cause as occasion hereafter shall require."[73] The judges, too, were solicited for their opinions, and the hopeful ones collected while Justice Doddridge was singled out as a neighbor whose recommendations would bear weight.

In the meantime the struggle itself proceeded. The Bishop remained unaware of the identity of the city's agent "albeit theie have used manie meanes to dog the tracke of my waie," but Prouze kept a close and accurate watch over the Bishop's maneuvers.[74] The Lord Keeper was favorably disposed to the issuance of the commission as was the King also. But Prouze and his legal advisors, who now included Noy, soon put their fingers on the weak spot in the Bishop's proposal. The 1537 charter of the county of Exeter was explicit that there should be eight justices, all of them aldermen. So Prouze now tackled the Attorney-General to whom the commission had been sent for legal opinion. He urged Mr. Attorney to hear the opinion of the Lord Chief Baron and Mr. Justice Hutton.[75] His efforts were rewarded, for both the Attorney-General and the Clerk of the Crown gave judgment against the legality of the proposed commission.[76] The first round was won but not the whole battle, for the Lord Keeper talked of issuing a commission with a nonobstante clause but this as Prouze pointed out would impeach not only the charter but "the Common Law of the Realme: wherein every good subjecte hathe an estate of inheritans" and a lawsuit turning on this point would probably end favorably to the city.[77] Prouze continued to revolve various schemes for proceedings, whether by petition to the King, or to the Council, but for the time being nothing seems to have happened.

The last letter in this sequence is of the following year and describes an interview with the King at Hampton Court. Prouze found some difficulty in presenting his petition from the Chamber for the King said he had heard the citizens were Puritans. However, he

[73] Letters 227 and 229.   [74] Letter 227.
[75] Letter 223.   [76] Letter 226.
[77] Letter 231.

made "a modest annsweare, which somewhat pacified the King."[78]
What the final outcome was cannot be said, but it is probable that
had the Bishop obtained his commission some evidence would remain in the city's records.[79] More important than the matter of the
case is the character of the struggle as revealed in these letters. The
Chamber moved with the deftness and assurance born of experience
to check its opponent. All the city's resources of influence were
tapped, London connections, justices on the Western circuit, and
as many great officers as could be induced to act for the city. At the
same time, the city's strategy turned on forcing the Bishop from the
favorable grounds of court favor to the more uncertain ones of law.
At the game of law the city stood on as good grounds as any
adversary (in this case better). Hence their limited funds of influence were drawn on not so much to obtain royal favor as to
secure a strong position at law, if possible, strong enough to prevent
a contest altogether. Undoubtedly this episode may stand as a model
for many others.

The second episode reveals much of the peculiar difficulties which
the city faced in its struggles with rivals. These rivals—bishop,
chapter, some county magnate or noble, or some other city—were
of varying status but the contest had ultimately to be fought out in
London. In many cases, probably in most, this meant resort to the
law courts, but as the case above illustrates, this was not so simple
as it may seem. Ultimately the law might provide the ground rules
by which the issues could be fought out within the arena of Westminster Hall. But very often the preliminaries of the controversy
involved a political contest quite as important as the judicial one
which followed. In cases going before the Council itself the whole
process retained this dual character, and, indeed, given the inchoate
character of seventeenth-century government, the distinction between political and judicial judgments was never in practice clear.
Hence the city had to engage in a scramble for favor in the court
circle of power. Here arose the difficulty, for Exeter held much too

---

[78] Letter 242, 17 April 1623.
[79] The city secured itself against such a danger in the future in the terms
of its new charter of 1627. See above, Chapter II.

modest a place in the political firmament to play at the dangerous game of court politics. Yet, somehow, an interest had to be created at court to protect and support the city's position against its rivals. Its agents had to pick their way with great care, avoiding all possible offence and currying favor in every quarter. By the use of gifts, pensions, flattery, and favors a credit balance of influence could be built up, to be drawn upon at need. But mere influence was at best a fragile weapon, for it meant constant reliance on men of power who might or might not respond to the city's urgings at a crucial moment. But these were all the weapons in the borough's armory, and dubious as they might be, they had to be used.

On the whole, they were well and skillfully utilized, as the city's success in freeing itself from outside influences, clerical and lay, during our century indicates. But the cost in time and effort was large. Beyond the major disputes which have been discussed in the text, there were many others of which only bare traces remain. There were suits with other cities over trading privilege, or with neighboring landowners over property rights in land or in the river's waters. In 1630 there was a formidable suit brought on by John Norden, then surveyor to the Prince of Wales, over the city's right to the Northernhay.[80] The list could be lengthened indefinitely; it is safe to say that there was hardly a year when the city was free from some impending suit at Westminster. This meant maintaining agents on the scene. The recorder was usually an effective representative, but very often he was joined by one or more citizen auxiliaries sent up by the Chamber. And these men, as the Prouze correspondence and other letters show, kept in close touch with the Chamber itself.

One great advantage the Chamber possessed was its own internal unity. Except for the Merchant Adventurers charter there was no major issue on which this unity was broken during our period. Consequently there developed a consistency of civic policy which was the basis of success. The men who conducted civic affairs acquired long experience and great skill although at heavy cost in time and probably in money. But they had their rewards in the

[80] ECM, Law Papers, Attorney-General v. Exeter.

advancement in civic prestige and influence which unquestionably took place in this century.

But not all state business was done in the Council. As everyone knows, Parliament was by now emerging as a potent rival. In this body Exeter had direct representation. What use was made of this advantage? The answer to this question involves first of all the matter of elections.

Exeter had been represented in Parliament since the earliest assemblies of the late thirteenth and early fourteenth centuries. The method of election in this period is not clear, but by the sixteenth century it had, like the other elements in the borough's constitutional structure, attained a fixed character. There were three stages in the elections.[81] At the first, the nomination of the burgesses was made. During the sixteenth century this was always done in the Chamber. Only two candidates were chosen. The only such choice which was actually recorded in the act book[82] is that of September 1553, when it was noted that John Ridgeway and Richard Hert had been nominated. Beside the name of each of the Twenty-Four and under the names of the two nominees there is written "ibid," so we may assume that a ballot was taken and unanimous agreement obtained. The next stage was the formal submission of the two names to the voters in open County Court which since 1537 was held at the Guildhall.[83] It is not clear who was entitled to vote in this election. Before 1537, the rule apparently was that only freemen of the city could vote; after that date freeholders claimed the right and they may have exercised it. In 1588, at least, it was to the freeholders that the Chamber referred its nominees,[84] but only in the seventeenth century did an open contest between freeholders and freemen arise. In the final stage of the election process the Sheriff of Exeter transmitted the names of the elected members to Chancery by sealed indenture.

Obviously the choice of the burgesses was made in the Chamber.

[81] Alexander, *Exeter Members*, 195.
[82] AB ii, 252.
[83] See AB ii, 352, for account of this.
[84] AB v, 96.

In 1566, for example, at the by-election to replace the lately deceased Thomas Williams, Sir Peter Carewe had "made motion and request to be burgess,"[85] and it was agreed in the Chamber that he should have the place upon condition that he be sworn freeman "and supply the office in his own person." Failing this, Mr. Periam was to "supply the same room according to order already agreed and concluded." Clearly these preliminary arrangements were made within the Chamber without any consultation outside. On the other hand, the formal election in the county court always took place. And at the end of the century the voters may have been somewhat restive. For the election of 1588 and again for that of 1593 there are significant entries in the act book. In 1588, Drew and Periam were proposed to be chosen "if the said freeholders who shall be then assembled for the said purpose shall so like or think it good."[86] In 1593, it was agreed that Hele and Periam should be "pronounced to the commons to be burgesses with addition unto them if they like better of any other persons nevertheless they may choose the same whom they like better."[87] The voters followed the Chamber's choice in both instances, but the latent discontent burst into the open thirty years later. The revolt was led by the sturdily independent alderman, Ignatius Jurdaine, the most eminent man in the city in the last generation before the Civil War. Jurdaine had already served in the Parliaments of 1621 and 1625, but he was not nominated by the Chamber in 1626.[88] In spite of this he was elected in the open county court. A rather peevish Chamber agreed to pay his wages because of his many past services to the city, but resolved that henceforth burgesses elected by the commons should be paid by them.

In 1627 the Chamber sought to regain control by nominating four candidates for the commons' choice.[89] Jurdaine was not among

---

[85] AB iii, 181.   [86] AB v, 96.
[87] AB v, 240.   [88] AB vii, 647.
[89] AB vii, 693. There was a rueful addendum to the order. If there were any objections to the official nominees, the sheriff was to do his best for the old custom.

them, but once again he was chosen by the commons, along with one of the official four. Two returns were made, but on petition Jurdaine was seated.[90] The Chamber was naturally unwilling to pay his wages, but an accommodation seems to have been reached by which the city would pay but later be recompensed from a general collection.[91] But these disputed elections did not settle the quarrel between freemen and freeholders over the franchise. The charter of 1627 limited it to freemen, and the freeholders did not make good their claim until 1689.

The men chosen as burgesses during this era reflect Exeter's pride in its parliamentary privilege and its determination to use that privilege to the direct advantage of the city. Of the thirty-nine men who served Exeter in Parliament between 1537 and 1640, twenty-five were citizens,[92] all of whom had held one or other of the city offices. Five others were recorders of the city, one of whom, Geoffrey Tothill, was a native and son of the mayor of 1552. Of the remaining nine only one was not a native of Devon. This was Robert Weston who came to Exeter as chancellor to Bishop Coverdale and served in the last Parliament of Edward VI. The other eight were all Devon gentry, three of them closely related to one of the major Exeter families.[93] Among the gentry one was the city's close friend, Sir Peter Carewe; another, John Grenville, customer of the port of Exeter; and a third, John Pollard, was a member of a Devon family who had provided Exeter with a recorder. Only two, Passmore and Williams, seem to have come from outside the Exeter circle, and both of them were natives of Devon. All of these outsiders appear in the sixteenth century. After 1603 the only burgess who was not actually a member of the Twenty-Four was Nicholas Duck, the recorder. Among the citizen burgesses, twenty out of the twenty-five

[90] For details of this contest see Alexander, *Exeter Members*, 195.

[91] AB vii, 729.

[92] The information in this paragraph comes from Alexander, *Exeter Members*.

[93] John Hull, MP 1540, great-grandson of Henry Hull (possibly son or grandson of mayor of 1491), uncle to Henry Hull, mayor, 1605; John Ridgeway, son of mayor of 1489–90; Edward Ameredith, whose father was MP in 1547, sheriff 1555, receiver 1–2, 2–3 P & M.

had served as mayor at least once; two of the remaining had been sheriff; while the others, John Hooker and Richard Hert, served respectively as chamberlain and town clerk. Of these burgesses two sat in four Parliaments; five sat three times, and five twice.

From the above figures it is clear that the city was firmly resolved to choose only Exeter citizens or someone who was closely connected with the Chamber, either by family or by official ties. For the most part the Chamber preferred to entrust its interests in Parliament to one of its own experienced members or to a permanent city officer. The only evidence of outside interference in an election is the abortive attempt of the Earl of Bedford in 1562, and, considering the choices made by the Chamber, it is safe to assert that outside influence was very infrequent.

The burden of Parliamentary membership was not light. As we shall see shortly, the burgess was expected to transact a good deal of miscellaneous city business along with his attendance in the House. His absence was likely to be fairly long, but he was well paid. In Henry VIII's reign the allowance was 2s. per diem,[94] but by 1558 the burgesses were being paid 3s. 4d.[95] In 1571, this had risen to 4s.,[96] and in the Parliament of 1589, 5s.[97] Apparently this was regarded as a little too high, for in 1598 it was lowered to 4s. and there remained.[98]

How the city used its Parliamentary privilege can be better illustrated by an examination of the duties of the burgesses. These were twofold: first, their service in the House; second, the transaction of various items of city business in London. These two aspects of their duties were closely mingled in the instructions which they were given. We may take those to Richard Prestwood in 1553 as an example.[99] His principal concern was the new canal. He was first of all to make suit for the gift of the church plate, not only that already taken by the city, but also the residue, for the use of the Haven. To

[94] AB ii, 115 and 146.   [95] AB ii, 317.
[96] AB iii, 267.   [97] AB v, 250.
[98] AB v, 410.   [99] HMC Rep., 32, Letter 31.

support his case he took along with him the records of Edward I's time respecting the original obstruction of the river. Moreover, if any bill concerning church plate were put into Parliament, he was "to cause friends to be made" so that a proviso might be included which would secure the Exeter parish plate to the Chamber for the canal. He was also to write a letter to the Lord Privy Seal (Russell) "in the favor of the Citie anserying his frendshipp to the havyn &c." Apparently the Chamber desired more information about the value of the plate in the city, for he was to ascertain this from the royal inventories. Local trade privileges were also high on his list of instructions. He was to secure confirmation of the citizens' right which prohibited any "foreigner" from selling cloth within the city unless it had been checked by the city alnagers. Prestwood was also to find out how the latter used cloth forfeited because it was not made according to statute. Another of his tasks was to make arrangements about the establishment of a common hall for the merchants' use, including a decision as to the rent. Besides these larger assignments there was a variety of smaller ones. He was to try to obtain the prisage wine for Exeter such as London already had, and to see the burgesses of Poole, Southampton, and Bristol because these towns did not allow Exeter merchants free entry of town custom. A tun of Gascon wine was to be delivered to Russell, while Cecil was to be approached concerning the "Black Roll" which the former burgess, Ameredith, had earlier left in his custody. Lastly, Prestwood was to sue for the rent of £2 10s. coming from Exe bridge for the use of the city.

A similar set of instructions is extant for the Parliament of 1562.[100] The burgesses, Williams and Tothill, were to press for a certification of the charter of orphans by Parliament. Without Parliamentary affirmation the charter lacked prescription and would die with the Queen. Second, they were to seek an act repealing the custom of gavelkind then used in Exeter. Two items in the instructions were connected with the economic privileges of the city. The first related to the Statute of Apprentices, which then limited apprenticeship to those whose parents could spend 20s. of freehold per annum. It was

[100] AB iv, unnumbered page.

desired to extend this provision to cover Exeter as well as London and Norwich, the only cities so favored under the original statute. The second was the renewal of the statute merchant of the staple in Exeter. Two acts of more general character were sought by the Chamber. One would amend the statute of highways so that each man would contribute according to his wealth and thus the poor "be not as heretofore charged as far forth as the rich." The other proposed an amendment of poor-relief laws which would give the justices power to use coercion against those who refused to contribute.

How Tothill fared in his assigned tasks is indicated in the letters which he sent back to Exeter. In one, dated January 1562–63,[101] he referred to two private bills then in process, one in the Lords and the other in the Commons. He thought it better not to put both in one house lest the house "wold nott be best contentyd with too bylles for our private Cyttye." He hoped that the orphans' bill would go up to the Lords and "the church bill"[102] come down from them simultaneously. A government bill, supported by the Master of the Rolls, was already put in regarding apprentices. He asks for £10 to be sent him as he has "retayned divers in the causes and must give money aboute the same."[103]

It is hard to say how frequently the Exeter burgesses were successful in pressing their private bills. We know of only five in our period. The earliest, in 1540, was the bill permitting clearance of the river; another in 1610 was connected with the weirs.[104] In 1549 the new charter granted by Edward VI was confirmed in Parliament.[105]

---

[101] HMC Rep., 51, Letter 66.

[102] It is not clear what the "church bill" was. Conceivably the Chamber was already agitating for a re-districting of the parishes.

[103] There is a third set of instructions for the year 1585 (AB iv, 458), which varies but little from the others. From the fragmentary letters remaining it seems likely that the burgesses sent weekly accounts of their activities and of the House's doings down to the Chamber, usually mingled with general political news (see Letters 203, 210, 268 for examples).

[104] *Statutes of the Realm*, 31 Henry VIII, c. 4; AB vi, 403, 431, and 414 (a bill for charges for the passing of the act). I have not seen a copy of the act.

[105] Hooker, *History*, II, 339.

In 1570 the city secured a revision of the ancient custom of gavelkind which prevailed there,[106] and in 1607 a bill was passed at the city's behest to protect the monopoly of the Merchant Adventurers' Company against the consequences of the bill of 1606 which provided for general free trade with Spain, France, and Portugal.[107]

The attitude of the city towards Parliament as an institution emerges quite clearly. They regarded it primarily as another center of power through which the city interests might be advanced. Hence most of the acts in which they were interested were purely private ones. Matters of wider import concerned them only insofar as they touched Exeter interests. This parochialism may have been yielding slowly in the early seventeenth century as the great constitutional issues emerged. The Chamber was in constant communication with the burgesses and although the letters of the latter deal largely with civic concerns they also include considerable information on larger questions. Copies of the Petition of Right, the Remonstrance of 17 June 1627, and the King's reply are all preserved in the city archives.[108] But in the main, Parliament continued to be, from the city's point of view, a convenient institution for pressing local interests. Attendance at the session was only part of the duties of the burgess. He had at the same time to execute all kinds of commissions for the city—the solicitation of support in high places, the settlement of legal matters, or discussions with other cities. Such a task demanded selection of experienced and trustworthy men, careful instruction, and constant correspondence.

As we have already indicated above, there was another aspect of the relationship between the officers of the Exeter community and the central government. They were also, as justices of the peace and of gaol delivery, civil servants of the Crown, its direct agents for the execution of policy. As such they combined the duties of officers of police, of finance, and of war, executing the specific orders of the royal council in these areas, as well as acting as general representatives of Crown authority in Exeter. No distinct line can, of

[106] *Statutes of the Realm*, 23 Elizabeth, c. 17.
[107] *Statutes of the Realm*, 3 James I, c. 6, and 4 James I, c. 9. For the unsuccessful bills on the re-districting of the parishes, see above.
[108] Letters 313 and 314.

course, be drawn between their functions of this type and those of leadership in the local community, but it is convenient to separate the two for purposes of analysis. There was, of course, a constant stream of instructions and reminders coming down from the Council, and there were frequent additions to the statute book which added new duties to those already exercised by the magistrates. But our interest here is merely in general types of action.

The deep and anxious concern of the Tudor Privy Council with the problem of public order is a matter of common historical knowledge, and it was, as we have seen, shared by the Exeter magistrates. How deep the latters' fear of social disturbance was can be seen in their action in 1549 when their religious preferences were made to yield to the threat of disorder. Again in 1554 under a religious regime of quite opposite color, they showed the same devotion to the maintenance of public authority. This devotion never wavered, although it was not to be so severely tried again. The maintenance of public order was, of course, as much a matter of local as of national concern, and no boundary can be drawn between cases of national as over against those of local interest. Nevertheless, across the whole range of cases which arose, a distinction can be made between those which were dealt with locally and those which, for one reason or another, went up to the royal Council for action. The former type we have already considered in Chapter IV; now we may survey some of the latter. The evidence is sketchy, and it permits us only to enumerate the kind of situations which arose without making possible any detailed account of them. The cases that involved Council intervention fall under several headings.

There were first those occasional outbursts of violence which so alarmed Westminster, no matter how trivial the cause. Thus, a riot between the episcopal officers and those of the city in 1547[109] brought down a peremptory command to the dean and chapter, not only to restrain their officers but also to send their bailiff up to London to give an account of his behavior. Similarly in 1552 a fray

[109] APC, II, 534 and 538.

between the servants of Canon Carewe and the city officers[110] led to Council injunctions both to the angry Carewes, Sir Peter and Canon George, as well as to the city, commanding a reconciliation after the guilty servant of the canon had made apology for his faults. Both the Council and the Exeter magistrates had a sense of proportion about public disorder, and when an apprentices' riot occurred in 1556[111] the former congratulated the mayor on his prompt action in apprehending the offenders and agreed to his recommendation of a light sentence of reprimand, which was addressed to the masters as well as to the servants. An insult to a royal monopoly holder, in this case the playing card patentee, was regarded with less complacency, and the magistrates were ordered to send up to London the Exeter inhabitants who had offered him violence.[112] Twice, the authority of the local justices was seriously disregarded. The first occasion was when one of the sons of Sir John Fulford, arrested in the city for debt, resisted and threatened the safety of the mayor and aldermen. A special commission of four, including Sir Gawen Carewe and William Periam, had to be appointed to examine the case and to guard against further disorder.[113] The second occasion was in January 1588–89 when a riot occurred at the Exeter sessions.[114] Two servants of William Fortescue of Preston in Devon were killed by servants of Sir William Courtenay. The Council believed that proceedings in this case had been "indirect and unlawful," and the decision of the jury of inquest hasty. The magistrates were directed not to bail the offenders without permission from the Council and not to try them until afforced by special commissioners from the Crown. The magistrates were slow in acting to reapprehend the offenders,[115] and four Devon gentry were joined in commission with them. Not even this was sufficient, however, and in May a peremptory rebuke was sent down[116] declaring that "you have seemed rather to follow your own wills and affections than any way our directions as we thought fit" and ordering them

---

[110] *Ibid.*, II, 38, 85, 101.
[112] *Ibid.*, X, 431.
[114] *Ibid.*, XVII, 64.
[116] *Ibid.*, XVII, 194.

[111] *Ibid.*, VI, 50.
[113] *Ibid.*, XII, 186.
[115] *Ibid.*, XVII, 110.

to sue out a commission of oyer and terminer in association with the justices of assize for trying the case.[117] In all these cases the Council's concern with outbreaks of violence of any kind[118] is evident, as is their determination to reinforce the justices' authority, or even, as in the last case, to compel their action. Neither the prestige nor the determination of the civic magistrates was always sufficient, especially where powerful local gentry were concerned.

Exeter was a port with much foreign trade, and another type of case involving Council intervention was that touching foreigners. Thus in 1573 a Portuguese imprisoned on private complaint[119] was ordered sent up to London, and in 1574 the French Ambassador made suit that two Frenchmen brought from Exeter might be tried for piracy in London and not sent back to the West. In this case the Council consulted the Judge of the Admiralty in Devon for advice.[120] In 1600 the Council had to intervene in favor of a Frenchman[121] named Raoul Berthelot, who, when he attempted to collect a debt owed him in Exeter, was robbed of the instrument of obligation by his debtor. The Council indignantly pointed out that this was not only a private wrong but a slander to the justice of the state and ordered immediate redress.

The problem of maintaining the public peace was well on its way to solution by 1600. After that date the number of cases of violence in which the Council intervened declined almost to the vanishing point, and as a consequence the strict supervision of the local magistrates from above was relaxed. A fundamental social problem had been faced and solved by the coöperation of central and local authority; habits of orderly public behavior were now sufficiently strong so that local magistrates could meet most emergencies.

[117] The culprit in this case was condemned, but on order of the Council sent to Ireland to serve under George Cary (of Devon). He was not to return to England without special license. See *Calendar of State Papers Domestic, Elizabeth, 1581–1590,* II, 664.

[118] The Council was also much concerned about coiners. Two such cases in Exeter were referred to the Council, which sent down orders for taking care of them. See *Acts of the Privy Council,* V, 154, and III, 356.

[119] APC, VIII, 102.   [120] *Ibid.,* VIII, 268.

[121] *Ibid.,* XXX, 272.

The Council concerned itself with economic regulation, but instances of intervention are not numerous. Very typical is one of
1630. On 8 November the Council wrote to say they had heard
salt was being engrossed and the price raised at Exeter.[122] The
Chamber promptly answered on 23 November that they could find
no forestallers, that the merchants bought salt in Rochelle at 8s. the
bushel and sold it in Exeter for 9s., the ordinary price in the western
parts.[123] In other chapters we have traced the Council's interest in
overseas trade, a matter which more often involved the Merchant
Adventurers Company than the Chamber.

Religion was, of course, a matter which interested the Council
mightily. In 1580, the mayor's diligence against Papists was
praised.[124] There is extant for the same year a certificate of the
recusants in Exeter sent up by the sheriff.[125] It included two names
only, and these men were not permanent residents of Exeter. Occasionally we find the mayor and aldermen examining persons suspected to be "evil affected in religion." In January 1592–93, the
bishop and the mayor were thanked for their diligence in such a
case and ordered to turn the suspect over to the justices of assize.[126]
In the preceding year a private accusation of religious unorthodoxy
had been heard by the bishop, mayor, and aldermen.[127] When these
examiners certified that the accusation was false, the Council ordered
the accusers held in prison until they acknowledged the wrong
which they had done.[128]

Of particular interest is one case in which the Council found it
necessary to investigate the behaviour of the mayor himself. The
mayor and gaoler of Exeter were accused of being privy to the
escape of a notorious pirate from Exeter gaol. A commission of
Devon gentry were ordered to investigate the charges, to question
both of the accused, and to hold them for further appearance.[129]
Apparently the decision was unfavorable to the mayor, Simon

---

[122] PRO, PC 2/40, v. 6, fol. 156. [123] SPD, 388/87.

[124] APC, VIII, 349. [125] PRO, SP 12/165/30.

[126] APC, XXIV, 7. [127] *Ibid.*, XXII, 104.

[128] *Ibid.*, XXII, 404. [129] *Ibid.*, XII, 93–94.

Knight, for he was bonded to appear before the Council on 23 August 1580.[130] This examination revealed little, and so the justices of assize were ordered to continue the investigation down in Devon.[131] It is evident from another document of almost the same date that there was not enough evidence in the case to proceed, and with the release of the gaoler, it was dropped.[132]

In one private case to which the Mayor, Bailiffs, and Commonalty were a party the Council felt moved to intervene. This was the affair of Valentine Tucker, for nineteen years the keeper of the Merchants Hall in the New Inn, whose lease was terminated by the Chamber in 1601.[133] Tucker appealed to the Council.[134] Their answer is interesting.[135] "Though we do not willingly meddle or interpose our authoritie in matters that concern contracts between men because the ordinary course of the law doth provide for the doing of justice and right therein" yet in this case they think it well to require the mayor and brethren to deal "well and conscionably" with Tucker. The bishop, dean, and two prebendaries were appointed to make arrangements with the mayor and brethren. Tucker's inopportune appeal did him little good. The decision of the ecclesiastical arbitrators was against him, and they required him to make submission to the city authorities.[136] At the same time the Chamber invoked the powerful influence of Sir Robert Cecil, and in the end the unfortunate man made his submission to the Twenty-Four, acknowledging that he had no estate in the inn and seeking forgiveness from the Chamber.[137]

We can take the statement of the Council quoted above as a statement of policy. In general, they could and did rely upon the vigorous and effective action of the Exeter magistrates as guardians of the public peace and arbiters of justice, but when local interest was involved or when the parties concerned were men of prestige greater than that of the civic authorities, the Council did not hesi-

[130] *Ibid.*, XII, 163.
[131] *Ibid.*, XII, 247.
[132] *Ibid.*, XII, 233.
[133] AB v, 524.
[134] AB v, 527.
[135] APC, XXXI, 48.
[136] AB v, 531.
[137] AB v, 535. Nevertheless he continued to hold an interest in the New Inn for some years afterwards.

tate to interpose their authority, either to accomplish their own ends or to protect individuals against the selfish interests of the local community. How successful these interventions were is uncertain. Clearly in the case of the escaped pirate and in the Tucker affair local obstinacy obstructed any effective action by the Council.

Only once did the Council have to remedy a complete dereliction of duty by the magistrates of Exeter. In 1625, the worst plague in a century visited the city. The newly elected mayor, Thomas Walker, refused to take up his office,[138] and at the same time many of the other magistrates fled the city along with most of the wealthier inhabitants.[139] Unemployment, famine, and sickness produced riots. Into this breach stepped the staunch old Puritan, Ignatius Jurdaine, mayor in 1617, who acted as deputy and carried the city through the worst of the emergency.[140] Walker had to be dragged back by an order of the Privy Council.[141] But he did not return until the beginning of January 1625–26. It took still another order of the Council to bring back many of the lesser officials,[142] while the overseer of the poor, John Levermore, had to be made to appear before the Council and formally submit before he returned to his post.[143] Yet, even in this worst failure not all the Chamber had abandoned their posts; a faithful few had maintained the honor of their house.

No less important and considerably more onerous were the burdens of military responsibility laid on the Exeter magistrates by the royal authorities. These duties were numerous. First of all came the ever-present task of maintaining the walls. Although such defenses as Exeter's would have been obsolete anywhere outside England in the late sixteenth century, their importance had been brought home in 1549. As the capital of the West and the center of royal power in Devon, the city must be prepared to defend itself against such out-

---

[138] AB vii, 624.   [139] PRO, SP 16/12/68.
[140] AB vii, 624.
[141] APC, Charles I, I, 217. Walker made the excuse he was not a property-owner in the city any longer, having made over the lease of his house to his son. He had been in the Chamber since 1581 and mayor twice previously.
[142] *Ibid.*, 312.   [143] *Ibid.*, 422.

breaks as that of the Prayer Book Rebellion and to act as a fortress for royal authority. Hence, throughout this period municipal expenditures on the wall are ever-recurrent. During the French wars of Henry VIII it was ordered by the Chamber that a benevolence be gathered among the commoners of the city for the maintenance of the walls.[144] At this time a new barbican was erected.[145] In 1558 the reconstruction of the North Gate was undertaken.[146] Usually, amounts spent on the walls are included in the general account, "Repairs, etc.," but for those years when a separate listing is made, the total spent amounts to £263. The year of largest expenditure was 1582–83 when £88 were laid out for repairs of the walls.[147] But the walls alone, without artillery, provided no adequate defense for the city. This, too, was likely to be an expensive item. In 1546, for instance, £39 had to be appropriated for new ordnance.[148] Artillery required a gunner, but he was a functionary appointed only in times of emergency. In 1559 the Chamber appointed a Dutchman named Jacob,[149] who received 40s. down, 12d. for each day he worked, and 18s. for his house rent. The city was the custodian of part of the Earl of Bedford's ordnance,[150] and, as we have seen, the Earl gave the city as a gift a piece of ordnance in 1558.

Besides the maintenance of the defenses, the city was responsible for the ancient obligation of arms. Each able-bodied citizen was expected to keep his arms in readiness; his particular equipment depended upon his rank and income. In Exeter the yearly review of arms and armor took place on St. John's Eve, Midsummer Day. Upon this occasion the mayor went forth, attended in state by the Chamber and by the various companies of the city, all arrayed in armor. One may guess that with time this event became more ceremonial than martial. More important, because checked by the royal government, were the musters proper. These inspections, held at frequent intervals under special commissions issued by the royal

[144] AB ii, 137.
[146] AB ii, 341.
[148] AB ii, 135.
[150] AB ii, 294.

[145] AB ii, 149.
[147] RR, 24–25 Elizabeth.
[149] AB ii, 228.

government, were directed by the Lord Lieutenant and his deputies. Since Exeter was a county in its own right, the commission always included the mayor and usually some aldermen. Hooker records in some detail the long-remembered muster of 1538,[151] probably one of more elaborate nature than usual. It was directed by the receiver, Robert Tucker, who had served in Spain. It was a matter of satisfaction to the citizens that one of their own number should be versed in martial exercises so that the muster was held "to the great pleasure of the beholders and the recommendation of himself Tucker. He wore his armor and had charge of the horse and was attended by his horsemen and with all thought meet for a captain." About 1,000 men were mustered in that year. Actually, only about half the able-bodied men in the city were enrolled in the companies and armed.[152] They were divided into four companies, one for each quarter, each headed by a captain, who was a member of the Twenty-Four. In full martial pomp he was assisted by a lieutenant, an ensign, three sergeants, four corporals, three drummers, and a clerk, altogether a most formidable array. In 1569 there were sixty-five citizens who were completely armed at their own cost. For the rest the city provided a rather motley assortment of weapons, harquebuses, pikes, and bills. By 1638 pikes and muskets were the weapons, 60 of the latter for 40 of the former. The mayor and several aldermen acted as deputy lieutenants, sometimes assisted by a country gentleman or two.

During the first thirty years of Elizabeth the city bore no heavier burdens than these, but the war years which followed saw a heavy increase in military obligations. In the latter part of 1587 preparations were already being made; the first evidence we have from Exeter is the demand of the Deputy Lieutenants of Devon for a contribution from the city towards the training of soldiers in the

---

[151] Book 51, fol. 344, sub anno 1538.
[152] See the muster return for 1638, PRO, SP 16/407/27, which lists the enrolled men separately from those able-bodied but not enrolled. There are rolls for 1569 (SP 12/57/2) and 1573 (SP 12/92/38). The former is much more complete.

shire.[153] The Chamber immediately wrote up to London to Burghley begging a discharge from this demand or else that "our offer made be accepted." What this offer was is not clear, but one may guess that they offered a contribution for the war at sea. In January 1588, a muster master, servant of Sir Thomas Dennys, was appointed.[154] The Council made no financial demand upon the city until 1 April following. On that date they sent down a circular letter to several principal ports demanding the furnishing of ships and pinnaces, appointed according to schedule, furnished with victuals, mariners, and necessary furniture, to be ready to join Drake or the Lord Admiral on 25 April. Exeter and Topsham were required to furnish three ships and one pinnace. (Among the other ports London was ordered to furnish eight ships and two pinnaces; Bristol, three and one; Dartmouth and Totnes, two and one between them.)[155] The city's response was speedy; on 11 April a letter was written announcing to the Council that one fine ship and a pinnace had been "stayed and fitted out per directions," but asking that the second ship be charged to the creeks of the port, which had refused to contribute because they were not included in the original letter.[156] Nothing was said of a third ship, and the city seems to have escaped this demand. In the meantime the Chamber had gone ahead with their preparations. On 29 April they ordered the payment of 200 marks to the owners of the pinnace "Gift of God" and £250 to the owners of the "Rose of Exeter."[157] On 4 May it was agreed that the mariners of these two vessels should enter into pay 30 April, while those of a third, the "Bartholomew of Exmouth," should be taken

---

[153] AB iv, 548.   [154] AB iv, 557
[155] APC, Elizabeth, XVI, 9. Southampton was required to provide two ships and one pinnace; Yarmouth, one of each; Hull, two ships and one pinnace; Ipswich and Harwich, two ships and one pinnace; Newcastle, three ships and one pinnace.
[156] *Calendar of State Papers Domestic, Elizabeth, 1581-90*, 2 vols. (London, 1865), II, 475.
[157] AB iv, 563. The owners of the latter were demanding more, and a conference was ordered held. On 4 May more was conceded to the owners of the "Rose" and £16 voted to Thomas Spicer and Abraham Combe, owners of the pinnace. See AB iv, 566.

on as of 29 April.[158] Other preparations were set for the same day, with the purchase of 100 lbs. of powder and the appointment of a committee to view a cast-iron piece offered at 10s. the hundred-weight.[159]

In the interim, letters had been dispatched to the Lord Treasurer and the Council begging that the country about the city be charged one half the costs of the ships.[160] To these pleas the Council yielded so far as to direct that the Earl of Bath, Lord Lieutenant of Devon and Exeter, should levy a contribution from the creeks and the hundreds near the port.[161] The Mayor of Exeter was to act as general collector, and any recalcitrants were to be hailed before the Lords of the Council.[162] By 3 June commissioners from the creek hundreds in Devon had been appointed to treat with the mayor about the contributions for the ships,[163] and on 10 June the Chamber ordered the levying of a rate in the city, directing the mayor and the three Deputy Lieutenants of Exeter to collect it.[164] Previously, as early as 24 April,[165] a collection had been made from eighty-nine of the most prominent citizens, who gave sums varying from £1 to £20 each, and totaling £373. The second collection, made in June,[166] was taken up among the humbler inhabitants in sums varying from 32s. to 2s. 6d. Fifty-five contributed to this, but the total was only about £40. Before the second collection was made, the Council had written down urging that the charges be levied so that the poor might be spared as much as was conveniently possible.[167] Their

---

[158] *Ibid.*   [159] *Ibid.*

[160] AB iv, 565, 2 May 1588.

[161] APC, Elizabeth, XVI, 54.

[162] The Chamber had to write to the Council again in July. Although the latter had commanded the creek parishes to contribute, the miners dwelling there refused to contribute, alleging an exemption from the Lord Warden of the Stannaries. The Chamber now requested a specific command that the miners contribute along with the other residents of the creek parishes. They also asked that they be relieved of one month's charges for victuals (they were now charged for four months' victuals for their three ships). The Council conceded both applications. See PRO, SP 12/212/53, 16 July 1588 and Endorsement.

[163] AB iv, 568.   [164] AB iv, 570.

[165] AB v, 1.   [166] AB iv, 555.

[167] APC, Elizabeth, XVI, 112, to Mayor of Exeter.

Lordships added that they doubted not that the wealthier would be willing "to relieve and ease their poor neighbours." In another letter written the same day they specified the sum to be levied in the adjoining hundreds as £600,[168] "which is not half the charge."

There followed through the summer numerous authorizations of payment for revictualing the city's ships. In June the town clerk was sent to London to treat with Walsingham about revictualing arrangements as ordered by the Lord Admiral,[169] while Richard Dorchester was sent to the fleet to carry out the task.[170] In early July the alarm seemed to have subsided, for the Chamber ordered the sale of rye—previously purchased in fear of invasion—in an effort to bring down the market price.[171] There is no direct mention of the battle in the Exeter records, but by 15 August the city, as parsimonious as the Queen, was seeking to recoup at least part of its expenses. Six barrels of gunpowder were ordered sold in order to recover the money contributed for their purchase.[172] Before the end of the month the mayor was ordered to survey the victuals, powder, etc., which remained and to sell them.[173] On the last day of the month order was taken to pay the mariners their last two months' wages, at the rate of 10s. per month, per mariner;[174] the same day, the goods left on the ships were ordered sold. The autumn was occupied with various accounting connected with the expedition. In November a committee was sent to see Sir William Courtenay[175] for £130 still owed by the country parishes; if they obtained no satisfaction Mr. Periam was to make suit to Secretary Walsingham for an order to the Devon justices. In December[176] freemen who had not paid their share of the contribution were threatened with imprisonment, while nonfreemen were to be bound to appear before the Council. In the meantime a dispute had broken out with George Rawley, the owner of one of the ships, and he had appealed to Walsingham. The Secretary wrote a letter which was a masterpiece

---

[168] *Ibid.*, to Bishop of Exeter, Sir William Courtenay, et al.
[169] AB iv, 571.   [170] AB iv, 572.
[171] AB iv, 576.   [172] AB v, 82.
[173] AB v, 84.   [174] AB v, 86.
[175] AB v, 103.   [176] AB v, 108.

of velvet-gloved threat.[177] Declaring that he regarded Rawley's claim as just, he added, "I have staied him from acquaynting their Lordships with your slackness herein upon the perswation I have that this my own letter shall sufficientlie prevaile with you without occasioning him to use any furthur sute, which would be to your molestacion." A final clearance of the Armada accounts was made with the payment of £384 to the city by the Queen's treasurer at Plymouth, Sir John Hawkins, in May 1589.[178] The city thus recovered from the royal government at least a part of the sums laid out for the expedition.

The remaining years of the reign were full of alarms of invasion, especially on the vulnerable coasts of the West. These cost the city considerable sums. Members of the Chamber apparently contributed to the Portuguese expedition of 1589 and recovered only 6s. 8d. in the pound on their investment.[179] In 1595 the Council commanded the city share with Barnstaple, Plymouth, Totnes, and Dartmouth the cost of fitting out four ships.[180] After considerable grumbling the city accepted an arrangement by which they were to fit out one ship by themselves, with the assistance of the creek parishes as in 1588.[181] It was a costly adventure, for £1,056 was laid out, the city paying the bulk of the bill.[182] When the ship returned to Portsmouth the Chamber hastily dispatched two members to recover any salable items, but they found themselves involved in a dispute with the owners, which was settled only by Council intervention.[183] The claims connected with this voyage dragged on for another two years, and in 1599 collections were still being made.[184]

Various subsidiary duties fell to the city also during wartime. One was the provision of military intelligence. As a coastal city with

[177] HMC Rep., 63, Letter 95.   [178] AB v, 129.
[179] AB v, 158.
[180] BM, Lansdowne MS., vol. 80, no. 41.
[181] AB v, 352.
[182] APC, Elizabeth, XXVI, 144. By September 1596 the creek parishes had contributed only £121, the city £570, and £365 was still outstanding. The Privy Council commanded the Earl of Bath to enforce collections from the creek parishes.
[183] AB v, 360 and 362.   [184] AB v, 439.

trading connections abroad, Exeter was a center of foreign communications, and it was the duty of the Exeter magistrates to sift out and forward any such information they could obtain. In 1596 four sailors brought home the news of the English victory at Cadiz, and after careful examination, the information, together with other news from Exeter merchants coming from Morlaix, was passed on by the mayor to the Council.[185] In 1599 a sailor who had served in the Spanish and Portuguese merchant marines and then escaped to England on an Exeter ship coming from Morlaix brought with him a Spanish proclamation, which the Mayor of Exeter forwarded to London.[186] Very frequently the information came directly through the Exeter merchants themselves returning from Brittany. In an age when such channels were the normal means of communication, the careful collection of news of this sort was an important task, and an added duty of importance for the already heavily laden Exeter magistrates.

Similarly the city was a center for the Queen's post service. The mayor was responsible for the provision of post horses and for the speedy forwarding of any dispatches coming up from Plymouth for London, or originating at Exeter. This was a yearly expense which fell in part on the city, and in a year like 1588 could amount to the sum of £40.[187] In 1589 a new rate was established by the Controller of the Queen's Posts, and it was ordered that some particular person be made responsible for the service in each town.[188] It is not clear when a postmaster was first appointed at Exeter, but there was certainly one by 1600.[189] This man was paid a certain sum by the city, for which he was to be responsible for all charges and duties connected with the royal post.[190]

The coming of peace in 1603 brought a welcome end to the exactions of the Spanish war; and for two decades the city was free from wartime responsibilities. Only the routines of muster and drill,

[185] *Calendar of State Papers Domestic, Elizabeth* (1595–97), IV, 258.
[186] *Ibid.*, V, 183.
[187] RR, 30–31 Elizabeth.
[188] HMC Rep., 64.
[189] AB v, 425 and 475.
[190] The post system at Exeter clearly did not function altogether efficiently

and the replenishing of gunpowder stores, remained to be carried out in peacetime. But the wars of the 1620's brought a close to this agreeable interval, and the demands made by the Stuart government were far heavier than those of the previous war. In 1621 an unprecedented order for 20 footmen for the army was made (out of a total of 300 for Devon). The city's protests were anguished, and with the aid of the Lord Lieutenant Bath they seem to have escaped.[191] But the effort was in vain, for in 1625 the city sent thirty men to the army at a cost of £52.[192]

In the meantime the old obligation of naval aid was also being pressed. In 1626 the government ordered the fitting out of two ships, each of 200 tons, furnished, victualed, and manned.[193] The city made desperate entreaties to be spared from such an obligation at a time of trade suspension and plague, and the Devon justices backed their plea.[194] The latter pointed out that the recent loans would not have been paid by the Devon towns had they not supposed them to be a final satisfaction of royal demands. Whether or not the city's petitions were granted we do not know; there is no record of ships being fitted out.

On top of these heavy impositions, the royal government added those of extraordinary taxation.[195] In 1622, the city had contributed to the benevolence £228;[196] in 1625, twenty-four wealthy citizens paid £136 in Privy Seal loans.[197] The heaviest demand was that of

---

in 1595, for there is a very angry letter of that year from Sir Thomas Gorges to Robert Cecil, in which the former relates that, though he arrived at Exeter in the evening, he was unable to obtain post-horses until 9:00 the next morning, and then "only such as carry wood up and down the town." Gorges urged Cecil to order the mayor to answer for such contempt. *Calendar State Papers Domestic, Elizabeth* (1595–97), IV, 73.

[191] PRO, SP 14/127/29.

[192] See *Calendar State Papers Domestic, Charles I, 1625–26*, 28, and ECM, Letter 285.

[193] PRO, SP 16/35/5 and 16/51/45.

[194] PRO, SP 16/60/64 and 72.

[195] The city had already voluntarily given £367 to the Winter Queen for the war in Bohemia. See Letter 195, 196, and 196-A.

[196] PRO, SP 14/131/63.

[197] See ECM, Free Loan Papers, no. 13.

the free loan of 1627 which cost the citizens at least £690.[198] This last was collected only after much delay and prodding by the magistrates. In July 1627 there were seventy-five defaulters, and in the following winter still twenty-six, assessed at about £80.

To add to Exeter's woes in these troubled years came the vexations of billeting.[199] Soldiers had been passing through the city since the fall of 1626,[200] but not until the following year were they quartered there.[201] About 160 of them were in the city for over a month and cost £277.[202] The Earl of Bedford and the Chamber jointly moved the Council to relieve Exeter of this burden, and this was granted on condition that Exeter pay for their maintenance elsewhere.[203] The Council also granted a commission of martial law to protect the citizens against the recurrent disorders caused by soldiers in transit.[204] During these years another £164 of city money was spent for military purposes as well as the £40 spent in London in negotiations for the removal of the troops.[205]

Peace came in 1630 but not an end to financial exactions. Exeter's assessment in the ship money loans was £350 (out of £1,280 levied on the Devon towns).[206] There seems to have been little difficulty in securing prompt payment of this money at Exeter until the very eve of the meeting of the Short Parliament. In 1639 there was a sharp letter to the Chamber from the Privy Council about shortages in collections, and a report of the following winter lists five defaulters, none of them apparently an Exeter citizen.[207]

---

[198] See PRO, SP 16/51/45; 16/66/26; 16/76/14; and 16/83/56 as well as ECM, Free Loan Papers.

[199] It should be remembered that along with these war levies Exeter had paid £500 in 1620 for an expedition against the pirates.

[200] AB vii, 647, 648.

[201] Letter 301 and AB vii, 684.

[202] Letter 301.

[203] APC, Charles I, Sept. 1627–June 1628, 144, 147. They were asked to pay for 100 men at 3s. 6d. a head each week according to the Acts of the Privy Council. ECM Letter 304 says 160 men.

[204] ECM, Letter 308.

[205] RR, 2–3, 3–4 Charles I and AB vii, 684.

[206] SPD, 12 Sept. 1635, 376/35 ccxcvii.

[207] PRO, SP 16/444/74 and PC 2/51 (Pt. 2), v. 17, f. 590.

War bore very heavily on the Exeter community during our century. Unfortunately for the city, all England's wars during this period involved Spain and France and thus disrupted Exeter's normal trade patterns. War taxation had to be financed at moments of trade depression. At the best such taxation was grievous, for besides the direct financial sacrifice, there was the tiresome task of squeezing money from reluctant citizens as well as the vexatious and tedious work of administering purchase and supply. We may be mildly amused at the penny-pinching devices of the Chamber, scrambling after stray barrels of gunpowder or remnants of ships' stores, but the fact remains that war was a very serious strain for so modest a trading community. We need not be surprised if there is little evidence of the high-spirited pride traditionally associated with the Armada year, but rather a worrying concern about money matters and an almost ludicrous effort to escape from the financial burden of war. This nascent irritation in the city hints at the possible limits of action by the royal government. The most faithful servants balked when the load became too heavy. The cautious policy of Elizabeth in avoiding any steps which might increase the financial needs of the Crown showed a clear insight into political reality. Correspondingly the far heavier demands made by the Stuarts, although reluctantly met, must have left a bad taste.

Our century was one of strong, centralized government. At Exeter as elsewhere its commands were obeyed and its policy executed, but underneath the respectful, almost reverential, obedience of the local officers, there were certain frictions. These officers labored under the sometimes painful anomalies of their position. The interests of the community of which they were leaders did not always coincide with royal policy. When this happened, they could not refuse to obey the unwelcome commands from above. But they did not lack an armory for resistance. Petition and remonstrance backed by the voices of city friends at court could win exemptions or concessions for the city. Such oblique forms of resistance did not aim at contradicting or reversing royal policy. Their purpose was purely local, a determination to win some exception from a general hardship for this particular city. But the cumulative effect may have been considerable in slowing the action of the central government. These efforts certainly reveal once again the resolute skill with which the community guarded its interests as far as it could, even against the irresistible commands of the state.

Chapter Ten

The Civic Community:
A Synthesis

The preceding chapters have formed a kind of itinerary of Exeter, in which we have traveled from point to point, viewing the community from many angles, exploring every corner and crevice of city life. This final chapter will be devoted to obtaining a single and comprehensive view, in an attempt to bring into one vision the whole mass of detail. A point of focus is required to give ordered structure to the picture. Looking back over the evidence, it is not difficult to see where that focus must lie. For wherever our exploration has taken us, regardless of the angle of view, one fact has constantly emerged as most prominent. This is the domination of community life by a small group of families, interlocked by personal and business ties, and monopolizing wealth, power, and prestige. So absolute was this monopoly that the rest of the city's inhabitants seem hardly to emerge from the shadows of history. At best they form a kind of chorus for the actions of this little group of leading actors. Undoubtedly the nature of the evidence heightens this impression and probably distorts our view somewhat. But there is little that can be done to remedy this, and perhaps we need not be too deeply disturbed. The ruling minority did in fact hold the stage of civic life, filling all the great roles and dictating every movement of the drama. Here, then, is the focus of our picture. By concentrating on the life of the ruling minority we can also hope to see, although not so clearly nor in so great detail, the proportions and lines of the whole community pattern.

We can begin by surveying the distribution of wealth in the city. Since economic and social privilege were practically identical in the community, this will enable us at the same time to block in the main social stratifications. The basis for such a calculation is the great subsidy of 1524–25,[1] the rolls of which are mostly intact for Exeter. Perhaps the most comprehensive levy of the century, it fell on nearly every level of the population, reaching to the 20s. a year wage earner. It was a comprehensive tax, falling on lands, goods, and wages, according to the nature of the subject's income. Only the latter two categories are of interest since few Exonians were taxed on land within the city. The provisions of the statute were simple. The government distinguished three primary groups. One, consisting of subjects assessed on £20 or more in goods, was to pay 1s. in the pound. Those assessed on goods under £20 but not less than £2 were to pay 6d. in the pound; wage earners receiving £1 or more a year were to pay a flat 4d. Payments were spread over four years. There were additional refinements for the wealthy; those assessed at £40 or over were to pay an "anticipation" a year in advance. Taxpayers worth £50 or more paid an extra shilling on the pound in the fourth year.

The figures in Table VII must be used with certain reservation. First of all, assessments above £40 are conventional and do not represent anything like real wealth. The rich were able to influence the assessors very effectively, and these figures therefore represent only relative levels of wealth. At the lower end of the scale, the assessment figures probably come pretty close to financial reality. Second, a large number of Exeter's inhabitants were so wretchedly poor as to be assessed *nil*, owners of nothing visible even to the assessor's sharp eyes. According to a rough calculation based on the preliminary survey of 1522 this group probably numbered over 30 per cent, perhaps not much under 40 per cent of the whole population.

---

[1] See PRO, E/179/96/171, 179/96/146–7, 179/96/155, 179/97/188. For the subsidy see *Statutes of the Realm*, III, 230, 14–15 Henry VIII, c. 26. Dr. Hoskins has drawn my attention also to the preliminary survey of 1522 (ECM, Book 156a) which contains the *nil* assessments.

TABLE VII.—*Distribution of Wealth, 1524–25*

	Assessments in goods												Assessments in wages					
	£300–100		£99–40		£39–20		£19–10		£9–5		£4–2		Over 20s.		20s.[a]		Number illegible	Total number
	No.	%	No.	%	No.	%	No.	%	No.	%	No.	%	No.	%	No.	%		
St Lawrence	1	2	2	4	6	12	3	6	4	8	10	20	8	16	16	32		50
St. Stephen	3	7	3	7	0	0	3	7	6	14	6	15	4	9	17	40		42
St. Martin	1	1.5	4	6	0	0	1	1.5	7	11	7	11	26	40	17	26	2	65
St. Paul	0	0	2	5	2	5	2	5	1	2	10	24	15	36	10	23		42
All Saints G. St.	1	3	3	9	2	6	5	15	1	3	3	9	5	15	13	40		33
St. Pancras	0	0	0	0	3	19	3	19	2	12	3	19	2	12	3	19		16
St. Kerian	1	4	0	0	0	0	2	8	2	8	1	4	1	4	4	17	13	24
St. Petrock	8	14	5	9	4	7	5	9	6	11	14	25	9	16	4	7		55
St. Mary Arches	6	25	4	17	2	8	2	8	0	0	4	17	3	13	2	8	1	24
St. John	0	0	0	0	0	0	7	15	6	13	12	25	9	20	13	28		47
All Saints on Walls	0	0	0	0	0	0	1	5	2	10	5	25	0	0	12	60		20
St. Mary Steps	0	0	0	0	1	5	0	0	1	5	7	35	0	0	11	55		20
St. George	2	3	2	3	6	10	7	12	7	12	7	12	11	20	13	23	2	57
St. David	1	2	3	6	2	4	2	4	0	0	8	17	15	32	13	27	3	47
St. Mary Major	0	0	2	1.5	9	6	7	5	14	10	25	17	59	40	27	18	3	146
Holy Trinity	1	1	1	1	3	3	7	7	12	13	23	24	6	6	37	37	5	95
St. Olave	4	9	0	0	2	4	5	11	2	4	11	23	3	7	13	30	5	45
St. Edmund and Exe I.	0	0	2	3	3	5	6	9	5	7	16	25	21	30	14	21		67
St. Sidwell	0	0	0	0	0	0	0	0	7	12	30	50	2	3	19	30	3	61
Totals	29	3	33	3.5	45	4.7	68	7.1	85	8.9	202	21	199	20.8	258	27	37[b]	956

[a] This total includes those assessed £1 in *goods*. They paid the same tax as those earning £1 per annum.

[b] 3.9 per cent.

Table VII distinguishes eight income levels, but the pattern can be somewhat simplified. In the 3 per cent assessed over £100 stand the great magnates of the city, men of commanding wealth. The not much larger group assessed between £40 and £100 were clearly among the well-to-do, an "upper-middle class" enjoying a privileged and comfortable place in society. Those above £20 were viewed by the government as belonging to the wealthier segment of its subjects; somewhere between £20 and £10 we pass from modest affluence to mere competence, and below £10 we are probably in the "lower-middle class." There is a notable increase in the numbers assessed below £5, and it is probably here that we reach the "poor" although there are gradations below this. Probably at this lowest economic level the distinction between assessment in wages and assessment in goods represents administrative convenience rather than real economic difference. It may not be unreasonable to lump together as a single economic group the whole great mass assessed at £4 or less.

The nature of the distribution is clear enough—an "upper class" containing 6 per cent of the population, a "middle class" containing at most 20 per cent. To put it another way, those assessed at £2 in goods (130), workers earning £2 or less a year, and those few (36) assessed at £1 in goods, make up 60 per cent of the taxed population; and a submerged 35 per cent are not even on the rolls. In terms of the assessed valuation of property, one half was owned by 3 per cent, and another 38 per cent owned by 16 per cent of the assessable population (Table VIII). Not only was wealth concentrated in the hands of a few, but the lot of more than half the population was grinding poverty. One understands more easily the compulsive fears of the ruling class toward any kind of public disturbance. In this grim society, the rich few might well dread the violence of the submerged many. The hearth tax returns for 1671–72, which correspond roughly to those for 1524–25, have led Professor Hoskins to conclude that "70% of the population could be classed as poor, about 19% as relatively comfortable, 8½% as prosperous, and 2½% as well-to-do."

In the absence of similar studies, it is not possible to compare

TABLE VIII.—*Distribution of Tax Assessments, 1524–25*

Amount of assessment (pounds)	Total value, assessed valuation (pounds)	Percentage of total city assessed valuation	Percentage of taxed population
100 or over	4,294	50	3
40–99	1,410	16.4	3.6
20–39	1,002	11.7	5
10–19	818	9.9	7.4
5–9	508	5.9	9.2
1–4	542	6.1	26
Total percentage of inhabitants taxed on goods			54.2
Total percentage of inhabitants taxed on wages			45.8
			100.0

Exeter effectively with other English cities. Hoskins' figures for Leicester[2] show a very different state of affairs since in that much smaller market town no inhabitants were assessed over £40. At Exeter on the other hand 60 per cent of the first year's payment on the subsidy was borne by those paying the "anticipation," that is, those assessed at over £40. (At Bristol the comparable figure was 72 per cent and at Norwich 73 per cent.) What this suggests is that the richer Exeter merchants had relatively few peers in the provinces, and those in a handful of larger cities. It is noteworthy that only six provincial cities paid over £500 in the first installment of the subsidy: Norwich, Coventry, Bristol, Salisbury, Exeter, and Ipswich, in that order.[3] Without doubt, in each case, the bulk of this sum came from the pockets of the small class of the very rich.

The geographical distribution of wealth within the city is also a matter of interest, especially when contrasted with the pattern which Dr. Hoskins has uncovered for the late seventeenth century.[4] In the early sixteenth century a nucleus of wealthy parishes was formed by three in the North quarter, St. Mary Arches, St. Petrock, and St.

[2] See *Studies in Social History*, 44.
[3] I owe to Dr. Hoskins the figures in this and the preceding paragraph.
[4] W. G. Hoskins, *Industry, Trade, and People in Exeter, 1688–1800* (History of Exeter Research Group, Monograph No. 6) (Manchester, 1935) 116 seq.

Olave. Not only was the percentage of well-to-do citizens high in these parishes (25 per cent in St. Mary Arches), but the percentage of the very poor was also small (only 8 per cent in St. Mary Arches and 7 per cent in St. Petrock). They were the center from which the city was governed as a subsidy roll of 1586 confirms.[5] Since this subsidy fell on a limited class, only the wealthier citizens are listed. No fewer than twelve members of the Twenty-Four came from St. Petrock; three more dwelt in St. Mary Arches; and another represented the small parish of St. Olave. At the other extreme of wealth were the peripheral parishes partly or wholly outside the walls. In All Saints on the Walls and St. Mary Steps more than half the inhabitants fell in the poorest category. In St. Sidwell only about a third fell in this category; half were assessed at between £2 and £4 in goods, and no one in the parish at above £8 in goods. The pattern was fundamentally the same as that revealed by Dr. Hoskins: a wealthy nuclear area centering on St. Petrock, surrounded by a ring of poorer districts.

The structure of power in the city faithfully mirrored economic realities. The same men commanded both wealth and power, and as we have seen in the preceding chapters, brought within their control every aspect of life in this tightly regulated community. The center of this structure was, of course, the Twenty-Four. The prerequisite to entrance into this body was commercial success. The biographies of the mayors of Exeter narrated by John Hooker reveal wide divergence of social origin, but all these careers are marked by one common achievement; each in his turn "grew to good wealth and riches" before entering the ranks of the privileged. Moreover, success in the business world determined not only entry into the Twenty-four, but also advance in the civic *cursus honorum*. Personal defects of character might hold a man back, as in the case of the haughty John Midwinter or the high-tempered John Levermore, but the real barrier to advancement was insufficiency of money. We have already seen how heavy was the financial burden of office and how difficult it was to escape after climbing the first rung or two on the ladder of dignities. The rule is well illustrated by the single

[5] PRO, Transcript, second part of Lay Subsidy granted 18 Elizabeth.

exception recorded in our period. In 1565 John Wolcott was elected mayor under unusual circumstances.[6] He had passed all the other offices twenty years before[7] but "by reason of his age and his small welthe it was not thought nor ment that ever the office of the mayroltie shold have fallen unto his lott." He had once been "a greate merchaunt and adventured verie mich, whereby he had greate welth; but yn the ende his losses were so greate that he was verie poore and lyved yn very meane estate." However, it fell out (for reasons which Hooker does not make clear) that Wolcott was chosen mayor. The Chamber thereupon ordered his house to be furnished up properly and an allowance made for his housekeeping. It is apparent enough that this was an exceptional occasion, and that ordinarily lack of wealth was a bar to high office.

Yet among the members of the Twenty-Four there was considerable variation in personal wealth. At the top of the scale stood figures like the elder Hurst, lord of seven manors in Devonshire and of much other land.[8] Even a relatively lesser member of the ruling circle, Christopher Spicer, who died in 1600 at a rather early age, left a net estate of about £4,200. But not all the members of the Twenty-Four boasted such prosperity as Spicer, much less such wealth as the Hursts. Thomas Spurway, a councillor who died in 1595, left less than a thousand pounds; Henry Maunder left only £342; while Hugh Pope, who begged release from the Twenty-Four in 1565, left but £191 on his death four years later.[9] Inequality of fortune probably meant inequality of influence at the council board.

Within the limited circle of the Twenty-Four there were yet narrower cliques, formed around some dominant figure like the elder Hurst, or built on the family alliances described below. These casual but effective groupings are reflected in an Act Book phrase of 1613: "whereas the Mayor, the Recorder, Mr. Howell, Mr. Prouze and other the *principall* of this house...."[10] The clerk un-

---

[6] ECM, Book 51, fol. 355.
[7] He was receiver in 1543.
[8] There is a copy of his will (PCC 3 Tashe) in the Exeter City Library.
[9] ECM, Inventory 76, 57, 2, 12.
[10] AB vii, 96, 11 Sept. 1613.

consciously records the sway of the dominant few in the Chamber. In a number of cases a kind of client relationship may have existed. Three councillors were admitted freemen of the city as apprentices of William Hurst; two served in the Twenty-Four in his lifetime. At least a dozen other such cases occurred in the latter half of the sixteenth century.

Very striking are the family relationships within the Twenty-Four, where a few interrelated families played a preponderant role. Two of the most important were the Hursts and the Periams. The former were represented in the Chamber by two members, but one brother, John, died after a short term of office. William Hurst lived to a great age and filled the mayoral chair no less than five times between 1524 and 1561. With his death the family disappeared from active participation in civic affairs. The Periams, on the other hand, occupied the mayoralty in three successive generations, and a Periam sat in the Chamber from 1523 to 1616. Their interests were early divided between London and Exeter; in 1557 John Periam was dismissed from the Twenty-Four because he had been absent from the city for a year and a quarter.[11] But in August 1559 he was re-elected to the Chamber and twice served as mayor.[12] His son, the second John, was elected mayor in 1587 while away in London and he had to be summoned by the city sergeant.[13] Previously, in 1585, he had refused the governorship of the Merchant Adventurers of Exeter on the grounds that he intended to reside permanently in London.[14] In 1587, however, he took the office, and until his death in 1616 the Periam family remained prominent in the city.

The three Martin brothers, sons of the mayor of 1533, and his wife Margaret, daughter of William Hurst, likewise established a considerable family interest in the civic government. This family was represented in the Twenty-Four from 1564 to 1635. Nicholas, the eldest, was mayor in 1574 and 1585; the next brother, Thomas, was mayor in 1581; while the third, William, held the office in 1590 and 1600. Several other families contributed more than one

---

[11] AB i, 313.
[13] AB iv, 520.
[12] AB ii, 357.
[14] Cotton, *Elizabethan Guild*, 35.

mayor during this period. The three Prestwoods—Thomas, his brother Richard, and the former's son, another Thomas—sat in the Chamber continuously from the early 1530's until the death of the younger Thomas in his mayoral year, 1576. The two Midwinter brothers, John and Robert, were members of the Twenty-Four for well over thirty years. The Spicers contributed three mayors while another member of the family, Christopher, died after having reached the receivership. The Smiths and the Chapells each gave three mayors to the city during this epoch. In short, 11 families held the office during 48 out of the 110 mayoral terms between 1530 and 1640. An examination of the Merchant Adventurers Company reveals that nine of these families provided governors for that body during twenty-one out of the forty-four yearly terms between 1559 and 1601.[15]

Moreover, the intimacy of personal association and of business connection was reinforced by family ties. We cannot set forth here, even if it could be drawn up, a table of genealogical relationships in the city, but a few can be pointed out. Marriage was not an unusual way of obtaining entrance into the ranks of the oligarchy itself. Thomas Spurway, for instance, the mayor of 1540, married the daughter of Geoffrey Lewis, the mayor of 1519, and with her money established himself in Exeter, where he prospered.[16] She outlived her husband and, ironically, married the gentle-born but impecunious Walter Staplehill, who duplicated his predecessor's career and in time rose to the mayoralty (1556). The elder Prestwood (mayor in 1550) founded his family fortunes in a similar fashion. Born in Worcester and apprenticed in London, he traveled to Exeter for his master; there met the widow of John Bodley, wooed and married her, and settled down to a prosperous career as a merchant in the Western capital.

The families constituting the inner circle of the oligarchy were also linked by marriage. The Hursts, for example, were allied to the

---

[15] *Ibid.*, 42–43.
[16] All biographical data on the mayors, except where otherwise noted, comes from John Hooker's *Commonplace Book* (ECM, Book 51, fol. 341 seq.).

Martins, the Yards, and the Drakes by marriages of William Hurst's daughters,[17] while his grandson married Mary Peter,[18] daughter of John Peter, the mayor of 1557, 1562, and 1575. The alliance with the Martins outlasted the death of Richard Martin (the husband of Margaret Hurst). William Hurst left legacies to William Martin and made him his executor.[19] In due course of time, the Hurst line failed (with Nicholas, the grandson of William Hurst), and the Hurst estate of Oxton passed to William Martin, the son of Nicholas and grandson of Richard Martin and Margaret Hurst. The Martins made other matrimonial alliances also. The same William mentioned above, who became Recorder of Exeter in 1605, married the daughter of Thomas Prestwood,[20] the mayor who died in office in 1576, so that, in his person, the fortunes of the Martins, the Hursts, and the Prestwoods were united.

The Periams also had their share of city alliances. The older William Periam married the daughter of John Blackaller, the mayor of 1530;[21] his son married one of two sisters, the other of whom became the wife of the older John Bodley (one of the merchants who aided Russell in 1549)[22] and mother of the founder of the Bodleian. The list of marital alliances within the city oligarchy could be extended at length. Grace Tothill, daughter of the mayor of 1552 and sister of the Recorder, married first James Walker (councillor 1561–63 and father of the mayor of 1625) and secondly Thomas Brewerton, the mayor of 1571 and 1580.[23] By her first husband she had two daughters. One married John Howell, the mayor of 1599; the other married George Smith, mayor three times, knighted by James I. Edward Hert, the town clerk from 1578 to 1620, married[24] the daughter of Richard Prouze, mayor in 1578 and 1589, while

---

[17] See 1 PM Chancery C 142/150/173 (transcript in archives of Devon and Cornwall Record Society, deposited in Exeter City Library).

[18] Genealogy (Pole 261) preserved in Exeter City Library in file headed "Hurst."

[19] See transcript of William Hurst's will in Exeter City Library.

[20] John Prince, *The Worthies of Devon* (London, 1810), 576.

[21] Genealogy in Exeter City Library under heading "Periam."

[22] Hooker, *History*, II, 83.

[23] Alexander, *Exeter Members*, 210.

[24] *Ibid.*, 209.

the latter's son, John (mayor 1608 and 1619), married the daughter of Eustace Oliver, a merchant who sat in the Twenty-Four from 1560 to 1571.[25] To continue such a list would only confuse the reader and labor a point already made. Enough has been said to indicate the elaborate family network which tied together the ruling circles of the city. We need not assume too much from this. Family ties can be divisive as well as cohesive, but the important fact is that the economic group dominant in the city was also bound together by more intimate relationships.

These data give sufficient evidence of the formal structure of the governing group in the city, but we should like to know more about them as individuals. Where did they come from? How wealthy were they and how was their wealth constituted? What were their religious opinions; their political and moral ones? What did they read? In short, what manner of men were they? Unfortunately, these questions are more rhetorical than real, for they cannot be answered in any satisfactory manner. We can only marshal available evidence.

The mayoral biographies which Hooker included in his *Commonplace Book* are a central source of information about the personal careers of these men. Above all they give us a good idea of their origins, both geographical and personal. Perhaps the most striking fact is the diversity of their backgrounds. Most of them either came from some place outside Exeter or else were the sons of newcomers. Indeed, most of the families we have just discussed, who came to dominate Exeter affairs during our period, were founded by outsiders. The first Periam came from Broadclyst in Devon; the first Hurst from Modbury in the same county.[26] The Martins were a Dorsetshire family;[27] the elder Prestwood was born in Worcester; the Midwinters at Ottery St. Mary. It is not possible to give a clear account of the other families mentioned above. Possibly the Spicers were an old city family; their name appears among the fourteenth-

[25] *Ibid.*, 210.   [26] *Ibid.*, 206.
[27] Prince, *Worthies*, 574.

century mayors.[28] The birthplaces of the other mayors whose biographies Hooker included were widely separated. Several towns in
Devon are represented;[29] still others came from farther afield, two
from Somerset, one each from Suffolk, Wales, and Cheshire. One,
Kirk, may have been an alien.[30] John Lynne, mayor in 1628, came
of a Cambridgeshire family.[31] While Devon provided the greater
number of these immigrants, there was a substantial proportion
coming from quite distant parts of the kingdom. Quite certainly a
large proportion of the Exeter governing class was not born in the
city but came from elsewhere seeking fortune.

It is hard to estimate the effects of this fact. If the situation provided a flow of new talent into the city, it may also have had the
effect of strengthening Exeter's conservatism as a community. These
newcomers, eager to win acceptance in a community firmly established in a pattern of deep-rooted customary ways, were all the more
willing to conform to the existing practice of the city. Their very insecurity increased their conservatism. On the other hand, the new
spirit of enterprise and venture which showed itself in Exeter during
this century may have owed something to the new citizens, who
were less confined within any customary framework of practice than
their native-born fellow citizens. At any rate Exeter, during the sixteenth century, drew ambitious men seeking commercial success
from a very wide area.

The social origins of the Exeter mayors were almost as diverse as
their geographical provenance. Virtually all classes in the realm
were represented. The first Martin, Richard, mayor in 1533, was the
second son of Sir Richard, a knight, of Athelhampton in Dorset;[32]
his mother was one of the Pawletts of Hinton St. George. Griffin
Ameredith, the city burgess in the first Parliament of Edward VI,

[28] Oliver, *History*, 229.

[29] Spurway came from Tiverton, Tucker from Moreton Hampstead, Staplehill from Tresham, Knight and Chaffe from Somerset, Bucknam from Suffolk,
Ameredith from Wales, and Richardson from Cheshire.

[30] In the 1524–25 subsidy, the number of aliens was 28 out of a total of 919.

[31] Alexander, *Exeter Members*, 194. Of a random list of 37 apprentices entering the weavers guild between 1615 and 1634, 20 were born outside Exeter,
all of them in the four western counties (Youings, *Tuckers Hall*, 78–79).

[32] Prince, *Worthies*, 574.

who died in 1557 just after holding the receivership, came of a Welsh family of great lineage but small lands. At the other extreme of the social scale stood the Periams. Although Hooker assures us that William, the mayor of 1532, was of good parentage, he goes on to reveal that his father was a franklin, and that the son was apprenticed as a capper. Moreover, he notes that Periam was of a rough and ready exterior and not used to polite society; perhaps his marriage to Mayor Blackaller's daughter helped here. When William Periam held the mayoralty he was careful to take the advice of those best qualified around him rather than to rely upon his own judgment. His rise in the social scale must have been as spectacular on the local scene as that of any Victorian industrial magnate.

Between these two extremes several backgrounds are represented. Some of the men, of course, like Henry Hamlyn, the founder of the Exeter cloth market, were born into merchant families (his father was mayor in 1500) and trained in the "art of merchandise." (His earlier life was spent abroad in Brittany as a merchant.) William Bucknam, the mayor of 1541, was the nephew of a former mayor, who himself came to Exeter from Suffolk and founded the family fortunes. The nephew, reared in the trade, prospered and added to his inherited wealth. The Midwinter brothers represent a slight variation of this type. They came of a dyer's family at Ottery St. Mary but shifted to "merchandising" and there made their fortunes. We have already mentioned those who began as apprentices of one of the older merchants and then made their own way to success. Simon Knight, the mayor of 1570 and 1579, began as an apprentice of Hurst, acting as his agent overseas before striking out on an independent career.

There was also a sprinkling of less conventional careers. Robert Tucker, mayor in 1543, came of "mean parentage" from Moreton Hampstead on the edge of Dartmoor. He had served in the Spanish campaign of 1512, but finding the military life not likely to lead to any permanent position, came home and married a widow who leased the barton of Duryard from the city. A fortunate dispute with one of the city servants resulted in an injury for which the city recompensed him, and with this money he set up as a baker and brewer, prospered, and was so well accepted in the higher social circles that he was chosen to represent the city at court when the grant of county status was sought. He won the favor even of King Henry himself. His family prospered with him, for his brother was the last Abbot of Buckland. Thomas Spurway, born at Tiverton, the second son of a good family, initially made his way in life as receiver to the Earls of Devon and bailiff of Exe Island. The fortunate marriage mentioned above saved him from ruin in the crash of the Courtenay fortunes, and the prestige which he had obtained in the Earl's service, added to his own talents, won him pre-eminence in civic affairs, although he seems not to have become an active merchant. Another figure who made his fortune outside the mercantile world was Thomas Chaffe, mayor in 1568 and 1576. Born in Somerset, he was brought to Exeter by his uncle, the bishop's register, sent to the cathedral school to be trained as a chorister, and then to the Exeter High School. Eventually he became assistant to his uncle and a proctor of the ecclesiastical courts of the diocese as well as register of the dean and chapter's peculiars. He was the only one of the ecclesiastical lay officials who appeared prominently in city affairs in this period.

The most fascinating aspect of the life of this world is the process of social acceptance that went on in the civic community. The city was a kind of neutral ground where scions of the gentry, the yeomanry, and of husbandmen met on equal terms to contend for the prize of economic success and the rewards of social prestige which followed it. Griffin Ameredith is an interesting case in point. A member of a proud but impoverished Welsh house, he sought to recoup his fortunes in the wars in France, but finding this unprofitable, took his pride in his hands and set up as a tailor in Exeter, preserving, however, the connections in good society to which his birth entitled him. He prospered and was able to enter the more dignified trade of draper merchant. Soon his wealth enabled him to invest in land, to send his son to Oxford and the Inns of Court, and to rise in the municipal hierarchy before death cut short his successes just as his turn as mayor came round. His son, Edward, abandoned trade and city life altogether and retired to his estate. He married the daughter of one of the Fortescues who was a baron of Exchequer, and became himself a justice of the peace in Devon.[33] The connection with the city was not dropped entirely, for he served as burgess for Exeter in the fourth Parliament of Elizabeth.[34] Ameredith's career was, of course, far from unique, for the ambition of every successful merchant was to become a landed gentleman. To quote Hooker, the merchants "do attain to great wealth and riches, which for the most part they do employ in purchasing land and little by little they do creep and seek to be gentlemen. . . ."[35] This was equally true of the impoverished younger son of good family, the citizen born and bred a merchant, or the ambitious farmer's son from some Devon village come to the provincial capital to make his fortune. All three types prospered at Exeter in this era.

Perhaps the most successful family was the Periams, who rose in three generations from the humblest origins to the highest ranks of legal officialdom. The second Periam was governor of the Merchant Adventurers at Antwerp. John as mayor of Exeter rose no higher in the official hierarchy than his father, but Sir William served as Lord Chief Baron and made a marriage alliance with the Bacons. They were the only Exeter family to rise to such spectacular success in the generations before 1600, but many others enjoyed satisfactory advances in social prestige. The hallmark of success was, of course, the acquisition of landed property. Instances of this are fairly numerous. The Hursts bought land at Oxton;[36] the Periams had two establishments, one at Fulford, the other at Creedy-Wiger.[37] The Ameredith estate was at Slapton.[38] John Peter bought land in Bowhay in the parish of Shillingford where his son (by Wilmot, the sister both of Sir William Petre and of the customer of Exeter) settled[39] and founded a county family. The Smiths built a mansion

[33] Alexander, *Exeter Members*, 208.
[34] *Ibid.*, 200.
[35] BM, Harleian MS. 5827, 3d.
[36] Transcript, Exeter City Library, PCC 58 Drake.
[37] Prince, *Worthies*, 626–627.
[38] Alexander, *Exeter Members*, 208.
[39] Prince, *Worthies*, 633.

just outside the city in Heavitree parish,[40] retired from business, and married in the right circles. General Monk was the grandson of Sir George Smith, mayor of Exeter. As we have noted, the Martins, besides the land they acquired for themselves, fell heirs to the Hurst estate of Oxton.

But these successful figures were hardly the rule. Much more common were the men who used their profits to invest in land, but were unable to achieve the complete transformation they sought. As a glance at Table IX will show, most of the Exeter merchants put some money into land, but very few had purchased enough to secure independence from mercantile pursuits.

Landed estate was not the only token of social success in the community. Many citizens found their triumphs not in their own advancement in the world but in that of their posterity. Even a modest income allowed parents to launch their children in an education which, if the children had talent, led to eminence in one of the learned professions. There was a considerable number of such instances in the city among the generation born late in the sixteenth century. Whether this was a particularly new phenomenon in English society is difficult to say. The careers of Wolsey and Gardiner illustrate the rise of provincial merchants' sons to high office in earlier times, but the rather large number of quite minor middle-class children who made modest but solid careers in the learned professions was significant of new opportunities for the lesser middle-class. The Hooker family affords a good instance. Both John and his nephew, the famous Richard, attended university. Of the latter's career we need not speak here. John,[41] our guide to so much of the matter recorded here, not only followed literary and antiquarian pursuits, but also filled a number of city administrative offices, sat in both the English and Irish Parliaments, and still found time to act as general agent to Sir Peter Carewe.

[40] Charles Worthy, *The History of the Suburbs of Exeter* (London and Exeter, 1892), 10.
[41] See Hooker's account of himself in Harleian MS. 5827, fol. 49.

The Bodleys[42] were another Exeter family of hardly less fame. Their fortunes were founded in the city, but they migrated to London. The founder of the Bodleian saw little of his native city, but his brother Lawrence came back to be canon in the cathedral and founder of a lectureship in the city churches. A child of more modest circumstances than either Richard Hooker or John Bodley was John Bridgeman. His parents kept the Bear Inn at South Street. Educated at Cambridge, he rose to be Bishop of Chester under the first Stuarts; his son, Orlando, was Lord Chief Justice and Lord Keeper under Charles II. John Barkham, nephew to Bridgeman the innkeeper, went to Oxford and similarly prospered in a clerical career, dying a prebendary of St. Paul's and Dean of Bocking. Another successful family was the Hakewills. The father married Thomasin, daughter of the second John Periam. Of their three sons one was a successful London lawyer, a second was Mayor of Exeter, and the third, George, became Archdeacon of Surrey and chaplain to the Prince of Wales but more famous as the author of the *Apology . . . of the Power and Providence of God.*

Medical practice was another road to professional success. Simon, the son of Thomas Baskerville, apothecary of Exeter who died in 1596 with the modest fortune of £324, was sent to Exeter College. Trained there as a physician, he was knighted while serving the Stuart kings in that capacity. A fellow student of Baskerville's at Oxford was Robert Vilvain, who returned to his native city to practice, apparently with considerable success, since he was able to give handsome endowments to the new school founded in the 1630's. He was a medical author of some renown, who published three works in London in 1654.

Law also offered opportunities for the ambitious. William, the eldest son of Nicholas Martin,[43] after the usual grammar-school education in Exeter, went to Pembroke College, Oxford, and then to the Inns of Court, returning to become Recorder of Exeter in 1605.

[42] The information on the Bodleys, Bridgemans, Barkhams, Hakewills, Baskervilles, and Vilvain comes from a collection of biographies written by George Oliver for *Trewman's Flying Post*, 1849–50, now assembled in the Exeter City Library.
[43] Prince, *Worthies*, 574–575.

He was more generally and unhappily famed as the author of a history of the kings of England which James thought derogatory both to his family and to his native Scotland. His cousin, Richard, the son of William Martin, rose even further in the law,[44] becoming Recorder of London in 1618. These instances do not complete the list of Exeter youth who obtained various kinds of advancement in the law, the Church, or medicine. They do make clear the range of opportunities available to even quite modest citizens of ambition and talent, and indicate the alternative avenues of advancement for those who could not enter the ranks of the landed gentry.

Social advancement requires money. What kind of resources had these rising citizens? Happily, there is an excellent source of information in the inventories of the orphans' court although, as always, not as much as we should like to have. Among the whole collection of inventories are many of ranking merchants, including more than twenty-five who sat in the Chamber. Gross estates of more than £5,000 were uncommon; only about a third of them amounted to more than £2,000; the remainder were about equally divided between those with a total between £1,000 and £2,000 and those under £1,000. John Modiford's fortune of over £13,000 is larger by £5,000 than the next in size. A royal agent, writing from Devon in 1625, estimated it at £30,000, and that of Alderman Thomas Walker at £70,000;[44a] assuming the same margin of error in both cases, the latter may have had as much as £25,000.

We have few comparative figures to assist us. Certainly Exeter fortunes are petty beside those of London, where the median personal estate of a merchant of this period was about £7,800. At Bristol, however, the average was almost the same as at Exeter, and at Newcastle far greater.[45] Yet the Exeter community belonged to a relatively small economic class; their peers, throughout the provinces, were probably not numerous. If not at the very top of provincial

[44] *Ibid.*, 576–577.

[44a] HMC, *Twelfth Report*, App., pt. 1 vol. I. (Cowper MSS), 213. We do not know the totals for the Periam or Hurst estates.

[45] W. G. Hoskins, "The Elizabethan Merchants of Exeter," in *Old Devon* (Newton Abbot, 1966; repr. from *Elizabethan Government and Society*, ed. S. Bindoff and J. Hurstfield, London, 1961), 82; Howell, *Newcastle upon Tyne*, 14–17.

TABLE IX.—*Selected Inventories (pounds) of Merchants, 1560–1640**

Merchants	Goods	Money	Accounts receivable		Plate	Leases	Miscellaneous	Adventures abroad	Household goods (exc. apparel)	Accounts payable	Net total
			Good	Bad							
William Horsam[a]	136		376	483	8			132	31	1188	-505
Thomas Cooke	1153		937	420	48	316			124	864	1716
John Webber	781		187	59					79	180	867
John Blight	474	23	63	110	59	241		80	88	390	638
William Martin	1168		1542	2634	368	1326		1877	321	1979	4623
Thomas Moggridge	408	913	1186	410	42			2222	183	436	4518
John Snellinge	121	135	365		25	253			130		1029
John Modyford	177	1326	10625	1540	123		1173[b]		386		13810
Anthony Walter	39		1698	138[c]	11				228		2103[c]
Horsey	924	764	520	64	11	250			116	43	2603

* These ten were selected because the fullest information is available about them. In spite of residual ambiguities, they give us the closest approximation of actual wealth which it is possible to arrive at. For this corrected version of the table, I am indebted to Professor Hoskins and to Mr. C. P. Stone, Deputy City Librarian. See also selected lists of merchant fortunes in Hoskins, "The Elizabethan Merchants of Exeter," 83–85.
a Names of merchants are spelled as in the original inventory.
b Capitalized value of annuities worth £103 a year.
c Possibly incomplete.

cities, Exeter stood well within the first range of provincial commercial wealth.

It would be interesting to know what annual incomes were, but it is not possible to do more than guess. The size of the mayor's salary, £120, is one clue. This was not intended to include his major entertainment expenses, which were provided for separately. Probably £120 was considered the basic sum necessary for a man of his dignity and substance. Another clue is afforded by the Moggridge will. Thomas Moggridge died leaving a net estate of about £4500. As a special favor the Orphans' Court allowed the widow Moggridge £107 a year for the maintenance of her three daughters.[46] An income of £100 a year was apparently considered suitable for a widow of wealth with three children. Probably £100 can be fixed as the lower limit of income for prosperous Exeter merchants.

Average incomes probably were a good deal higher. For instance, there is the case of John Hayne, a substantial but not eminent merchant, whose financial diary for the years 1631–43 survives.[47] Married, with four children, and a staff of two servants (one the children's nurse), Hayne's annual expenditures average about £160 from 1636 through 1642. About £25 of this went for house rent; £3 a fortnight went to his wife for her household purse. Their one domestic cost £2 10s. a year in wages, the children's nurse about £4.

Compare these figures with those for the Devon gentry, of the same period given by Hoskins in *Devonshire Studies*.[48] Many of the smaller gentry of the county enjoyed between £50 and £100 a year from their estates. Doubtless they also received invisible income from their farms, but it would seem that a middling Exeter merchant could command somewhat more income per annum than his contemporary in the country.

It is useful to compare these incomes with others in the city. The mayor's cook received £8 a year with livery; the lecturers in the

[46] ECM, Book 144, p. 178.
[47] See TDA, 33 (1901) 187–269, T. N. Brushfield, "The Financial Diary of a Citizen of Exeter, 1631–43."
[48] W. G. Hoskins and H. P. R. Finberg, *Devonshire Studies* (London, 1952), "The Estates of the Caroline Gentry," 334–365.

churches, £40 to £60; the schoolmaster, £30; no clergyman in the city received more than £20; no canon in the cathedral enjoyed as much as £100. A laborer was paid from 1s. to 14d. a day in the 1630's.[49] If he worked three hundred days a year, he would earn about £15.

The composition of fortunes is more significant than the totals (see Table IX). One is immediately struck by their fragility and by their lack of liquidity. Invariably much of the estate consists of accounts receivable or stock on hand. Usually cash is a relatively small item. (The men listed all died leaving minor children and hence were probably still in the prime of life. Their estates represent going businesses rather than the settled investments of retirement.) Such circumstances point up the plight of the seventeenth-century businessman. In the absence of banks or negotiable stocks he had no safe place in which to deposit surplus funds or lay away reserves. Investment in land was one possibility, but land was not easily convertible. Plate was another alternative, and usually he had some investment of this kind, which could quickly be turned into money. But the bulk of his fortune remained in debts owed him or in goods on hand, and both were terribly susceptible to the fluctuations of the market and the great uncertainties of overseas trade. And quite naturally he, in turn, often owed large sums to other merchants.

Both social ambition and economic security urged him to invest in land, and the wills of these men make it clear that land was the investment by which they trusted to provide for their families. The lands are frequently divided carefully among the various children by legacy. Bequests of money might not be payable when the time came, but land was something more solid. Usually the land was purchased as investment and not worked by the merchant himself, but it was not uncommon to have a small holding where some livestock was kept and which provided for the family's household needs. Occasionally there was an establishment in the country besides the house in the city. But land, although an important item, was hardly ever the prime element in the estate.

Other forms of investment were even more uncommon. One mer-

[49] See account books attached to Receivers' Rolls.

chant, the wealthy John Modiford,[50] whose estate seems to have been in excellent order, did not choose land for investment, but instead had purchased annuities. These were charges on lands, payable annually for either a term of years or a term of lives. The income was about £103 a year, which the accessors capitalized at £1,173. One other more imaginative merchant, Thomas Martin, varied the usual type of investment by taking shares in an East India Company venture.[51] There was some investment in city property although not so much as one would expect. This group may not be entirely representative in this regard, for at the purchase of the monastic estates several merchants made rather large investments of this kind.

But accounts receivable remained the big item in almost every estate. The appraisers divided them as "sperate" and "desperate" or sometimes added a third category of doubtful. The "desperate" accounts were often alarmingly large; credit must have been very shaky at the best. Usually the debtors are to be found in the Devon or Cornwall towns, and doubtless carried running accounts. Some, however, were located overseas, and a very few in London. There was, of course, no discounting agency through which these accounts could be made liquid.

Altogether, these Exeter mercantile fortunes were of extremely fragile character, subject to every breath of commercial or political disturbance, and in the absence of discount banks, not very liquid. The extreme distaste for any form of taxation becomes even more understandable when we consider how small the liquid resources of these men were. The financial burdens imposed by civic office must also have borne very heavily. Nor could the hope of passing on a fortune to the next generation lighten the burden of the present. The custom of Exeter required that one third of the estate go to the widow; another third had to be divided equally among all the children; the remainder was at the disposal of the testator. Under these conditions it was hard to pass on a fortune intact to a single heir. The great Modiford fortune was broken up among eleven children. The time for the foundation of a great house like that of

[50] ECM, Book 144, p. 178.   [51] ECM, Inventory 132.

the Barings, established in Exeter a century or more later, had not yet come.

But in spite of the uncertainties of trade, politics, war, and plague, the daily life of these families went forward, and here again the inventories enable us to catch a glimpse of it. The keynote of life was comfort rather than luxury. The merchants' houses in the heart of the old city were roomy but hardly grand and still contained the shop and warehouse. A garden and court gave air and light. Within, there was an air of bourgeois ease. The inventories note with care the soft feather beds, the piles of fresh linen, the dully gleaming pewter, the shining plate, neatly embroidered cushions, and heavy curtains—all the accoutrements of domestic comfort and pleasure but not tokens of splendor or mere adornment.

The nucleus of the dwelling quarters was the hall,[52] which contained a fireplace and a few chairs and often served as the family dining room, for only the very rich boasted a separate chamber for eating. Table boards on trestles and stools were provided for the meal. The other principal living room was the parlor, comfortably fitted out with chairs and cushions, and, like the hall, boasting painted cloths or tapestries on the walls and possibly a few pictures or maps on the walls. The tapestries and cushions and the carpets on the floor often came from abroad. Below stairs there would also be the kitchen with its array of pewter and iron ware, table, settle, and stools. There might be a spence, a buttery, and below, a cellar, while a passage led out to the garden, court, and stable. Above stairs would be the sleeping chambers provided with feather beds and bolsters, presses for clothes, and chairs. There might be four or five bedchambers, sometimes served by a gallery, where the armor and weapons of the master stood. Sometimes there were two floors above the living quarters, the servants' bedrooms being in the highest. Glass in the windows was frequently to be found, but was still uncommon enough to be listed separately. The parlor and hall usually boasted wainscoting. Furniture was a relatively modest item in a household inventory. A few presses and chests, some tableboards

---

[52] These paragraphs are founded on evidence selected from the various inventories. In many cases household goods was listed room by room.

and stools, and the bedsteads usually exhausted the list. Comfort and adornment were provided by plentiful hangings, curtains, carpets, and cushions with a few looking glasses and pictures on the walls. Pewter, plate, and linen were often more considerable items in the inventories.

Here as in other matters Exeter merchants stand well below the metropolitan splendor of London, but substantially above the standard of living of townsmen of Leicester, for example.[53] Their houses were larger (three stories instead of two) and there is a mild note of extravagance in dining furniture, in fine embroidery, and in glass. The Exonians could afford the space and adornment which were lacking among the poorer and soberer Leicester burghers. In Exeter the rich merchants still lived in the heart of the city (although there was sometimes a family farmhouse outside the walls). The era of suburban mansions began perhaps at the end of our era when the Smiths built their new mansion in Heavitree parish.

So far we have dealt with the way of life of the ruling oligarchy. What about the poorer citizens? The differences were of size rather than kind. Where the merchants measured their fortunes in thousands, a soapboiler or brewer measured his in hundreds. The composition of their wealth was not substantially different. Their leases consisted of a tenement or two or a field in Duryard; their accounts receivable were locally owed rather than owed abroad or in country towns. Similarly, their domestic establishments were smaller copies of the great merchants', fewer rooms, fewer luxuries, but still modest comfort. A weaver's house, for instance,[54] contained a hall, but here used for sleeping as well as daytime activity, two sleeping chambers and a kitchen, besides the shop. Painted cloths adorned the walls of hall and one sleeping chamber; cushions softened the hardness of the bench and the two chairs in the hall. But this weaver with a gross estate of £90 was still higher in the social scale than a joiner with barely £4 of goods.[55] Here at the bottom of the social scale one

---

[53] See Hoskins in *Studies in Social History*, 58.
[54] ECM, Inventory 31.
[55] ECM, Inventory 60.

room had to suffice, and a mere scattering of furnishings, but even so there was the comfort of a feather bed and bolster, sheets, and coverlet. The estates listed in the inventories were those of free-men, and certainly do not plumb the depths of poverty in the city, but still they indicate that the lower-middle class enjoyed at least some of the amenities of life.

The citizens had their occasions of pomp and display, especially those in the Chamber, the city's service, or one of the companies. And a man of substance had at all times to present an appropriately dignified appearance. Hence the wardrobes of the citizens were often well furnished. A member of the Twenty-Four such as Alexander Germyn[56] had three gowns, one somber black, faced with satin, guarded with velvet and lined with baize; another of scarlet, and of course his robe of scarlet, lined with taffeta. Alderman Martin, who died in 1620, had a wardrobe worth £75.[57] Even a baker with a gross estate of only £65 boasted £8 in apparel.[58]

One would, of course, like to know something not only of the material environment of the Exeter merchants but also of their intellectual and spiritual milieu. Here it is more difficult to speak. We can say a little of their amusements, something of their reading. Beyond that it is not safe to go. The amusements afforded the citizens seem to have been those of every English town in the period. There had never been any great guild or civic feast day, and the Midsummer muster was the only regular occasion when the citizens went forth in state. Fairs provided some entertainment, but there were also more regular events, as the office of the "bull-ring man" shows. He was to be present whenever any bull or bear was to be beaten. On one such occasion in 1581 the graver citizens were much edified by an accident which befell the spectators at "the vayne pastyme of bearebeating."[59] It was a Sabbath when, as Hooker thought, they might better have been keeping the solemnity of the day. They had their punishment, for the scaffold on which they stood fell, killing seven of the beholders. There was also gentler

[56] ECM, Inventory 99.   [57] ECM, Inventory 132.
[58] ECM, Inventory 176.   [59] ECM, Book 51, fol. 361.

entertainment for the citizenry. The city maintained a group of waits who sang every weekday in the streets, and attended the mayor on great occasions. The city even provided instruments for them, and they received a yearly wage and livery. Traveling players were frequent visitors,[60] and most of the famous companies of the day played at Exeter. There seems to have been a local performance entitled "Robin Hood and Lyttel John" which took place once a year for the benefit of St. John Bow church. Sentiment about players varied with each mayor. As early as 1585 a company was forbidden[61] to play but dismissed with a fee. The Puritanical mayors of 1622 and 1632 forbade plays altogether, and other mayors of the 1630's gave them money to leave. At home music provided entertainment and many wealthier households boasted a set of virginals.

Naturally, the most common reading matter in an Exeter home was the English Bible, but this was not so until the last generation of the sixteenth century, and a Bible was not a universal possession of the seventeenth-century families. But books are a common entry on inventories after 1600. Often the titles are not specified; when they are they usually resemble those owned by Thomas Chappell (mayor in 1588)[62] which included a Bible, a chronicle, three service books, and one book of "Sickman Souls." To this one might add Foxe's *Book of Martyrs*, and the abridgements of the statutes. But ownership of books was a very common thing even in quite modest households by 1640. There is an inventory for one of the Exeter booksellers who died in 1615, with a stock of several thousand books, heavily weighted on the side of divinity, but containing a few histories and Bodin's *De Republica*.[63]

A most amazing instance is that of Henry James, a successful merchant and a member of the Twenty-Four, who died in 1579 possessed of around sixty books,[64] seemingly his own private library. If this is so, his tastes were certainly catholic and his knowledge of

[60] See TDA, 81–82 (1949–50), 241 seq., Cecily Radford, "Three Centuries of Play-Going in Exeter."
[61] AB iv, 456.
[62] ECM, Inventory 43.
[63] ECM, Book 144, p. 129.
[64] ECM, Inventory 29.

languages creditable. Besides both English and Latin Bibles, his theological works included Cranmer on the sacraments, Erasmus' *Paraphrases,* and a concordance of Scripture. His taste for the classics ran mostly to Cicero and Virgil but he also owned volumes of Horace, Terence, Lucian, and Aulus Gellius. He possessed a dictionary of Greek and an English translation of Aesop. More modern authors included in his collection were Lorenzo Valla and Sir Thomas Elyot. The library was completed by a collection of the statutes, four "singing books," and a stock of unidentified works, some of which were in French. The catalogue tantalizes the imagination, but affords little ground for speculation. James must have been an exceptional man, but still it is significant to find such a lay intellectual at all.

Hooker was a man of importance of whom we know far more, who stood as the representative of a new order. It is unlikely that in any earlier generation he could have found a place in provincial life. With a university education (Oxford and Strasbourg), he did not pursue a clerical or even a professional career, but returned to his native city to become a civic official. It was now possible for a lay intellectual to make his living and to find an important place in Exeter. Aside from his capacity for business he must have been immensely useful to the Exeter magnates, for he had the fluency and coherence of expression which they lacked, and could give voice to their sentiments in language of appropriate dignity and sophistication. His skill can be seen, for instance, in the struggle over the Merchants Adventurers charter. As a leader of public opinion he was unexcelled, for he never clashed with the ruling causes of the day and yet his opinions were honest and ardent. His warm Protestantism tempered by a reverent regard for authority was an ideal combination for the temper of the Tudor magistracy. Such a figure, orthodox in opinion yet no mere mouthpiece of authority, was an imperative need in a society beginning to develop a self-conscious but still unexercised public opinion on a variety of topics. For Hooker himself his position must have been a happy one, for he had standing in the community and an outlet for his intellectual energies in his keen antiquarianism. His pride in Exeter's past was both enthusiastic and informed, but something of it must have been felt by his less educated contemporaries, for it fitted well into the pattern of civic pride and enterprise. We cannot underestimate the role of this native-born intellectual in stimulating the whole movement of civic development during our century.

The early seventeenth century produced no intellectual equal in importance or stature to Hooker. Probably the most prominent leader of the generation before the Civil War was a man of very different stripe, the bold and tenacious alderman, Ignatius Jurdain.[65] Unlike Hooker he was something of a rebel, prepared to defend his principles without regard for established interests. Thus he took up the cause of the freeholders in the Parliamentary elections of 1626 and later challenged the royal anger and episcopal indignation by his letter on the *Book of Sports*. But he was no mere agitator; the truly heroic strain in his character emerged in the courageous leadership which he gave the city in the crisis of 1625. In the absence of the mayor and in the general breakdown of social order under the scourge of plague, he provided for the helpless sufferers through the worst months of the winter, liberally drawing upon his own pocket. The courage he showed then arose from his own intense religious convictions, gained when he underwent the characteristic conversion of the Puritan some fifty years earlier. The citizens recognized his services by the pension which the Chamber paid him in the last years of his life. Jurdain, with his austere morality and fearless temper, is as characteristic of the generation which founded the new schools and supported the lectureships, as Hooker is of the more worldly minded but not less energetic Elizabethans.

General social attitudes in the city were probably as orthodox as its entertainments in the Elizabethan period. The dispute over the Merchant Adventurer charter reveals something of the frame of reference of the ruling group. The speech with which Hooker concluded the reading of the Council's letters in January 1560 reflected the standard opinions of the age, and we cannot doubt that the elders of the city gravely nodded approval to the Chamberlain's

[65] See TDA, 29 (1897), 350–377, Frances Rose-Troup, "An Exeter Worthy and his Biographer."

words.[66] Two points, he declared, were the heads of his argument: "thone concerninge obedience and thother touching concorde and unitye, which too are of such force and effycacie, that therby all comon welthes and all estates are preserved and kept, and without them all are turned to utter ruyn and desolacion." The first point was illustrated by many instances, not only Biblical and historical, but drawn also from Exeter's own experience in 1549 and from the recent rebellion of Sir Thomas Wyatt. He then expounded the second head of his argument, with much cogent reasoning on the advantages of harmony and unity in any corporate body. The pith of his reasoning was found in the exhortation with which he concluded his first point, "Wherefore let us all well remember, as well for the dewtie we owe unto God, the obedience unto the prince and love to this our Comon welthe and Citie that with all humbleness and obedience wee do quietlie submitt our selfs to the Government of the higher powers and magistrates."[67] These three powers, conceived as stages of a single hierarchical order, summarized the framework of authority to which the inarticulate loyalties of the governors of Exeter were given. But we cannot doubt that the most important one was the last. For them, as their arguments earlier in the dispute over the charter revealed, the civic corporation was endowed with the same *natural* authority as the prince or the hereditary orders of society. If such an attitude provoked them to wrathful resistance when any threat faced them, it also provided them with a deep self-confidence in all their own works, which formed the psychological foundation of their bold and restless enterprise. Nor were their inferiors disposed to question this dispensation. Although they might grumble on occasion and frequently sought to avoid the more irksome regulations imposed by their governors, they too accepted their humble status as the course of nature.

These general attitudes did not change during our century. But an additional element entered into the fabric of public opinion in the seventeenth century—the new religious spirit. We have observed its manifestations in earlier chapters; it is only necessary here to recall

[66] Printed in Cotton, *Elizabethan Guild*, 99–107.
[67] *Ibid.*, 101.

the tone of seriousness, almost of solemnity, which seems to pervade the generation of Charles I, here in Exeter as elsewhere. The change was not fundamental, since regulation of moral and spiritual life had always been reckoned part of the task of governance, but it was now approached with additional concern and with a notable increase of activity.

This brief account of its ethos exhausts what detailed information we can collect about the civic aristocracy and provides an opportunity to embark upon a series of more abstract reflections about the Exeter community. The civic aristocracy's climate of political opinion and their haughty self-assurance re-emphasize once again their dominant position in the city. These also point up the nature of the civic community of Exeter.

In exploring these matters it is useful to compare the local community with the national. The latter was conceived as comprehending the whole body of the nation, "all sorts and conditions of men," even though its governance was entrusted to a relatively few men hereditarily endowed with the right to rule. The community of Exeter, on the other hand, was a consciously exclusive one, including at the most the body of freemen. Here again, a smaller body of citizens was entrusted with full authority to govern the whole community. In this case the selection was not hereditary, but was based on business success. This fact, coupled with the explicit exclusiveness of the civic body, gave to it its particular characteristics. In conception it retained the notion of a corporate social body. Hooker gave voice to this idea when he defined a "civitas" (in particular Exeter) as "a multitude of people assembled and Collected to the ende to Contynewe and lyve together in a Comon societie yeldinge Dutefull obedience unto the superiors and mutuall love to a nother...."[68] He expressed the idea more concisely in his favorite phrase "this our Comon welthe and Citie" while the legal formula was "The Mayor, Bailiffs, and *Commonalty* of Exeter."[69] This tradition of a common social loyalty embracing at least the body of freemen had little real meaning by the sixteenth century although it remained a frame of

[68] Hooker, *History*, III, 787.   [69] My italics.

reference to which appeal was made on occasions of disagreement. Moreover, this tradition had no place for the "hote Citesen or a foryner." It thus excluded the majority of the city's inhabitants, and of the minority who enjoyed citizen status, only a few could share the sweets of power or indeed participate at all in the direction of the community's life. The result was that the civic community of Exeter was in essence the small oligarchy among whom the offices of government circulated. In them was embodied the true corporate spirit of the city. We have already described the tight internal structure of this group as well as their calm self-confidence in their right to rule, while our whole study has been an account of their activity as governors of Exeter. It is the general characteristics of this group with which the concluding pages of the study will be concerned.

In the first place the civic leaders were marked off as parvenus in a society recognizing an hereditary social hierarchy. As officers of the city and of the Crown, they were vested with all the delegated legal powers which the landowning gentry enjoyed, and were thus the official equals of the latter. Nevertheless, they did not enjoy the intangible but all-important prestige of birth. Moreover, as merchants they followed a calling which stood a stage lower in dignity than that of the landowner. Around the latter there still lingered an aura of feudal splendor, and he frequently added to his dignity of birth the distinction of a military career. The merchant magistrates were not only denied this advantage, but stood at a positive disadvantage in the performance of the military duties which fell upon them. The slight but real inferiority of their status vis-à-vis the county magnates was never so apparent as in time of war. But even in time of peace there were a thousand little ways in which the magistrate born to office asserted his pre-eminence over the citizen who had climbed there. The rather too self-conscious pomp and display of the civic dignitaries in all their panoply of scarlet and purple, as well as their acute sensitiveness to any breach of decorum by one of their own number, were small but meaningful instances of the same insecurity of status.

On the level of political action the inequality between the civic and county magistrates was evident again in the entrée to the court and to high official circles which the latter alone possessed. The same difference was probably reflected in the attitudes of the lower classes towards their superiors, although here our evidence is slight. It is worth noting that the servants of the Earl of Bedford at his house in Exeter did not hesitate to knock down an alderman, and on several other occasions riots broke out in the city among the serving-men of the Devon gentry. A few scattered interrogations in Hooker's collection in Act Book iv also reveal occasional flashes of sullen envy felt by the lower classes towards the self-made men who governed them. Yet it would not do to overemphasize the insecurity of status of the civic magistrates. At Exeter there was never any breakdown of authority or even the threat of one; on the contrary in 1549 when the thoroughly angry countrymen of Devon and Cornwall ignored their natural-born rulers and broke out into open rebellion, the Exeter magistrates were able to maintain their authority successfully. The inequalities of status had important effects for individual merchants, however, and powerfully influenced their personal goals.

But, to discern fully the nature of the merchant oligarchy of Exeter—the civic community of Exeter by our definition—one must understand its function as a social unit. The bewildering complexity of the duties which were carried out by the members of the civic oligarchy in the variety of their official capacities obscures somewhat the basic character of their association. Therefore, it is necessary to sort out the various functions of the group and to arrange them in intelligible order. Here we must distinguish carefully between those actions which their position as officials and their status as governors of society compelled them to undertake, and those they initiated themselves for their own particular corporate ends.

Under the former heading fall their routine but important tasks in maintaining public order, organizing defense, and providing for the poor and the unemployed. But under the latter are comprehended the really major undertakings of the civic corporation during this epoch. They include the building of the canal, the struggle over Topsham, the founding of the new wholesale markets, and the

10

establishment of the Merchant Adventurers Company. The goal of all these enterprises was the same, the expansion of economic opportunity for the Exeter merchants; the whole elaborate apparatus of the civic corporation was directed to one end: the making of money. For the merchant in the privileged top stratum of Exeter society his membership in the civic community was primarily valuable because it provided him the opportunity of building a fortune. Indeed, the essential character of the borough (as distinct from the civic community) was an economic—or rather, a commercial—one. That which distinguished a citizen, a freeman, from a "foryner" was his right to do business within the city jurisdictions. And the small community of wealthier merchants was really defined in the same economic terms. For entry into the circle depended upon business success or, at least, the acquisition of wealth by one means or another. From one point of view, this group, which enjoyed both the privileges of the borough and privileged status within it, were as much a chartered monopoly as the Russia Company. They enjoyed the same exclusive rights to trading, in the very advantageously situated markets of Exeter, that the Muscovy merchants enjoyed in that distant land.

Nevertheless, it would be unfair to overemphasize the purely economic function of the community. We need only recall the extensive governmental tasks performed by the same merchants in their official capacities. This role was of high importance, for it enabled the merchant to enjoy the sweets of power which, next to wealth, he most anxiously sought. Not many actually succeeded in founding a county family, but a much larger number realized dreams of power and consequence within the city. But we must be careful not to ascribe merely selfish motives to these men. They were not great men in the English scene; they were not possessed of princely wealth; but within the limited arena of their activity they responded well to the demands of their situation. The pomp and display of civic life has its mildly comic side; an alderman is always thought a fit subject for mirth. But the large conception of their status that the governors of Exeter held bore fruit of various kinds. Not only did they patiently execute the demands placed upon them by the Crown; not only did they meet the exigencies of local life; they voluntarily and generously worked to improve the condition of their little world. Bourgeois in origin and ambition, they nevertheless lived by a high and rigorous code of social responsibility. Not only in legal power and status but also in social standards, these civic magistrates approximated the world of the country gentlemen.

Beyond this there is the important problem of the place of the civic community within the social structure of England. That social structure was, in the main, hierarchical, and movement upward from stratum to stratum was not easy. Class status was hereditary, and the traditional values of such a society were opposed to ascent from the level in which one was placed by natural circumstance. The borough presented a marked contrast to this structure. Here was a society based on quite another set of values, in which status was measured not by birth but by commercial success. Here rapid ascent from humble to exalted social position was not only an acceptable but a common phenomenon.

How then could such a community exist within the framework of an aristocratic society? To answer that we need take in account the accommodations that were made on both sides. As we have already seen, within the borough the dominant social class had come to equate its position with that of the hereditary gentry of the shires. Not only did they conceive their position as being equally a natural condition of the social order, but in fact they exercised the same legal powers within the civic jurisdictions as the gentry without. The gentry in turn conceded to them at least a measure of equality, and the close relations between many merchant families and the county families prevented the erection of any insurmountable barriers. Thus, by tacit agreement, an approximation of the status of superior class was created for the inferior group by glossing over the underlying differences and thus a mutually friendly relationship (though not one of true social equality) was made possible.

Nevertheless, even after allowance has been made for this accommodation, the fact remains that the two societies, that of the borough and that of the county (or, if you please, of the nation), were fundamentally different. The counties were merely separate geographic areas, while the walls of a city enclosed not only territory but another social world. The importance of these social enclaves cannot be overestimated. They acted as release valves for all the pressure of social tension built up within an aristocratic society. Within the walls of the city the normal values of English society were, in effect, abrogated, and the relations of individual to individual placed, to a certain extent, on a different footing. Here all the reshuffling which individual circumstance renders necessary in any society could take place with relative ease. The portionless younger son could obtain the fortune necessary to support his hereditary dignity; the ambitious yeoman could ascend even to the higher rungs of the social ladder; or, perhaps more rarely, the obscure husbandman could make the same social advance. In Exeter alone we have seen evidences of all these types in our century. The importance of the borough communities in providing social mobility within a society otherwise rather rigidly constructed is obvious. Tensions which might otherwise have been dangerous to the whole order of society were relieved, while the flow of talent into higher circles was measurably facilitated.

This condition, however, gave a rather peculiar character to the borough oligarchies. They did not assure permanent social position to anyone. The chances of competitive economic life made it unlikely that any family could retain its dominance indefinitely, but more than that, most of the members of the oligarchy regarded it merely as an intermediate stage in their passage to higher and more secure status as county gentry. Thus although the borough was a part of the official hierarchy of government, the merchants were not part of a correspondingly distinct social class. They did, of course, participate as merchants in the great complex of families who made up the governing classes of the kingdom, but their position, compared with that of the landed gentry, remained anomalous. The constant defection of their most talented members and the nature of the social ambitions they all shared, made this inevitable.

Our initial conclusions have pointed up the fluid, changing aspects of Exeter life during this period. Obviously they are easier to describe; they are, in some measure, the historian's particular concern;

but our picture would be badly described if we did not insist on the essentially conservative, indeed, traditionalist, character of the city's life. In examining the merchant oligarchy we have necessarily concentrated on the element in the city's population which was most restless, both in its social ambitions and in its commercial enterprise. In the course of this examination we have also abstracted the actions of the oligarchy for purposes of analysis and thus in some measure torn them from their historical context. This again may have had the consequence of understating the importance of the ancient pattern of customary life in the city. Hence in our final considerations we need to turn again to the point where we began, the long, historic past of the city.

Probably the most important aspect of Exeter's history in the sixteenth century was the continuity of medieval custom. The evidence for it has been a minor but persistent theme in every chapter of this study. It is a truism to point out the authoritarian character of customary societies, and we have seen much evidence of such authoritarianism in sixteenth-century Exeter. More important, to a certain extent the period witnessed a renewed emphasis on the traditional character of civic society. At a time when the borough in general was declining in importance as an economic unit and probably as a center of social loyalty, the governors of Exeter reasserted the particularist nature of the city, both by strengthening their market monopoly in locally produced goods and by obtaining a monopoly of overseas trade. At the same time they continued to regulate rigorously all aspects of social life. These policies were obviously related in large part to the defense of the oligarchy's privilege, but they also had the effect of reaffirming the autonomous character of the community and making more effective its control over the lives of the individual inhabitants of the city. The foundation of the Merchant Adventurers Company was another stimulant to this trend, for it organized the major overseas trade of the city in terms more reminiscent of the past than anticipatory of the future. By a kind of historical paradox, the merchants took advantage of the traditional economic order of the city to provide themselves with an opportunity for increasing their individual wealth. The entrepreneurial drive which is conventionally pictured as being peculiarly individualistic in its manifestations was here, for a time at least, clothed in quite traditional garb. Nevertheless, there can be no doubt that the underlying motive in the foundation of the Merchant Adventurers Company was personal gain rather than a drive for group protection such as characterized the true guilds of the early Middle Ages. As far as the bulk of the inhabitants was concerned, however, the era was not one of significant change.

The customary life of the city, centuries old already in most of its dominant patterns, went on unchanged. The citizens bought and sold and went about the affairs of their lives in much the same way as their ancestors had done. The structure of the society in which they lived remained unchanged; neither opinions nor institutions altered. The one exception was, of course, in religious matters, but even here the change must have seemed to the average passively religious man of minor importance. At any rate the citizens adapted themselves without undue friction to all the religious alterations of the century, and it was only after 1600 that the new current of Puritanism began to dilute the older religious indifference. The ruling classes, however much ambition and boldness they displayed in commercial affairs, remained strong conservatives in all other matters, governing their conduct steadily by the example of the royal government and of the dominant gentry. Although we may, with the hindsight of four hundred years, regard them as innovators within their community, we must not forget that they were stalwart conservatives in their own age.

We cannot, in concluding, offer any very striking assertions about the community we have been studying. As we have repeated frequently, for Exeter this period was not one of marked change or rapid development. Rather it was a time for the consolidation and exploitation of newly appointed legal privilege and of opening economic opportunity. The foundations of the great prosperity of the eighteenth century were laid by a bold and confident merchant oligarchy which, at the same time, readily undertook the burdens of government imposed by the Tudor monarchy. The central ambition of these men was commercial prosperity, and in pursuit of that goal they undertook a series of boldly conceived and executed enterprises. In other realms of activity they remained highly conservative, even traditionalist in outlook, and zealous defenders of existing authority. It is the contrast between this steady traditionalism in political and social matters, on the one hand, and an expansive and vigorous empiricism in economic matters, on the other, that characterizes the Exeter of our century.

Appendices

Appendix I

1577	George Perryman		1608	John Prouze
1578	Richard Prouze		1609	Hugh Crossing
1579	William Chapell, Simon Knight		1610	Walter Borough
			1611	John Lant
1580	Thomas Brewerton		1612	William Newcombe
1581	Thomas Martin		1613	Geoffrey Waltham
1582	Michael Germyn		1614	Thomas Walker
1583	Geoffrey Thomas		1615	John Marshall
1584	John Davy		1616	John Shere
1585	Nicholas Martin		1617	Ignatius Jurdain
1586	George Smith		1618	Thomas Martin
1587	John Periam		1619	John Prouze
1588	Thomas Chapell		1620	Hugh Crossing
1589	Richard Prouze		1621	Walter Borough
1590	William Martin		1622	John Modiford
1591	Michael Germyn		1623	John Gupwell
1592	Nicholas Spicer		1624	Thomas Crossing
1593	Thomas Spicer		1625	Thomas Walker
1594	John Davy		1626	John Tailor
1595	John Chapell		1627	John Acland
1596	John Levermore		1628	John Lynne
1597	George Smith		1629	Nicholas Spicer
1598	John Periam		1630	Thomas Flaye
1599	John Howell		1631	Nicholas Martin
1600	William Martin		1632	John Hakewill
1601	Thomas Walker		1633	Gilbert Sweet
1602	Richard Beavis, to 26th Aug., William Martin		1634	Francis Crossing
			1635	Adam Bennett
1603	Nicholas Spicer		1636	Roger Mallack
1604	John Davy		1637	Thomas Crossing
1605	Henry Hull		1638	James Tucker
1606	Richard Dorchester		1639	Robert Walker
1607	Sir George Smith, Knight		1640	John Penny

Appendix II

There is a variety of different ways in which these data could be utilized:

(1) Assume that about 36 per cent of the names are missing (this is the percentage of *nil* returns listed for the fifteen parishes in the incomplete 1522 return). If we use 950 as a base we swell the probable total to 1,486; if 1,000, to 1,562. Hoskins, regarding the list as of household heads, uses a multiplier of 4.5, to take account not only of children under 16 years but also of servants (*Provincial England*, 72). This would give a lower total of 6,687, a higher one of 7,029.

(2) A variant on this procedure is suggested in a recent letter from Professor Hoskins. Looking at the Coventry figures for 1522 and 1524, he finds a higher proportion of untaxed— about 50 per cent. We might then assume that only half the Exeter population are included in the list of 1524–25 and double that number (to 1,900 or 2,000) before using a multiplier of 4.5. On this calculation we should have a total population of from 8,550 to 9,000.

(3) We might take an entirely different line, as suggested by Dr. Julian Cornwall (*Economic History Review*, 13, No. 1 [April 1970], 37). Working wth these same subsidy returns for the counties of Rutland and Buckingham, he suggests another method of calculation: augment figures drawn from 1524 and 1525 (as those for Exeter are) in the ratio 3:2 to cover omissions. He then assumes a population under age 16 of 40 per cent. Hence his formula, applied to Exeter, would produce a total of 1,486 (or 1,562) x $\frac{3}{2}$ x 3.333. The results would be 7,430 to 7,810.

I do not see any clear reason for choosing one of these methods over another. Hoskins' method assumes that we are dealing with households, but the evidence is not clear on this point since servants within households may have been taxed individually. Cornwall's method makes an assumption about the proportion of under-16's which is impossible to substantiate since we have no clues to birth rates in Exeter before 1520.

These estimates leave us assuming an urban population somewhere between 7,500 and 8,500 in the 1520's.

Appendix III

The inadequacy of information makes it difficult to plot out changes in the movement of Exeter's foreign trade across the century. In general it was the French market which absorbed the largest share of Exeter's exports and provided the bulk of imports. We know that this market was badly disarranged by the long period of civil war in the last decades of the sixteenth century but we lack consecutive figures to give us a clear picture. Similarly the Spanish market, second in importance, was cut off by the break of Anglo-Spanish relations which preceded actual war and must have been virtually wiped out for a couple of decades. But again lack of statistical information prevents our giving precise descriptions.

The peaceful decades following James I's accession probably mark a peak of prosperity for our century. The port books for 1624 (PRO E 190/945/8, summarized in Stephens, *Exeter*, 10) present a fairly full picture of the distribution of exports just before war with France and plague at home struck a disastrous blow at Exeter's export economy from which it had not fully recovered by 1640. In 1624 slightly more than two thirds of cloth exports were going to France; the great bulk of the remaining third to Spanish ports, about equally divided between mainland destinations and the Atlantic Islands. In that year total customs collections at Exeter were higher than at any other provincial port except Hull.

Within a year the picture changed radically and disastrously. The plague years 1625 and 1626 saw a virtual collapse of civil government and wholesale social disorganization. At the same time war with Spain (1625) curtailed the Spanish trade by about two thirds (*ibid.*, 14). And in 1626 and 1627 war with France followed, striking a death blow at the very heart of the export trade. Heavy demands on the city for wartime taxation, plus billeting and transportation costs for soldiers, enlarged the scope of the disaster. Trade figures reflect these accumulated catastrophes; both exports and imports were negligible in 1628 and major improvement is not recorded until about 1632. Even in the mid-1630's, figures for both exports and imports failed to reach the levels of 1624 (*ibid.*, 18 and 20, figs. I and II). Piracy was now a major problem, not relieved until the convoy system of 1636 was set up.

Moreover, trade was now beginning to flow in a new direction. Commercial relations with France did not return to normal after the peace of 1629 and Exeter's efforts to establish a regulated company in cooperation with London did not win Privy Council backing. A few more far-sighted merchants realized that the long-term solution demanded a search for new markets, and from about 1635 on exports began to move for the first time in some volume to the Netherlands. By 1638 more than half of Exeter's exports went to markets other than France; about a quarter of the total of all exports was now being shipped to the Low Countries. We have seen how this triggered a dispute with the London Merchant Adventurers and how the Exeter merchants came off victors in that contest. The trade with the Low Countries marked not only a shift in market but also in commodity (*ibid.*, 27–32). In the 1620's Devon clothiers had introduced a new fabric originally called Spanish cloth because it was a mixture of local and Spanish wool. By the 1630's the Spanish fiber had been replaced by Irish wool. This cloth, paying less duty than broadcloth, sold so well in the Netherlands that it occasioned the London Merchant Adventurers' intervention.

At the close of the century Exeter export trade went through a severe crisis, triggered by the plague in the 1620's and extended by Charles I's wars until 1630. Even after that disturbances in the French market and endemic piracy in the waters off the English coast retarded recovery. But the long-run effects were healthy ones since Exeter merchants were pushed into an exploration for new markets from which they had long held back, and their establishment in the Low Countries' market heralded what was to be the golden age of Exeter overseas commerce.

Bibliographical Essay

This study is based in large part on the manuscripts in the possession of the City of Exeter. There exist two calendars, a manuscript one in the City Library and a more complete printed one, published by the Historical Manuscripts Commission. The printed calendar offers a full and reasonably detailed account of the collection.

The Exeter archives form one of the richest civic collections of manuscripts in England, reaching back to the thirteenth century. Those relevant to the sixteenth and seventeenth centuries fall into two groups—the official records of the Chamber of Exeter, and the private collections made by John Hooker, the Chamberlain, during his long tenure of that office.

The official documents for this period are represented by two major categories. The first of these, the Act Books, begin in 1508. They contain the minutes of the Chamber meetings and to a large extent supersede the Mayor's Court Rolls in which the activities of the Mayor and Twenty-Four had been noted down earlier. Although the Act Books provide us with information about all of the varied activities of the Chamber, the entries are frequently disappointingly brief. Often they merely record a final decision without any indication of antecedent action. Again, one finds instructions for certain actions, but he is unable to uncover any later indication as to whether they were accomplished or not. This difficulty is gradually ameliorated as the century progresses. Each Act Book is larger than its predecessor, and by the end of the century the volume of detail in each entry is quite considerable. The importance of these books cannot be overestimated, for they provide a skeleton account of the whole activity of the Chamber as well as much specific detail.

The regular chronological order of the Act Book is broken only in Act Book IV. Here the first 194 folios are devoted to a collection of miscellaneous entries made by John Hooker. They run in time from 1559 to 1576 and include a large number of topics. The largest part of these entries consists of brief accounts of cases in the justice court, in major part vagrancy and morals charges or those connected with serious disturbance of the public peace. But there are also many entries on the canal and on public events of the period.

The second major category of public documents is the Receiver's Rolls. These long parchment rolls were made up yearly according to a fixed formula. Receipts were listed in detail, down to the actual rentals of individual tenements in the city or individual relief fines. The one exception to this rule was the city manors. Only the net totals, taken from the manor account rolls, were included on the city receiver's rolls. The expenditures, which appeared on the back of the roll, were not broken down in such detail, nor were the account headings so consistently followed from year to year, on the income side. After 15 Elizabeth, however, small account books appeared and these provide more detail on expenditure. Totals of income and expenditure and the deficit, if any, appear at the bottom of the roll.

Among the other public documents there is a great variety of material. About two hundred of the miscellaneous letters in the collection are relevant to our period. Most of these letters are abstracted in the Historical Manuscripts Commission Report or in *Notes and Gleanings* for 1891. Many of them are of great value, but frequently they represent only one or two links in a chain of correspondence and we are left to guess at the missing parts. The collection of miscellaneous bound volumes contains much useful matter. Both the poor accounts and the accounts of the purchase of monastic lands are included in them. Even richer in material is Book 185, which contains the extensive series of papers relating to the great dispute over the Merchant Adventurers Company. The miscellaneous rolls of the city include the merchant hall rates and lists of wages set by the justices.

The records of the Orphans' Court are preserved in fair detail in a series of bound volumes. More important, however, are the inventories of estates made for the Orphans' Court. There are nearly two hundred relevant to our period, and the wealth of detail provided by them includes all sorts of information about the lives and habits of individuals. The Orphans' Court documents also contain a number of wills, mostly those of citizens of lesser consequence. The huge collection of deeds dating from very early times is of less use for our period than for earlier ones. Nevertheless, the deeds relating to the monastic property, to Trew's contract, and to the Topsham cranage are all very useful.

The second major category of sixteenth-century material is John

Hooker's collections. This indefatigable antiquary not only supervised the very extensive contemporary official records but also prepared several collections of miscellaneous documents, many of which are memoranda written by him on various points of city administration. There are also the more elaborate general accounts of the city which Hooker wrote, and his Annals. Most of these documents are collected in two bound books of manuscript in the Exeter City Muniments. The first (Book 52) has been published by the Devon and Cornwall Record Society, in two volumes. It begins with a long history of the city which includes a long eye-witness account of the Rebellion of 1549 and the siege of Exeter. The balance of the printed volumes is filled with a medley of documents, mingled with brief descriptive accounts written by Hooker himself. To catalogue all the diverse subjects which are considered in the two volumes would be both tedious and unprofitable. It is sufficient to note that much of our information on the civic constitution, the city markets and fairs, the struggle over Topsham, the suit with London, and a host of lesser matters comes from this collection.

The second bound manuscript volume is that called the Commonplace Book (Book 51). The main contents of this volume are Hooker's Annals. They are a year-by-year listing of events in Exeter, done in the traditional medieval annal form. They are of particular value for the period of his own lifetime, for they include biographical sketches of many of the mayors as well as much anecdotal material. Some passages from this manuscript have been selected and published by Professor W. J. Harte. There is a third volume, the so-called Freeman's Book (Book 55), which Hooker compiled, at least in part. It takes its name from the lists of yearly freemen's admissions, but it includes many other items, such as an account of the quarrel with John Levermore or the fight with Bedford's servants. Besides these collections of Hooker, there is another manuscript volume of his in the British Museum (Harleian MS. 5827). Entitled "Synopsis Chorographical of Devon," it is a model for later similar works. Besides an elaborate general essay on the county and its inhabitants, Hooker has included some interesting biographies (among them his own) and transcriptions of numerous official documents.

Other printed documents which have been utilized in this study are Miss Cresswell's *Edwardian Inventories* and Cotton's *Elizabethan Guild*. The former is a transcription of the church goods inventories preserved in the Exeter City Muniments as well as in the Public Record Office. The latter is a brief account of the Merchant Adventurers Company, written in 1873, which also includes as an appendix many transcriptions from the company's papers. These transcriptions are quite complete. The company's papers run only to 1600.

Besides the collections in the custody of the City of Exeter, there are two other useful sources of information at Exeter. One of these is the Bishop's Register. Available to students only at half a guinea per diem and very badly housed it is not really available for thorough investigation. The second source is the collection of information on Exeter families in the City Library. These files, organized according to families, are valuable for the genealogies, transcripts of wills and deeds, and other information not easily accessible. Particularly notable are the newspaper articles on eminent Exonians which Dr. George Oliver, the nineteenth-century antiquarian, wrote for *Trewman's Flying Post*. These have been collected in one volume in the City Library.

Outside of Exeter itself, the Public Record Office and the British Museum proved to be sources of additional information. The State Papers Domestic and the Acts of the Privy Council furnished numerous details and some matters of major importance, but the most important documents concerning Exeter which are preserved in the Public Record Office are the Port Books. They begin in 1565, although only about half a dozen books prior to 1640 are complete. Yet these few provide information of major importance about the city's economic life. The Subsidy Rolls are of little value for our purposes with the exception of that of 14-15 Henry VIII. In the British Museum, besides the Hooker manuscript mentioned above, the Harleian and Lansdowne collections contain a number of important letters from the Chamber to Burghley, and correspondence of his concerning the city.

Secondary Works

The bibliography of Exeter is not a rich one. There is a long list of titles but only a few of them are worth serious attention. Besides Hooker, Exeter boasts two antiquarians of note. One of these was Richard Isacke, chamberlain in the seventeenth century, who published his *Antiquities of Exeter* in 1677. As he relied on Hooker, his value is limited, but there are occasional items of interest which are not to be found elsewhere. This same author compiled a list of the principal benefactors of the city (*An Alphabetical Register, &c.*), published in 1736 by his son. It is our principal source of information for most of the benefactions made during the sixteenth and earlier centuries.

The second of the Exeter antiquarians whose work has been used in this study is Dr. George Oliver. His *History of Exeter* appeared in two editions, the first in 1821, the second posthumously in 1861. The second is the better edition. The actual text is not very useful, for it suffers from the common defect of nineteenth-century local history in that it is focused on national rather than local affairs. The Appendices, however, especially the account of the canal, and the lists of city officers, are very valuable. This same writer also prepared the exhaustive and valuable *Monasticon Diocesis Exoniensis*, which assembles in one cover a vast amount of material on ecclesiastical history up to the Reformation. The only other history of the city which needs mention is E. A. Freeman's *Exeter* in the Historic Towns series. Admittedly written from second-hand sources, it is not a work of much value to the serious historian. One other nineteenth-century work requires mention. This is the careful little study of the building of Exeter canal written by P. C. de la Garde and published in *Archaeologia* in 1840.

In our own times an important contribution to the study of Exeter affairs has been made by the History of Exeter Research Group. The six monographs published by them are all of a high quality. Those which are particularly relevant to this study are Wilkinson and Easterling's *Medieval Council of Exeter*, Little and Easterling's *Franciscans and Dominicans of Exeter*, and Curtis' *Disputes between the City and Cathedral of Authorities*. Hoskins' excellent monograph *Industry, Trade, and People in Exeter, 1688–1800*, which deals with a later period than ours, has not only provided useful information but has also served as a model of organization and analysis.

The volumes of the *Transactions of the Devonshire Association* have been used with profit as well as those of the *Devon and Cornwall Notes and Queries*. Of particular value are Alexander's *Exeter Members of Parliament* in the *Transactions* and the series on the rectors of Exeter churches in *Notes and Queries*.

The briefness of this bibliography emphasizes the unsatisfactory state of local history studies in general. Only with the History of Exeter Research Group's monographs do we find the application of modern historical technique to the city's history. Hitherto local history has been the preserve either of the antiquarian or the popularizer. Much of the work of the former has been very useful, but what is now necessary is the additional efforts of professional historians devoted to the particular problems of local history rather than those of national history. And, indeed, one may add, only when the work of the local historians is well done, will the general historians be able to confirm many of their present hypotheses.

Bibliography

PRIMARY MATERIALS (MANUSCRIPT)

The City and County of the City of Exeter
Books
   The Act Books, vols. II–VIII (1508–1640).
   Book 51 (John Hooker's Commonplace Book)
   Book 55 (The Freeman's Book)
   Books 141–145 (Book-proceedings of the Orphans' Court)
   Book 157 (A Book of the Accounts of the Poor, 1563–1572)
   Book 184a
   Book 184b   (Accounts of the Purchase of Monastic Lands)
   Book 184c
   Book 185 (Merchant Adventurers' Papers, 1558–1559)
Rolls and Miscellaneous Papers
   The Receiver's Rolls (32–33 Henry VIII—16–17 Charles I)
   Miscellaneous Roll 31 (Acts, Orders, Tables of Rates, &c., respecting
      the Merchants' Cloth Hall, 1602)
   Inventories
   Books of the Receiver's Accounts
   Law Papers
   Transcripts
Deeds
Letters
   (See under Historical Manuscripts Commission Report for calendar
      of the Letters.)
Exeter City Library
   "Clipping" Files on Devon families, particularly the bound volume
      of newspaper articles on eminent Exonians written by Dr. George
      Oliver for *Trewman's Flying Post.*
The Lord Bishop of Exeter
   The Bishop's Register, vols. XVI–XXV (1552–1640)
The Public Record Office
   State Papers, Domestic (Edward VI–Charles I)

See *Calendar of State Papers, Domestic*, vols. I–VI and addenda, London, 1856–72.

Acts of the Privy Council
See *Acts of the Privy Council of England*, ed. J. R. Dasent, 32 volumes, London, 1890–1907, and MSS. volumes.

The Port Books (Exeter)
See Class, Exchequer, King's Remembrancer.

The Subsidy Rolls (Exeter)
See Class, Exchequer, King's Remembrancer.

British Museum
See the calendars of the Lansdowne Manuscripts and of the Harleian Manuscripts. See particularly Harleian MS. 5827 (*Synopsis Chorographical of Devonshire* by John Hooker).

PRIMARY MATERIALS (PRINTED)

Cotton, William. *An Elizabethan Guild of the City of Exeter*, Exeter, 1873. The Appendices of this work are transcriptions from the papers of the Merchant Adventurers Company.

Cresswell, Beatrix F. *The Edwardian Inventories for the City and County of Exeter* (Alcuin Club Collection XX), London and Milwaukee, U.S.A., 1916. These are transcripts of the inventories of church property made by the royal commissioners in 1552.

De la Garde, Philip Chilwell. "On the Antiquity and Invention of the Lock Canal of Exeter," published in *Archaeologia*, XXVIII (1840), 7–26.

Dymond, Robert. *History of the Parish of St. Petrock*, Plymouth, 1882.

Early Tours in Devon and Cornwall, ed. by Richard Pearse Chope (issued as appendix to *Devon and Cornwall Notes and Queries*), Exeter, 1918.

Freeman, E. A. *Exeter* (Historic Towns Series, ed. E. A. Freeman and W. Hunt), London and New York, 1890.

Harte, Walter J. *Gleanings from the Common-Place Book of John Hooker, relating to the City of Exeter, 1485–1590*, Exeter, 1926.

History of Exeter Research Group Monographs, I–VI. See particularly:
Little, A. G. and Easterling, R. C. *The Franciscans and Dominicans of Exeter* (Monograph No. 3), Exeter, 1927.
Wilkinson, B. and Easterling, R. C. *The Medieval Council of Exeter* (Monograph No. 4), Manchester, 1931.

Curtis, M. E. *Some Disputes between the City and the Cathedral Authorities of Exeter* (Monograph No. 5), Manchester, 1932.

Hoskins, W. G. *Industry, Trade and People in Exeter, 1688–1800* (Monograph No. 6), Manchester, 1935.

Holmes, W. *A Translation of a charter granted . . . by Charles I; likewise some abstracts and quotations from charters and grants to the city of London*, Exeter, 1785.

Hooker, John. *Life of Sir Peter Carewe*, edited by Sir Thomas Phillips and published in *Archaeologia*, XXVIII (1840), 96–151. There was another edition, edited by Sir John Maclean and published as a separate book, London, 1857.

Hoskins, W. G. and Finberg, H. P. R. *Devonshire Studies*, London, 1952.

Isacke, Richard. *An Alphabetical register of divers persons, who by their last wills, grants, feoffments, and other deeds, have given tenements, rents, annuities, and moneys toward the relief of the poor of the county of Devon and city and county of Exon; and likewise to many other cities and towns in England*, printed by Samuel Isacke, London, 1736.

The Description of the Citie of Excester by John Vowell alias Hooker, ed. by W. J. Harte, J. W. Schopp, and H. Tapley-Soper, 2 volumes numbered Parts II and III (Devon and Cornwall Record Society), Exeter, 1919. This is a transcription of Book 52 in the Exeter City Muniments. Part I: *Index*, Exeter, 1947.

Harte, W. J. *Gleanings from the Common Place Book of John Hooker*, Exeter, 1927 (?). These are brief selections from the Hooker manuscript (Book 51).

——— *Gleanings from the Manuscripts of Richard Isacke's Antiquities of Exeter*, Exeter, 1929. This includes some matter not included in the printed editions of Isacke's work.

Historical Manuscripts Commission. *Report on the Records of the City of Exeter* (Cd. 7640), London, 1916. This is a calendar of the Exeter City Muniments, based on the manuscript calendar in the Muniment Room, but considerably expanded. Most of the Letters are either abstracted or quoted at length, and this portion of the work is particularly useful.

SECONDARY WORKS

This does not pretend to be an exhaustive bibligraphy of works relating to Exeter. It represents only those works which were actually used in the preparation of this study.

BOOKS

Accounts and Papers, vol. 16 (LXV of 1909 *Parliamentary Papers*), #37: "Endowed Charities (County Borough of Exeter)."

Bibliotheca Devonensis, a Catalogue of Books relating to Devon, ed. J. Davidson, Exeter, 1852. (Supplement issued in 1861.)

Boggis, R. J. E. *A History of the Diocese of Exeter*, Exeter, 1922.

Britton, John. *The History and Antiquities of the Cathedral Church of Exeter*, London, 1826.

Cotton, William. *An Elizabethan Guild of the City of Exeter*, Exeter, 1873.

Cresswell, Beatrix F. *Exeter Churches* (issued as appendix to *Devon and Cornwall Notes and Queries*), Exeter, 1908.

—— *History of Weavers, Tuckers, and Shearmen of Exeter*, Exeter, 1930.

Isacke, Samuel. *Remarkable Antiquities of the City of Exeter*, published in three editions, London, 1677, 1724, and 1734. The last was used in this study.

Jenkins, Alexander. *History and Description of the City of Exeter and its Environs*, Exeter, 1806.

Prince, John. *Damnonii orientales illustres: or the worthies of Devon. A work wherein the lives and fortunes of the most favous divines, statesmen, swordmen, physicians, writers, and other prominent persons...are memorized*. Exeter, 1701 and London, 1810. The latter edition was used in this study.

Moore, Thomas. *History of Devonshire from the earliest period to the present*, 2 volumes, London, 1829–31.

Oliver, George. *History of Exeter*, Exeter, 1821, and Exeter and London, 1861. The latter edition was used in this study.

—— *Monasticon Diocesis Exoniensis*, Exeter, 1846.

Pickard, Ransom. *Population and Epidemics of Exeter in Pre-census Times*, Exeter, 1947.

Pole, Sir William. *Collections towards a description of the county of Devon,* London, 1791. (Pole lived from 1561 to 1635.)

Polwhele, Richard. *The History of Devonshire,* Exeter, 1793–1806.

Reynolds, Herbert. *A Short History of the Ancient Diocese of Exeter,* Exeter, 1895.

Risdon, Tristram. *Chorographical Description of Devon and Exeter,* London, 1714.

Rose-Troup, Frances. *The Western Rebellion of 1549,* London, 1913.

Studies in Social History, ed. by J. H. Plumb, London and New York, 1955.

Worth, R. N. *History of Devonshire,* London, 1886.

Worthy, Charles. *The History of the Suburbs of Exeter,* London and Exeter, 1892.

PERIODICALS

Devon and Cornwall Notes and Queries, 1901 seq.

Notes and Gleanings, 1888–92.

Transactions of the Devonshire Association for the Advancement of Science, Literature, and Art, 1863 seq.

Western Antiquary, 1882–95.

ADDENDA

Hoskins, E. G. *Devon,* London, 1954.

———"The Elizabethan Merchants of Exeter," in *Old Devon,* Newton Abbot, 1966; reprinted from *Elizabethan Government and Society,* ed. S. Bindoff and J. Hurstfield, London, 1961.

———*Exeter in the Seventeenth Century.* Devon and Cornwall Record Society, n.s.2, Torquay, 1957.

———*Provincial England,* London, 1965.

———*Two Thousand Years in Exeter,* Exeter, 1960.

Howell, Roger. *Newcastle upon Tyne and the Puritan Revolution,* Oxford, 1967.

Parry, H. Lloyd. *The Founding of Exeter School,* Exeter and London, 1913.

Seaver, Paul. *The Puritan Lectureships,* Stanford: Stanford University Press, 1970.

Youings, Joyce A. *Tuckers Hall, Exeter,* Exeter, 1968.

Index